Why the Tool?

Tools have been important to the success of the human race since the dawn of time. Unlike other species, humans are adept at building and using tools to accomplish specific and important tasks. In the modern era, software tools are the latest innovation in moving humanity forward in the tools frontier. Microsoft is proud to continue to innovate and provide new software tools and contribute to an improved society for all.

The Saw

The modern handsaw is a descendant of the original true saw, a great innovation developed during the Bronze Age (3000 B.C.) and Iron Age (1200 B.C.). For early toolmakers, meteoric iron was the most convenient source of metal to be pounded and worked into tools such as the handsaw. Throughout time, Egyptians and Romans have contributed to the development and refinement of the handsaw. Today, the handsaw is an effective woodcutting instrument consisting of a thin, wide steel blade with teeth permitting cutting both on the pull and push strokes. The teeth are designed to be non-clogging, thus the "M" shaped design with gaps, or gullets, between them to allow space for the cuttings. Control of the handsaw by the operator is excellent, permitting great accuracy while being operated.

MICROSOFT C#
LANGUAGE
SPECIFICATIONS

Microsoft
.net

Based on Beta Content

PUBLISHED BY
Microsoft Press
A Division of Microsoft Corporation
One Microsoft Way
Redmond, Washington 98052-6399

Library of Congress Cataloging-in-Publication Data
Microsoft C# Language Specifications / Microsoft Corporation.
     p. cm.
   Includes index.
   ISBN 0-7356-1448-2
   1. C (Computer program language)   2. Microsoft C.   I. Microsoft Corporation.

 QA76.73.C15 M514   2001
 005.13'3--dc21   2001030477

Printed and bound in the United States of America.

    4 5 6 7 8 9   QWE   6 5 4 3 2 1

Distributed in Canada by Penguin Books Canada Limited.

A CIP catalogue record for this book is available from the British Library.

Microsoft Press books are available through booksellers and distributors worldwide. For further information about international editions, contact your local Microsoft Corporation office or contact Microsoft Press International directly at fax (425) 936-7329. Visit our Web site at mspress.microsoft.com. Send comments to *mspinput@microsoft.com.*

Acquisitions Editor: Juliana Aldous
Project Editor: Denise Bankaitis

Body Part No. X08-19539

Contents

Preface

If you are holding this book in your hands, no doubt you want information about Microsoft .NET and you want it now. You have heard about how .NET will allow developers to create programs that will transcend device boundaries and fully harness the connectivity of the Internet in their applications. You have read in the news journals that Microsoft will soon be releasing a new programming language called C# that is derived from C and C++ and is part of Visual Studio.NET. You are curious about .NET, what Microsoft has planned, and how you can be a part of it.

This book contains some of the most requested topics on Microsoft .NET available through the Microsoft Developer Network (MSDN)—Microsoft's premier developer resource. *Microsoft C# Language Specifications* is one book in a series that includes *The Microsoft .NET Framework, The Microsoft .NET Framework Developer Specifications, Web Applications in the Microsoft .NET Framework,* and *Microsoft VisualStudio.NET*. Within this series, you'll find important technical articles from *MSDN Magazine* and MSDN Online as well as subject matter overviews and white papers from Microsoft and industry experts. You will also find transcripts of key speeches and interviews with top Microsoft product managers. We have also included the documentation and specifications for the new C# language and other key documents. And code…lots and lots of code.

Who Is This Book For?

This book is for developers who are interested in being on the cutting edge of new technologies and languages. It's for developers who are eager to learn, want to stay ahead of the curve, and aren't willing to wait until everything is in place and wrapped up in a pretty package. If you fit these criteria, order a pizza and settle in—this book is for you.

What's in This Book?

This book contains the complete C# specification written by Anders Hejlsberg and Scott Wiltamuth. C# is a modern object-oriented language that enables programmers to quickly and easily build solutions for the Microsoft .NET platform. The framework provided allows C# components to serve as Web services that are available across the Internet, from any application running on any platform. The language enhances developer productivity while eliminating programming errors that can lead to increased development costs. C# brings rapid Web development to the C and C++ programmer while maintaining the power and flexibility required by developers.

This specification is in beta form and is not final. In some cases, you might come across headings with no associated information. These incomplete sections represent areas of the specification that are still being built. That said, the specification does provide a good introduction to the C# language. By reading this book, you will learn about the features of C# and gain an understanding of its concepts and definitions. The specification will help familiarize you with the language and vocabulary of C# and provide a good peek at what is under the hood.

A Warning

Microsoft is offering this material as a first look, but remember that it's not final. Be sure to read any warnings posted on MSDN before installing any beta products. Visit MSDN regularly, and check for updates and the latest information.

About MSDN

MSDN makes it easy to find timely, comprehensive development resources and stay current on development trends and Microsoft technology. MSDN helps you keep in touch with the development community, giving you opportunities to share information and ideas with your peers and communicate directly with Microsoft. Check out the many resources of MSDN.

MSDN Online

More than just technical articles and documentation, MSDN Online (*msdn.microsoft.com*) is *the* place to go when looking for Microsoft developer resources. On MSDN Online, you can

- Search the MSDN Library and Knowledge Base for technical documentation
- Visit an online Developer Center for resource listings on popular topics
- View and download sample applications and code, or make and review comments through the Code Center
- Participate in peer developer forums such as Newsgroups, Peer Journal, Members Helping Members, and Ratings & Comments
- Find technical seminars, trade shows, and conferences sponsored or supported by Microsoft and then easily register online

MSDN Publications

MSDN Publications (*msdn.microsoft.com/magazines*) offers print and online publications for current information on all types of development. The following is a list of just a few of the publications MSDN produces.

- *MSDN Magazine*—a monthly magazine featuring real-world solutions built with Microsoft technologies, as well as early looks at upcoming products and new directions, such as Microsoft .NET
- *The .NET Show* (MSDN Show)—a regular series of webcasts about Microsoft's hottest technologies
- *MSDN Online Voices*—an online collection of regular technical columns updated each week
- *MSDN News*—a bimonthly newspaper of technical articles and columns for MSDN subscribers

MSDN Subscriptions

With an MSDN subscription (*msdn.microsoft.com/subscriptions*), you can get your hands on essential Microsoft developer tools, Microsoft .NET Servers, Visual Studio.NET, and Microsoft operating systems. Available on CD and DVD as well as online through MSDN Subscriber downloads, an MSDN subscription also provides you with

- Monthly shipments of the latest Microsoft Visual Studio development system, Microsoft .NET Enterprise Servers, Microsoft operating systems, and Visio 2000
- The latest updates, SDKs, DDKs, and essential programming information

1. Introduction

C# is a simple, modern, object oriented, and type-safe programming language derived from C and C++. C# (pronounced "C sharp") is firmly planted in the C and C++ family tree of languages, and will immediately be familiar to C and C++ programmers. C# aims to combine the high productivity of Visual Basic and the raw power of C++.

C# is provided as part of Microsoft Visual Studio 7.0. In addition to C#, Visual Studio supports Visual Basic, Visual C++, and the scripting languages VBScript and JScript. All of these languages provide access to the Microsoft .NET platform, which includes a common execution engine and a rich class library. The Microsoft .NET platform defines a "Common Language Subset" (CLS), a sort of lingua franca that ensures seamless interoperability between CLS-compliant languages and class libraries. For C# developers, this means that even though C# is a new language, it has complete access to the same rich class libraries that are used by seasoned tools such as Visual Basic and Visual C++. C# itself does not include a class library.

The rest of this chapter describes the essential features of the language. While later chapters describe rules and exceptions in a detail-oriented and sometimes mathematical manner, this chapter strives for clarity and brevity at the expense of completeness. The intent is to provide the reader with an introduction to the language that will facilitate the writing of early programs and the reading of later chapters.

1.1 Getting started

The canonical "hello, world" program can be written as follows:

```
using System;
class Hello
{
   static void Main() {
      Console.WriteLine("hello, world");
   }
}
```

The source code for a C# program is typically stored in one or more text files with a file extension of .cs, as in hello.cs. Using the command-line compiler provided with Visual Studio, such a program can be compiled with the command line directive

```
csc hello.cs
```

which produces an executable program named hello.exe. The output of the program is:

```
hello, world
```

Close examination of this program is illuminating:

- The `using System;` directive references a namespace called `System` that is provided by the Microsoft .NET Framework class library. This namespace contains the `Console` class referred to in the `Main` method. Namespaces provide a hierarchical means of organizing the elements of a class library. A "using" directive enables unqualified use of the types that are members of the namespace. The "hello, world" program uses `Console.WriteLine` as a shorthand for `System.Console.WriteLine`.

- The `Main` method is a member of the class `Hello`. It has the `static` modifier, and so it is a method on the class `Hello` rather than on instances of this class.

- The main entry point for a program—the method that is called to begin execution—is always a static method named `Main`.

- The "hello, world" output is produced through the use of a class library. The language does not itself provide a class library. Instead, it uses a common class library that is also used by languages such as Visual Basic and Visual C++.

  For C and C++ developers, it is interesting to note a few things that do *not* appear in the "hello, world" program.

- The program does not use a global method for `Main`. Methods and variables are not supported at the global level; such elements are always contained within type declarations (e.g., class and struct declarations).

- The program does not use either "`::`" or "`->`" operators. The "`::`" is not an operator at all, and the "`->`" operator is used in only a small fraction of programs. The separator "`.`" is used in compound names such as `Console.WriteLine`.

- The program does not contain forward declarations. Forward declarations are never needed, as declaration order is not significant.

- The program does not use `#include` to import program text. Dependencies among programs are handled symbolically rather than textually. This system eliminates barriers between programs written in different languages. For example, the `Console` class could be written in another language.

1.2 Types

C# supports two kinds of types: **value types** and **reference types**. Value types include simple types (e.g., `char`, `int`, and `float`), enum types, and struct types. Reference types include class types, interface types, delegate types, and array types.

Value types differ from reference types in that variables of the value types directly contain their data, whereas variables of the reference types store references to objects. With reference types, it is possible for two variables to reference the same object, and thus possible for operations on one variable to affect the object referenced by the other variable. With value types, the variables each have their own copy of the data, and it is not possible for operations on one to affect the other.

The example

```
using System;
class Class1
{
    public int Value = 0;
}
class Test
{
    static void Main() {
        int val1 = 0;
        int val2 = val1;
        val2 = 123;
        Class1 ref1 = new Class1();
        Class1 ref2 = ref1;
        ref2.Value = 123;
        Console.WriteLine("Values: {0}, {1}", val1, val2);
        Console.WriteLine("Refs: {0}, {1}", ref1.Value, ref2.Value);
    }
}
```

shows this difference. The output of the program is

```
Values: 0, 123
Refs: 123, 123
```

The assignment to the local variable val1 does not impact the local variable val2 because both local variables are of a value type (the type int) and each local variable of a value type has its own storage. In contrast, the assignment ref2.Value = 123; affects the object that both ref1 and ref2 reference.

The lines

```
Console.WriteLine("Values: {0}, {1}", val1, val2);
Console.WriteLine("Refs: {0}, {1}", ref1.Value, ref2.Value);
```

deserve further comment, as they demonstrate some of the string formatting behavior of Console.WriteLine, which in fact takes a variable number of arguments. The first argument is a string, which may contain numbered placeholders like {0} and {1}. Each placeholder refers to a trailing argument with {0} referring to the second argument, {1} referring to the third argument, and so on. Before the output is sent to the console, each placeholder is replaced with the formatted value of its corresponding argument.

Developers can define new value types through enum and struct declarations, and can define new reference types via class, interface, and delegate declarations. The example

```csharp
using System;
public enum Color
{
    Red, Blue, Green
}
public struct Point
{
    public int x, y;
}
public interface IBase
{
    void F();
}
public interface IDerived: IBase
{
    void G();
}
public class A
{
    protected virtual void H() {
        Console.WriteLine("A.H");
    }
}
public class B: A, IDerived
{
    public void F() {
        Console.WriteLine("B.F, implementation of IDerived.F");
    }
    public void G() {
        Console.WriteLine("B.G, implementation of IDerived.G");
    }
    override protected void H() {
        Console.WriteLine("B.H, override of A.H");
    }
}
public delegate void EmptyDelegate();
```

shows an example or two for each kind of type declaration. Later sections describe type declarations in greater detail.

1.2.1 Predefined types

C# provides a set of predefined types, most of which will be familiar to C and C++ developers.

The predefined reference types are `object` and `string`. The type `object` is the ultimate base type of all other types. The type `string` is used to represent Unicode string values. Values of type `string` are immutable.

The predefined value types include signed and unsigned integral types, floating point types, and the types `bool`, `char`, and `decimal`. The signed integral types are `sbyte`, `short`, `int`, and `long`; the unsigned integral types are `byte`, `ushort`, `uint`, and `ulong`; and the floating point types are `float` and `double`.

The `bool` type is used to represent boolean values: values that are either true or false. The inclusion of `bool` makes it easier to write self-documenting code, and also helps eliminate the all-too-common C++ coding error in which a developer mistakenly uses "=" when "==" should have been used. In C#, the example

```
int i = …;
F(i);
if (i = 0)  // Bug: the test should be (i == 0)
  G();
```

is invalid because the expression `i = 0` is of type `int`, and `if` statements require an expression of type `bool`.

The `char` type is used to represent Unicode characters. A variable of type `char` represents a single 16-bit Unicode character.

The `decimal` type is appropriate for calculations in which rounding errors caused by floating point representations are unacceptable. Common examples include financial calculations such as tax computations and currency conversions. The `decimal` type provides 28 significant digits.

The table below lists the predefined types, and shows how to write literal values for each of them.

Type	Description	Example
object	The ultimate base type of all other types	`object o = null;`
string	String type; a string is a sequence of Unicode characters	`string s = "hello";`
sbyte	8-bit signed integral type	`sbyte val = 12;`
short	16-bit signed integral type	`short val = 12;`
int	32-bit signed integral type	`int val = 12;`
long	64-bit signed integral type	`long val1 = 12;` `long val2 = 34L;`

Type	Description	Example
byte	8-bit unsigned integral type	`byte val1 = 12;` `byte val2 = 34U;`
ushort	16-bit unsigned integral type	`ushort val1 = 12;` `ushort val2 = 34U;`
uint	32-bit unsigned integral type	`uint val1 = 12;` `uint val2 = 34U;`

ulong	64-bit unsigned integral type	`ulong val1 = 12;`
		`ulong val2 = 34U;`
		`ulong val3 = 56L;`
		`ulong val4 = 78UL;`

float	Single-precision floating point type	`float val = 1.23F;`
double	Double-precision floating point type	`double val1 = 1.23;` `double val2 = 4.56D;`
bool	Boolean type; a `bool` value is either true or false	`bool val1 = true;` `bool val2 = false;`
char	Character type; a `char` value is a Unicode character	`char val = 'h';`
decimal	Precise decimal type with 28 significant digits	`decimal val = 1.23M;`

Each of the predefined types is shorthand for a system-provided type. For example, the keyword `int` refers to the struct `System.Int32`. As a matter of style, use of the keyword is favored over use of the complete system type name.

Predefined value types such as `int` are treated specially in a few ways but are for the most part treated exactly like other structs. Operator overloading enables developers to define new struct types that behave much like the predefined value types. For instance, a `Digit` struct can support the same mathematical operations as the predefined integral types, and can define conversions between `Digit` and predefined types.

The predefined types employ operator overloading themselves. For example, the comparison operators `==` and `!=` have different semantics for different predefined types:

- Two expressions of type `int` are considered equal if they represent the same integer value.
- Two expressions of type `object` are considered equal if both refer to the same object, or if both are `null`.
- Two expressions of type `string` are considered equal if the string instances have identical lengths and identical characters in each character position, or if both are `null`.

The example

```
class Test
{
    static void Main() {
        string s = "Test";
        string t = string.Copy(s);
        Console.WriteLine(s == t);
        Console.WriteLine((object)s == (object)t);
    }
}
```

produces the output

```
True
False
```

because the first comparison compares two expressions of type string, and the second comparison compares two expressions of type object.

1.2.2 Conversions

The predefined types also have predefined conversions. For instance, conversions exist between the predefined types int and long. C# differentiates between two kinds of conversions: ***implicit conversions*** and ***explicit conversions***. Implicit conversions are supplied for conversions that can safely be performed without careful scrutiny.
For instance, the conversion from int to long is an implicit conversion. This conversion always succeeds, and never results in a loss of information. Implicit conversions can be performed implicitly, as shown in the example

```
using System;
class Test
{
    static void Main() {
        int intValue = 123;
        long longValue = intValue;
        Console.WriteLine("{0}, {1}", intValue, longValue);
    }
}
```

which implicitly converts an int to a long.

In contrast, explicit conversions are performed with a cast expression. The example

```
using System;
class Test
{
    static void Main() {
        long longValue = Int64.MaxValue;
        int intValue = (int) longValue;
        Console.WriteLine("(int) {0} = {1}", longValue, intValue);
    }
}
```

uses an explicit conversion to convert a `long` to an `int`. The output is:

```
(int) 9223372036854775807 = -1
```

because an overflow occurs. Cast expressions permit the use of both implicit and explicit conversions.

1.2.3 Array types

Arrays may be single-dimensional or multi-dimensional. Both "rectangular" and "jagged" arrays are supported.

Single-dimensional arrays are the most common type, so this is a good starting point. The example

```
using System;
class Test
{
    static void Main() {
        int[] arr = new int[5];
        for (int i = 0; i < arr.Length; i++)
            arr[i] = i * i;
        for (int i = 0; i < arr.Length; i++)
            Console.WriteLine("arr[{0}] = {1}", i, arr[i]);
    }
}
```

creates a single-dimensional array of `int` values, initializes the array elements, and then prints each of them out. The program output is:

```
arr[0] = 0
arr[1] = 1
arr[2] = 4
arr[3] = 9
arr[4] = 16
```

The type `int[]` used in the previous example is an array type. Array types are written using a non-array-type followed by one or more rank specifiers. The example

```
class Test
{
    static void Main() {
        int[] a1;          // single-dimensional array of int
        int[,] a2;         // 2-dimensional array of int
        int[,,] a3;        // 3-dimensional array of int
        int[][] j2;        // "jagged" array: array of (array of int)
        int[][][] j3;      // array of (array of (array of int))
    }
}
```

shows a variety of local variable declarations that use array types with `int` as the element type.

Array types are reference types, and so the declaration of an array variable merely sets aside space for the reference to the array. Array instances are actually created via array initializers and array creation expressions. The example

```
class Test
{
    static void Main() {
        int[] a1 = new int[] {1, 2, 3};
        int[,] a2 = new int[,] {{1, 2, 3}, {4, 5, 6}};
        int[,,] a3 = new int[10, 20, 30];
        int[][] j2 = new int[3][];
        j2[0] = new int[] {1, 2, 3};
        j2[1] = new int[] {1, 2, 3, 4, 5, 6};
        j2[2] = new int[] {1, 2, 3, 4, 5, 6, 7, 8, 9};
    }
}
```

shows a variety of array creation expressions. The variables a1, a2 and a3 denote *rectangular arrays*, and the variable j2 denotes a *jagged array*. It should be no surprise that these terms are based on the shapes of the arrays. Rectangular arrays always have a rectangular shape. Given the length of each dimension of the array, its rectangular shape is clear. For example, the length of a3's three dimensions are 10, 20, and 30 respectively, and it is easy to see that this array contains 10*20*30 elements.

In contrast, the variable j2 denotes a "jagged" array, or an "array of arrays". Specifically, j2 denotes an array of an array of `int`, or a single-dimensional array of type `int[]`. Each of these `int[]` variables can be initialized individually, and this allows the array to take on a jagged shape. The example gives each of the `int[]` arrays a different length. Specifically, the length of j2[0] is 3, the length of j2[1] is 6, and the length of j2[2] is 9.

The element type and shape of an array—including whether it is jagged or rectangular, and the number of dimensions it has—are part of its type. On the other hand, the size of the array—as represented by the length of each of its dimensions—is not part of an array's type. This split is made clear in the language syntax, as the length of each dimension is specified in the array creation expression rather than in the array type. For instance the declaration

```
int[,,] a3 = new int[10, 20, 30];
```

has an array type of `int[,,]` and an array creation expression of `new int[10, 20, 30]`.

For local variable and field declarations, a shorthand form is permitted so that it is not necessary to re-state the array type. For instance, the example

```
int[] a1 = new int[] {1, 2, 3};
```

can be shortened to

```
int[] a1 = {1, 2, 3};
```

without any change in program semantics.

The context in which an array initializer such as `{1, 2, 3}` is used determines the type of the array being initialized. The example

```
class Test
{
    static void Main() {
        short[] a = {1, 2, 3};
        int[] b = {1, 2, 3};
        long[] c = {1, 2, 3};
    }
}
```

shows that the same array initializer syntax can be used for several different array types. Because context is required to determine the type of an array initializer, it is not possible to use an array initializer in an expression context.

1.2.4 Type system unification

C# provides a "unified type system". All types—including value types—derive from the type `object`. It is possible to call object methods on any value, even values of "primitive" types such as `int`. The example

```
using System;
class Test
{
    static void Main() {
        Console.WriteLine(3.ToString());
    }
}
```

calls the `object`-defined `ToString` method on an integer literal.

The example

```
class Test
{
    static void Main() {
        int i = 123;
        object o = i;      // boxing
        int j = (int) o;   // unboxing
    }
}
```

is more interesting. An `int` value can be converted to `object` and back again to `int`. This example shows both *boxing* and *unboxing*. When a variable of a value type needs to be converted to a reference type, an object *box* is allocated to hold the value, and the value is copied into the box. *Unboxing* is just the opposite. When an object box is cast back to its original value type, the value is copied out of the box and into the appropriate storage location.

This type system unification provides value types with the benefits of object-ness without introducing unnecessary overhead. For programs that don't need `int` values to act like objects, `int` values are simply 32-bit values. For programs that need `int` values to behave like objects, this capability is available on demand. This ability to treat value types as objects bridges the gap between value types and reference types that exists in most languages. For example, a `Stack` class can provide `Push` and `Pop` methods that take and return `object` values.

```
public class Stack
{
    public object Pop() {…}
    public void Push(object o) {…}
}
```

Because C# has a unified type system, the `Stack` class can be used with elements of any type, including value types like `int`.

1.3 Variables and parameters

Variables represent storage locations. Every variable has a type that determines what values can be stored in the variable. *Local variables* are variables that are declared in methods, properties, or indexers. A local variable is usually defined by specifying a type name and a declarator that specifies the variable name and an optional initial value, as in:

```
int a;
int b = 1;
```

but it is also possible for a local variable declaration to include multiple declarators. The declarations of `a` and `b` can be rewritten as:

```
int a, b = 1;
```

A variable must be assigned before its value can be obtained. The example

```
class Test
{
    static void Main() {
        int a;
        int b = 1;
        int c = a + b;

        …
    }
}
```

is invalid because it attempts to use the variable `a` before it is assigned a value. The rules governing definite assignment are defined in section 5.3.

A *field* (section 10.4) is a variable that is associated with a class or struct, or an instance of a class or struct. A field declared with the `static` modifier defines a *static variable*, and a field declared without this modifier defines an *instance variable*. A static field associated with a type, whereas an instance variable is associated with an instance. The example

```
using System.Data;
class Employee
{
    private static DataSet ds;
    public string Name;
    public decimal Salary;
    ...
}
```

shows an `Employee` class that has a private static variable and two public instance variables.

Formal parameter declarations also define variables. There are four kinds of parameters: value parameters, reference parameters, output parameters, and parameter arrays.

A *value parameter* is used for "in" parameter passing, in which the value of an argument is passed into a method, and modifications of the parameter do not impact the original argument. A value parameter refers to its own variable, one that is distinct from the variable of the corresponding argument. This variable is initialized by copying the value of the corresponding argument. The example

```
using System;
class Test {
    static void F(int p) {
        Console.WriteLine("p = {0}", p);
        p++;
    }
    static void Main() {
        int a = 1;
        Console.WriteLine("pre: a = {0}", a);
        F(a);
        Console.WriteLine("post: a = {0}", a);
    }
}
```

shows a method `F` that has a value parameter named `p`. The example produces the output:

```
pre: a = 1
p = 1
post: a = 1
```

even though the value parameter `p` is modified.

A *reference parameter* is used for "by reference" parameter passing, in which the parameter acts as an alias for a caller-provided argument. A reference parameter does not itself define a variable, but rather refers to the variable of the corresponding argument. Modifications of a reference parameter directly and immediately impact the corresponding argument. A reference parameter is declared with a `ref` modifier. The example

```
using System;
class Test {
    static void Swap(ref int a, ref int b) {
        int t = a;
        a = b;
        b = t;
    }
    static void Main() {
        int x = 1;
        int y = 2;

        Console.WriteLine("pre: x = {0}, y = {1}", x, y);
        Swap(ref x, ref y);
        Console.WriteLine("post: x = {0}, y = {1}", x, y);
    }
}
```

shows a `Swap` method that has two reference parameters. The output of the program is:

```
pre: x = 1, y = 2
post: x = 2, y = 1
```

The `ref` keyword must be used in both the declaration of the formal parameter and in uses of it. The use of `ref` at the call site calls special attention to the parameter so that a developer reading the code will understand that the argument could change as a result of the call.

An *output parameter* is similar to a reference parameter, except that the initial value of the caller-provided argument is unimportant. An output parameter is declared with an `out` modifier. The example

```
using System;
class Test {
    static void Divide(int a, int b, out int result, out int remainder) {
        result = a / b;
        remainder = a % b;
    }
    static void Main() {
        for (int i = 1; i < 10; i++)
            for (int j = 1; j < 10; j++) {
                int ans, r;
                Divide(i, j, out ans, out r);
                Console.WriteLine("{0} / {1} = {2}r{3}", i, j, ans, r);
            }
    }
}
```

shows a `Divide` method that includes two output parameters—one for the result of the division and another for the remainder.

For value, reference, and output parameters, there is a one-to-one correspondence between caller-provided arguments and the parameters used to represent them. A *parameter array* enables a many-to-one relationship: many arguments can be represented by a single parameter array. In other words, parameter arrays enable variable length argument lists.

A parameter array is declared with a `params` modifier. There can be only one parameter array for a given method, and it is always the last parameter specified. The type of a parameter array is always a single dimensional array type. A caller can either pass a single argument of this array type, or any number of arguments of the element type of this array type. For instance, the example

```
using System;
class Test
{
    static void F(params int[] args) {
        Console.WriteLine("# of arguments: {0}", args.Length);
        for (int i = 0; i < args.Length; i++)
            Console.WriteLine("\targs[{0}] = {1}", i, args[i]);
    }
```

(continued)

(continued)

```
static void Main() {
    F();
    F(1);
    F(1, 2);
    F(1, 2, 3);
    F(new int[] {1, 2, 3, 4});
}
}
```

shows a method F that takes a variable number of int arguments, and several invocations of this method. The output is:

```
# of arguments: 0
# of arguments: 1
    args[0] = 1
# of arguments: 2
    args[0] = 1
    args[1] = 2
# of arguments: 3
    args[0] = 1
    args[1] = 2
    args[2] = 3
# of arguments: 4
    args[0] = 1
    args[1] = 2
    args[2] = 3
    args[3] = 4
```

Most of the examples presented in this introduction use the WriteLine method of the Console class. The argument substitution behavior of this method, as exhibited in the example

```
int a = 1, b = 2;
Console.WriteLine("a = {0}, b = {1}", a, b);
```

is accomplished using a parameter array. The WriteLine method provides several overloaded methods for the common cases in which a small number of arguments are passed, and one method that uses a parameter array.

```
namespace System
{
    public class Console
    {
        public static void WriteLine(string s) {…}
        public static void WriteLine(string s, object a) {…}
        public static void WriteLine(string s, object a, object b) {…}
        …
        public static void WriteLine(string s, params object[] args) {…}
    }
}
```

1.4 Automatic memory management

Manual memory management requires developers to manage the allocation and de-allocation of blocks of memory. Manual memory management is both time consuming and difficult. In C#, **automatic memory management** is provided so that developers are freed from this burdensome task. In the vast majority of cases, automatic memory management increases code quality and enhances developer productivity without negatively impacting either expressiveness or performance.

The example

```
using System;
public class Stack
{
    private Node first = null;
    public bool Empty {
        get {
            return (first == null);
        }
    }
    public object Pop() {
        if (first == null)
            throw new Exception("Can't Pop from an empty Stack.");
        else {
            object temp = first.Value;
            first = first.Next;
            return temp;
        }
    }
```

(continued)

(continued)

```
public void Push(object o) {
    first = new Node(o, first);
}
class Node
{
    public Node Next;
    public object Value;
    public Node(object value): this(value, null) {}
    public Node(object value, Node next) {
        Next = next;
        Value = value;
    }
}
}
```

shows a `Stack` class implemented as a linked list of `Node` instances. Node instances are created in the `Push` method and are garbage collected when no longer needed. A `Node` instance becomes eligible for garbage collection when it is no longer possible for any code to access it. For instance, when an item is removed from the `Stack`, the associated `Node` instance becomes eligible for garbage collection.

The example

```
class Test
{
    static void Main() {
        Stack s = new Stack();
        for (int i = 0; i < 10; i++)
            s.Push(i);
        s = null;
    }
}
```

shows a test program that uses the `Stack` class. A `Stack` is created and initialized with 10 elements, and then assigned the value `null`. Once the variable `s` is assigned null, the `Stack` and the associated 10 `Node` instances become eligible for garbage collection. The garbage collector is permitted to clean up immediately, but is not required to do so.

The garbage collector underlying C# works by moving objects around in memory, but this motion is invisible to most C# developers. For developers who are generally content with automatic memory management but sometimes need fine-grained control or that extra iota of performance, C# provides the ability to write "unsafe" code. Such code can deal directly with pointer types and object addresses, C# requires the programmer to *fix* objects to temporarily prevent the garbage collector from moving them.

This "unsafe" code feature is in fact a "safe" feature from the perspective of both developers and users. Unsafe code must be clearly marked in the code with the modifier unsafe, so developers can't possibly use unsafe language features accidentally, and the compiler and the execution engine work together to ensure that unsafe code cannot masquerade as safe code. These restrictions limit the use of unsafe code to situations in which the code is trusted.

The example

```
using System;
class Test
{
   unsafe static void WriteLocations(byte[] arr) {
      fixed (byte *p_arr = arr) {
         byte *p_elem = p_arr;
         for (int i = 0; i < arr.Length; i++) {
            byte value = *p_elem;
            string addr = int.Format((int) p_elem, "X");
            Console.WriteLine("arr[{0}] at 0x{1} is {2}", i, addr, value);
            p_elem++;
         }
      }
   }
   static void Main() {
      byte[] arr = new byte[] {1, 2, 3, 4, 5};
      WriteLocations(arr);
   }
}
```

shows an unsafe method named WriteLocations that fixes an array instance and uses pointer manipulation to iterate over the elements. The index, value, and location of each array element is written to the console. One possible output of the program is:

```
arr[0] at 0x8E0360 is 1
arr[1] at 0x8E0361 is 2
arr[2] at 0x8E0362 is 3
arr[3] at 0x8E0363 is 4
arr[4] at 0x8E0364 is 5
```

but of course the exact memory locations may be different in different executions of the program.

1.5 Expressions

C# includes unary operators, binary operators, and one ternary operator. The following table summarizes the operators, listing them in order of precedence from highest to lowest:

Section	Category	Operators
7.5	Primary	`(x)  x.y  f(x)  a[x]  x++  x--  new` `typeof  sizeof  checked  unchecked`
7.6	Unary	`+  -  !  ~  ++x  --x  (T)x`
7.7	Multiplicative	`*  /  %`
7.7	Additive	`+  -`
7.8	Shift	`<<  >>`
7.9	Relational	`<  >  <=  >=  is`
7.9	Equality	`==  !=`
7.10	Logical AND	`&`
7.10	Logical XOR	`^`
7.10	Logical OR	`|`
7.11	Conditional AND	`&&`
7.11	Conditional OR	`||`
7.12	Conditional	`?:`
7.13	Assignment	`=  *=  /=  %=  +=  -=  <<=  >>=  &=  ^=  |=`

When an expression contains multiple operators, the **precedence** of the operators controls the order in which the individual operators are evaluated. For example, the expression x + y * z is evaluated as x + (y * z) because the * operator has higher precedence than the + operator.

When an operand occurs between two operators with the same precedence, the **associativity** of the operators controls the order in which the operations are performed:

- Except for the assignment operators, all binary operators are **left-associative**, meaning that operations are performed from left to right. For example, x + y + z is evaluated as (x + y) + z.

- The assignment operators and the conditional operator (?:) are **right-associative**, meaning that operations are performed from right to left. For example, x = y = z is evaluated as x = (y = z).

Precedence and associativity can be controlled using parentheses. For example, x + y * z first multiplies y by z and then adds the result to x, but (x + y) * z first adds x and y and then multiplies the result by z.

1.6 Statements

C# borrows most of its statements directly from C and C++, though there are some noteworthy additions and modifications. The table below lists the kinds of statements that can be used, and provides an example for each.

Statement	Example

Statement lists and block statements	```static void Main() {```
	 ``` F();```
	 ``` G();```
	 ``` {```
	 ``` H();```
	 ``` I();```
	 ``` }```
	 ```}```

Labeled statements and goto statements	```static void Main(string[] args) {```
	 ``` if (args.Length == 0)```
	 ``` goto done:```
	 ``` Console.WriteLine(args.Length);```
	
	 ```done:```
	 ``` Console.WriteLine("Done");```
	 ```}```

Local constant declarations	```static void Main() {```
	 ``` const float pi = 3.14;```
	 ``` const int r = 123;```
	 ``` Console.WriteLine(pi * r * r);```
	 ```}```

Local variable declarations	```static void Main() {```
	 ``` int a;```
	 ``` int b = 2, c = 3;```
	 ``` a = 1;```
	 ``` Console.WriteLine(a + b + c);```
	 ```}```

Expression statements	```static int F(int a, int b) {```
	 ``` return a + b;```
	 ```}```
	
	 ```static void Main() {```
	 ``` F(1, 2); // Expression statement```
	 ```}```

Statement	Example
| `if` statements | ```csharp
static void Main(string[] args) {
    if (args.Length == 0)
        Console.WriteLine("No args");
    else
        Console.WriteLine("Args");
}
``` |
| `switch` statements | ```csharp
static void Main(string[] args) {
    switch (args.Length) {
        case 0:
            Console.WriteLine("No args");
            break;
        case 1:
            Console.WriteLine("One arg ");
            break;
        default:
            int n = args.Length;
            Console.WriteLine("{0} args", n);
            break;
    }
}
``` |
| `while` statements | ```csharp
static void Main(string[] args) {
    int i = 0;
    while (i < args.length) {
        Console.WriteLine(args[i]);
        i++;
    }
}
``` |
| `do` statements | ```csharp
static void Main() {
    string s;
    do { s = Console.ReadLine(); }
    while (s != "Exit");
}
``` |
| `for` statements | ```csharp
static void Main(string[] args) {
    for (int i = 0; i < args.length; i++)
        Console.WriteLine(args[i]);
}
``` |
| `foreach` statements | ```csharp
static void Main(string[] args) {
    foreach (string s in args)
        Console.WriteLine(s);
}
``` |

Statement	Example
break statements	```static void Main(string[] args) {
int i = 0;
while (true) {
if (i > args.Length)
break;
Console.WriteLine(args[i++]);
}
}```
continue statements	```static void Main(string[] args) {
int i = 0;
while (true) {
Console.WriteLine(args[i++]);
if (i > args.Length)
continue;
break;
}
}```
return statements	```static int F(int a, int b) {
    return a + b;
}

static void Main() {
    Console.WriteLine(F(1, 2));
    return;
}``` |
| throw statements and try statements | ```static int F(int a, int b) {
    if (b == 0)
        throw new Exception("Divide by zero");
    return a / b;
}

static void Main() {
    try {
        Console.WriteLine(F(5, 0));
    }
    catch(Exception e) {
        Console.WriteLine("Error");
    }
}``` |

Statement	Example
checked and unchecked statements	```static void Main() {
int x = 100000, y = 100000;
Console.WriteLine(unchecked(x * y));
Console.WriteLine(checked(x * y));   // Error
Console.WriteLine(x * y);   // Error
}```
lock statements	```static void Main() {
A a = …
lock(a) {
a.P = a.P + 1;
}
}```
using statements	```using System;
class Resource: IDisposable
{
public void F() {
Console.WriteLine("Resource.F");
}
public void Dispose() {…}
…
}
static void Main() {
using(Resource r = new Resource()) {
r.F();
}
}```

1.7 Classes

Class declarations define new reference types. A class can inherit from another class, and can implement interfaces.

Class members can include constants, fields, methods, properties, indexers, events, operators, constructors, destructors, and nested type declarations. Each member has an associated accessibility, which controls the regions of program text that are able to access the member. There are five possible forms of accessibility. These are summarized in the table below.

Form	Intuitive meaning
public	Access not limited
protected	Access limited to the containing class or types derived from the containing class
internal	Access limited to this program
protected internal	Access limited to this program or types derived from the containing class
private	Access limited to the containing type

The example

```
using System;
class MyClass
{
   public MyClass() {
      Console.WriteLine("Constructor");
   }
   public MyClass(int value) {
      MyField = value;
      Console.WriteLine("Constructor");
   }
   ~MyClass() {
      Console.WriteLine("Destructor");
   }
   public const int MyConst = 12;
   public int MyField = 34;
   public void MyMethod(){
      Console.WriteLine("MyClass.MyMethod");
   }
   public int MyProperty {
      get {
         return MyField;
      }
      set {
         MyField = value;
      }
   }
   public int this[int index] {
      get {
         return 0;
      }
      set {
```

(continued)

(continued)

```
        Console.WriteLine("this[{0}] = {1}", index, value);
    }
}  public event EventHandler MyEvent;
public static MyClass operator+(MyClass a, MyClass b) {
    return new MyClass(a.MyField + b.MyField);
}
internal class MyNestedClass
{}
}
```

shows a class that contains each kind of member. The example

```
class Test
{
    static void Main() {
        // Constructor usage
        MyClass a = new MyClass();
        MyClass b = new MyClass(123);
        // Constant usage
        Console.WriteLine("MyConst = {0}", MyClass.MyConst);
        // Field usage
        a.MyField++;
        Console.WriteLine("a.MyField = {0}", a.MyField);
        // Method usage
        a.MyMethod();
        // Property usage
        a.MyProperty++;
        Console.WriteLine("a.MyProperty = {0}", a.MyProperty);
        // Indexer usage
        a[3] = a[1] = a[2];
        Console.WriteLine("a[3] = {0}", a[3]);
        // Event usage
        a.MyEvent += new EventHandler(MyHandler);
        // Overloaded operator usage
        MyClass c = a + b;
    }
    static void MyHandler(object sender, EventArgs e) {
        Console.WriteLine("Test.MyHandler");
    }
    internal class MyNestedClass
    {}
}
```

shows uses of these members.

1.7.1 Constants

A *constant* is a class member that represents a constant value: a value that can be computed at compile-time. Constants are permitted to depend on other constants within the same program as long as there are no circular dependencies. The rules governing constant expressions are defined in constant expression section 7.15. The example

```
class Constants
{
    public const int A = 1;
    public const int B = A + 1;
}
```

shows a class named Constants that has two public constants.

Even though constants are considered static members, a constant declaration neither requires nor allows a static modifier. Constants can be accessed through the class, as in

```
class Test
{
    static void Main() {
        Console.WriteLine("{0}, {1}", Constants.A, Constants.B);
    }
}
```

which prints out the values of Constants.A and Constants.B.

1.7.2 Fields

A *field* is a member that represents a variable associated with an object or class. The example

```
class Color
{
    internal ushort redPart;
    internal ushort bluePart;
    internal ushort greenPart;
    public Color(ushort red, ushort blue, ushort green) {
        redPart = red;
        bluePart = blue;
        greenPart = green;
    }
    ...
}
```

shows a `Color` class that has internal instance fields named `redPart`, `greenPart`, and `bluePart`. Fields can also be static, as shown in the example

```
class Color
{
    public static Color Red = new Color(0xFF, 0, 0);
    public static Color Blue = new Color(0, 0xFF, 0);
    public static Color Green = new Color(0, 0, 0xFF);
    public static Color White = new Color(0xFF, 0xFF, 0xFF);
    ...
}
```

which shows static fields for `Red`, `Blue`, `Green`, and `White`.

Static fields are not a perfect match for this scenario. The fields are initialized at some point before they are used, but after this initialization there is nothing to stop a client from changing them. Such a modification could cause unpredictable errors in other programs that use `Color` and assume that the values do not change. **_Readonly fields_** can be used to prevent such problems. Assignments to a readonly field can only occur as part of the declaration, or in a constructor in the same class. Thus, the `Color` class can be enhanced by adding the readonly modifier for the static fields:

```
class Color
{
    internal ushort redPart;
    internal ushort bluePart;
    internal ushort greenPart;
    public Color(ushort red, ushort blue, ushort green) {
        redPart = red;
        bluePart = blue;
        greenPart = green;
    }
    public static readonly Color Red = new Color(0xFF, 0, 0);
    public static readonly Color Blue = new Color(0, 0xFF, 0);
    public static readonly Color Green = new Color(0, 0, 0xFF);
    public static readonly Color White = new Color(0xFF, 0xFF, 0xFF);
}
```

1.7.3 Methods

A *method* is a member that implements a computation or action that can be performed by an object or class. Methods have a list of formal parameters (which may be empty), a return value (or `void`), and are either static or non-static. ***Static methods*** are accessed through the class. ***Non-static methods***, which are also called ***instance methods***, are accessed through instances of the class. The example

```csharp
using System;
public class Stack
{
   public static Stack Clone(Stack s) {…}
   public static Stack Flip(Stack s) {…}
   public object Pop() {…}
   public void Push(object o) {…}
   public override string ToString() {…}

   …

}
class Test
{
   static void Main() {
      Stack s = new Stack();
      for (int i = 1; i < 10; i++)
         s.Push(i);
      Stack flipped = Stack.Flip(s);
      Stack cloned = Stack.Clone(s);
      Console.WriteLine("Original stack: " + s.ToString());
      Console.WriteLine("Flipped stack: " + flipped.ToString());
      Console.WriteLine("Cloned stack: " + cloned.ToString());
   }
}
```

shows a `Stack` that has several static methods (`Clone` and `Flip`) and several instance methods (`Push`, `Pop`, and `ToString`).

Methods can be overloaded, which means that multiple methods may have the same name so long as they have unique signatures. The signature of a method consists of the name of the method and the number, modifiers, and types of its formal parameters. The signature of a method specifically does not include the return type. The example

```csharp
class Test
{
   static void F() {
      Console.WriteLine("F()");
   }
```

(continued)

(continued)

```
static void F(object o) {
    Console.WriteLine("F(object)");
}
static void F(int value) {
    Console.WriteLine("F(int)");
}
static void F(int a, int b) {
    Console.WriteLine("F(int, int)");
}
static void F(int[] values) {
    Console.WriteLine("F(int[])");
}
static void Main() {
    F();
    F(1);
    F((object)1);
    F(1, 2);
    F(new int[] {1, 2, 3});
}
}
```

shows a class with a number of F methods. The output of the program is

```
F()
F(int)
F(object)
F(int, int)
F(int[])
```

1.7.4 Properties

A *property* is a member that provides access to an attribute of an object or a class. Examples of properties include the length of a string, the size of a font, the caption of a window, the name of a customer, and so on. Properties are a natural extension of fields. Both are named members with associated types, and the syntax for accessing fields and properties is the same. However, unlike fields, properties do not denote storage locations. Instead, properties have accessors that specify the statements to execute in order to read or write their values.

Properties are defined with property declarations. The first part of a property declaration looks quite similar to a field declaration. The second part includes a get accessor and/or a set accessor. In the example below, the Button class defines a Caption property.

```
public class Button
{
    private string caption;
    public string Caption {
        get {
            return caption;
        }
        set {
            caption = value;
            Repaint();
        }
    }
}
```

Properties that can be both read and written, like the `Caption` property, include both get and set accessors. The get accessor is called when the property's value is read; the set accessor is called when the property's value is written. In a set accessor, the new value for the property is given in an implicit parameter named `value`.

Declaration of properties is relatively straightforward, but the true value of properties shows itself in use rather than in declaration. The `Caption` property can be read and written in the same way that fields can be read and written:

```
Button b = new Button();
b.Caption = "ABC";        // set; causes repaint
string s = b.Caption;     // get
b.Caption += "DEF";       // get & set; causes repaint
```

1.7.5 Events

An *event* is a member that enables an object or class to provide notifications. A class defines an event by providing an event declaration, which resembles a field declaration, though with an added `event` keyword, and an optional set of event accessors. The type of this declaration must be a delegate type.

In the example

```
public delegate void EventHandler(object sender, System.EventArgs e);
public class Button
{
   public event EventHandler Click;
   public void Reset() {
      Click = null;
   }
}
```

the Button class defines a Click event of type EventHandler. Inside the Button class, the Click member corresponds exactly to a private field of type EventHandler. However, outside the Button class, the Click member can only be used on the left hand side of the += and -= operators. The += operator adds a handler for the event, and the -= operator removes an handler for the event. The example

```
using System;
public class Form1
{
   public Form1() {
      // Add Button1_Click as an event handler for Button1's Click event
      Button1.Click += new EventHandler(Button1_Click);
   }
   Button Button1 = new Button();
   void Button1_Click(object sender, EventArgs e) {
      Console.WriteLine("Button1 was clicked!");
   }
   public void Disconnect() {
      Button1.Click -= new EventHandler(Button1_Click);
   }
}
```

shows a Form1 class that adds Button1_Click as an event handler for Button1's Click event. In the Disconnect method, the event handler is removed.

For a simple event declaration such as

```
public event EventHandler Click;
```

the compiler automatically provides the implementation underlying the += and -= operators.

An implementer who wants more control can do so by explicitly providing add and remove accessors. The Button class could be rewritten to include add and remove accessors as follows:

```
public class Button
{
    private EventHandler handler;
    public event EventHandler Click {
        add { handler += value; }
        remove { handler -= value; }
    }
}
```

This change has no effect on client code, but allows the Button class more implementation flexibility. For example, the event handler for Click need not be represented by a field.

1.7.6 Operators

An *operator* is a member that defines the meaning of an expression operator that can be applied to instances of the class. There are three kinds of operators that can be defined: unary operators, binary operators, and conversion operators.

The following examples defines a Digit type that represents decimal digits—integral values between 0 and 9.

```
using System;
public struct Digit
{
    byte value;
    public Digit(byte value) {
        if (value < 0 || value > 9) throw new ArgumentException();
        this.value = value;
    }
    public Digit(int value): this((byte) value) {}
    public static implicit operator byte(Digit d) {
        return d.value;
    }
    public static explicit operator Digit(byte b) {
        return new Digit(b);
    }
    public static Digit operator+(Digit a, Digit b) {
        return new Digit(a.value + b.value);
    }
    public static Digit operator-(Digit a, Digit b) {
        return new Digit(a.value - b.value);
```

(continued)

(continued)

```
    }
    public static bool operator==(Digit a, Digit b) {
        return a.value == b.value;
    }
    public static bool operator!=(Digit a, Digit b) {
        return a.value != b.value;
    }
    public override bool Equals(object value) {
        return this == (Digit) value;
    }
    public override int GetHashCode() {
        return value.GetHashCode();
    }
    public override string ToString() {
        return value.ToString();
    }
}
class Test
{
    static void Main() {
        Digit a = (Digit) 5;
        Digit b = (Digit) 3;
        Digit plus = a + b;
        Digit minus = a - b;
        bool equals = (a == b);
        Console.WriteLine("{0} + {1} = {2}", a, b, plus);
        Console.WriteLine("{0} - {1} = {2}", a, b, minus);
        Console.WriteLine("{0} == {1} = {2}", a, b, equals);
    }
}
```

The `Digit` type defines the following operators:

- An implicit conversion operator from `Digit` to `byte`.
- An explicit conversion operator from `byte` to `Digit`.
- An addition operator that adds two `Digit` values and returns a `Digit` value.
- A subtraction operator that subtracts one `Digit` value from another, and returns a `Digit` value.
- The equality (`==`) and inequality (`!=`) operators, which compare two `Digit` values.

1.7.7 Indexers

An *indexer* is a member that enables an object to be indexed in the same way as an array. Whereas properties enable field-like access, indexers enable array-like access.

As an example, consider the Stack class presented earlier. This class might want to expose array-like access so that it is possible to inspect or alter the items on the stack without performing unnecessary Push and Pop operations. The Stack is implemented as a linked list, but wants to provide the convenience of array access.

Indexer declarations are similar to property declarations, with the main differences being that indexers are nameless (the "name" used in the declaration is this, since this is being indexed) and that indexers include indexing parameters. The indexing parameters are provided between square brackets. The example

```csharp
using System;
public class Stack
{
    private Node GetNode(int index) {
        Node temp = first;
        while (index > 0) {
            temp = temp.Next;
            index--;
        }
        return temp;
    }
    public object this[int index] {
        get {
            if (!ValidIndex(index))
                throw new Exception("Index out of range.");
            else
                return GetNode(index).Value;
        }
        set {
            if (!ValidIndex(index))
                throw new Exception("Index out of range.");
            else
                GetNode(index).Value = value;
        }
    }
    ...
}
```

(continued)

(continued)

```
class Test
{
    static void Main() {
        Stack s = new Stack();
        s.Push(1);
        s.Push(2);
        s.Push(3);
        s[0] = 33;  // Changes the top item from 3 to 33
        s[1] = 22;  // Changes the middle item from 2 to 22
        s[2] = 11;  // Changes the bottom item from 1 to 11
    }
}
```

shows an indexer for the `Stack` class.

1.7.8 Instance constructors

An ***instance constructor*** is a member that implements the actions required to initialize an instance of a class.

The example

```
using System;
class Point
{
    public double x, y;
    public Point() {
        this.x = 0;
        this.y = 0;
    }
    public Point(double x, double y) {
        this.x = x;
        this.y = y;
    }
    public static double Distance(Point a, Point b) {
        double xdiff = a.x - b.x;
        double ydiff = a.y - b.y;
        return Math.Sqrt(xdiff * xdiff + ydiff * ydiff);
    }
    public override string ToString() {
        return string.Format("({0}, {1})", x, y);
    }
}
```

```
class Test
{
    static void Main() {
        Point a = new Point();
        Point b = new Point(3, 4);
        double d = Point.Distance(a, b);
        Console.WriteLine("Distance from {0} to {1} is {2}", a, b, d);
    }
}
```

shows a `Point` class that provides two public constructors. One `Point` constructor takes no arguments, and the other takes two `double` arguments.

If no constructor is supplied for a class, then an empty constructor with no parameters is automatically provided.

1.7.9 Destructors

A *destructor* is a member that implements the actions required to destruct an instance of a class. Destructors cannot take parameters, cannot have accessibility modifiers, and cannot be called explicitly. The destructor for an instance is called automatically during garbage collection.

The example

```
using System;
class Point
{
    public double x, y;
    public Point(double x, double y) {
        this.x = x;
        this.y = y;
    }
    ~Point() {
        Console.WriteLine("Destructed {0}", this);
    }
    public override string ToString() {
        return string.Format("({0}, {1})", x, y);
    }
}
```

shows a `Point` class with a destructor.

1.7.10 Static constructors

A *static constructor* is a member that implements the actions required to initialize a class. Static constructors cannot take parameters, cannot have accessibility modifiers, and cannot be called explicitly. The static constructor for a class is called automatically when the class is loaded.

The example

```
using System.Data;
class Employee
{
   private static DataSet ds;
   static Employee() {
      ds = new DataSet(…);
   }
   public string Name;
   public decimal Salary;
   …
}
```

shows an `Employee` class with a static constructor that initializes a static field.

1.7.11 Inheritance

Classes support single inheritance, and the type `object` is the ultimate base class for all classes.

The classes shown in earlier examples all implicitly derive from `object`. The example

```
class A
{
   public void F() { Console.WriteLine("A.F"); }
}
```

shows a class A that implicitly derives from `object`. The example

```
class B: A
{
   public void G() { Console.WriteLine("B.G"); }
}
class Test
{
   static void Main() {
      B b = new B();
      b.F();          // Inherited from A
      b.G();          // Introduced in B
```

```
        A a = b;          // Treat a B as an A
        a.F();
    }
}
```

shows a class B that derives from A. The class B inherits A's F method, and introduces a G method of its own.

Methods, properties, and indexers can be ***virtual***, which means that their implementation can be overridden in derived classes. The example

```
using System;
class A
{
    public virtual void F() { Console.WriteLine("A.F"); }
}
class B: A
{
    public override void F() {
        base.F();
        Console.WriteLine("B.F");
    }
}
class Test
{
    static void Main() {
        B b = new B();
        b.F();
        A a = b;
        a.F();
    }
}
```

shows a class A with a virtual method F, and a class B that overrides F. The overriding method in B contains a call `base.F()` which calls the overridden method in A.

A class can indicate that it is incomplete, and is intended only as a base class for other classes by including the abstract modifier. Such a class is called an ***abstract class***. An abstract class can specify ***abstract members***—members that a non-abstract derived class must implement. The example

```
using System;
abstract class A
{
   public abstract F();
}
class B: A
{
   public override F() { Console.WriteLine("B.F"); }
}
class Test
{
   static void Main() {
      B b = new B();
      B.F();
      A a = b;
      a.F();
   }
}
```

introduces an abstract method F in the abstract class A. The non-abstract class B provides an implementation for this method.

1.8 Structs

The list of similarities between classes and structs is long—structs can implement interfaces, and can have the same kinds of members as classes. Structs differ from classes in several important ways, however: structs are value types rather than reference types, and inheritance is not supported for structs. Struct values are stored either "on the stack" or "in-line". Careful programmers can sometimes enhance performance through judicious use of structs.

For example, the use of a struct rather than a class for a Point can make a large difference in the number of memory allocations performed by a program. The program below creates and initializes an array of 100 points. With Point implemented as a class, the program instantiates 101 separate objects—one for the array and one each for the 100 elements.

```
class Point
{
    public int x, y;
    public Point(int x, int y) {
        this.x = x;
        this.y = y;
    }
}
class Test
{
    static void Main() {
        Point[] points = new Point[100];
        for (int i = 0; i < 100; i++)
            points[i] = new Point(i, i*i);
    }
}
```

If `Point` is instead implemented as a struct, as in

```
struct Point
{
    public int x, y;
    public Point(int x, int y) {
        this.x = x;
        this.y = y;
    }
}
```

then the test program instantiates just one object—the one for the array. The `Point` instances are allocated in-line within the array. This optimization can be mis-used. Using structs instead of classes can also make a program slower and fatter, as passing a struct instance as a value parameter causes a copy of the struct to be created. There is no substitute for careful data structure and algorithm design.

1.9 Interfaces

An interface defines a contract. A class or struct that implements an interface must adhere to its contract. Interfaces can contain methods, properties, indexers, and events as members.

The example

```
interface IExample
{
   string this[int index] { get; set; }
   event EventHandler E;
   void F(int value);
   string P { get; set; }
}
public delegate void EventHandler(object sender, EventArgs e);
```

shows an interface that contains an indexer, an event E, a method F, and a property P.

Interfaces may employ multiple inheritance. In the example

```
interface IControl
{
   void Paint();
}
interface ITextBox: IControl
{
   void SetText(string text);
}
interface IListBox: IControl
{
   void SetItems(string[] items);
}
interface IComboBox: ITextBox, IListBox {}
```

the interface IComboBox inherits from both ITextBox and IListBox.

Classes and structs can implement multiple interfaces. In the example

```
interface IDataBound
{
   void Bind(Binder b);
}
public class EditBox: Control, IControl, IDataBound
{
   public void Paint() {…}
   public void Bind(Binder b) {…}
}
```

the class EditBox derives from the class Control and implements both IControl and IDataBound.

In previous example, the `Paint` method from the `IControl` interface and the `Bind` method from `IDataBound` interface are implemented using public members on the `EditBox` class. C# provides an alternative way of implementing these methods that allows the implementing class to avoid having these members be public. Interface members can be implemented using a qualified name. For example, the `EditBox` class could instead be implemented by providing `IControl.Paint` and `IDataBound.Bind` methods.

```
public class EditBox: IControl, IDataBound
{
    void IControl.Paint() {…}
    void IDataBound.Bind(Binder b) {…}
}
```

Interface members implemented in this way are called ***explicit interface members*** because each member explicitly designates the interface member being implemented. Explicit interface members can only be called via the interface. For example, the `EditBox`'s implementation of the `Paint` method can be called only by casting to the `IControl` interface.

```
class Test
{
    static void Main() {
        EditBox editbox = new EditBox();
        editbox.Paint(); // error: no such method
        IControl control = editbox;
        control.Paint(); // calls EditBox's Paint implementation
    }
}
```

1.10 Delegates

Delegates enable scenarios that C++ and some other languages have addressed with function pointers. Unlike function pointers, delegates are object-oriented, type-safe, and secure.

Delegates are reference types that derive from a common base class: `System.Delegate`. A delegate instance encapsulates a method—a callable entity. For instance methods, a callable entity consists of an instance and a method on the instance. For static methods, a callable entity consists of a class and a static method on the class.

An interesting and useful property of a delegate is that it does not know or care about the type of the object that it references. Any object will do; all that matters is that the method's signature matches the delegate's. This makes delegates perfectly suited for "anonymous" invocation. This is a powerful capability.

There are three steps in defining and using delegates: declaration, instantiation, and invocation. Delegates are declared using delegate declaration syntax. The example

```
delegate void SimpleDelegate();
```

declares a delegate named `SimpleDelegate` that takes no arguments and returns `void`.

The example

```
class Test
{
   static void F() {
      System.Console.WriteLine("Test.F");
   }
   static void Main() {
      SimpleDelegate d = new SimpleDelegate(F);
      d();
   }
}
```

creates a `SimpleDelegate` instance and then immediately calls it.

There is not much point in instantiating a delegate for a method and then immediately calling via the delegate, as it would be simpler to call the method directly. Delegates show their usefulness when their anonymity is used. The example

```
void MultiCall(SimpleDelegate d, int count) {
   for (int i = 0; i < count; i++)
      d();
   }
}
```

shows a `MultiCall` method that repeatedly calls a `SimpleDelegate`. The `MultiCall` method doesn't know or care what type method that is the target method for the `SimpleDelegate`, what accessibility this method has, or whether the method is static or non-static. All that matters is that the signature of the target method is compatible with `SimpleDelegate`.

1.11 Enums

An enum type declaration defines a type name for a related group of symbolic constants. Enums are used for "multiple choice" scenarios, in which a runtime decision is made from a fixed number of choices that are known at compile-time.

The example

```
enum Color
{
   Red,
   Blue,
   Green
}
class Shape
{
   public void Fill(Color color) {
      switch(color) {
         case Color.Red:

            ...
            break;
         case Color.Blue:

            ...
            break;
         case Color.Green:

            ...
            break;
         default:
            break;
      }
   }
}
```

shows a `Color` enum and a method that uses this enum. The signature of the `Fill` method makes it clear that the shape can be filled with one of the given colors.

The use of enums is superior to the use of integer constants—as is common in languages without enums—because the use of enums makes the code more readable and self-documenting. The self-documenting nature of the code also makes it possible for the development tool to assist with code writing and other "designer" activities. For example, the use of `Color` rather than `int` for a parameter type enables smart code editors to suggest `Color` values.

1.12 Namespaces and assemblies

The programs presented so far have stood on their own except for dependence on a few system-provided classes such as the `System.Console` class. It is far more common for real-world programs to consist of several different pieces. For example, a corporate application might depend on several different components, including some developed internally and some purchased from independent software vendors.

Namespaces and ***assemblies*** enable this component-based system. Namespaces provide a logical organizational system. Namespaces are used both as an "internal" organization system for a program, and as an "external" organization system—a way of presenting program elements that are exposed to other programs.

Assemblies are used for physical packaging and deployment. An assembly acts as a container for types. An assembly may contain types, the executable code used to implement these types, and references to other assemblies.

There are two main kinds of assemblies: ***applications*** and ***libraries***. Applications have a main entry point and usually have a file extension of `.exe`; libraries do not have a main entry point, and usually have a file extension of `.dll`.

To demonstrate the use of namespaces and assemblies, this section revisits the "hello, world" program presented earlier, and splits it into two pieces: a library that provides messages and a console application that displays them.

The library will contain a single class named `HelloMessage`. The example

```
// HelloLibrary.cs
namespace Microsoft.CSharp.Introduction
{
   public class HelloMessage
   {
      public string Message {
         get {
            return "hello, world";
         }
      }
   }
}
```

shows the `HelloMessage` class in a namespace named `Microsoft.CSharp.Introduction`. The `HelloMessage` class provides a read-only property named `Message`. Namespaces can nest, and the declaration

```
namespace Microsoft.CSharp.Introduction
{...}
```

is shorthand for several levels of namespace nesting:

```
namespace Microsoft
{
   namespace CSharp
   {
      namespace Introduction
      {...}
   }
}
```

The next step in the componentization of "hello, world" is to write a console application that uses the `HelloMessage` class. The fully qualified name for the class— `Microsoft.CSharp.Introduction.HelloMessage`—could be used, but this name is quite long and unwieldy. An easier way is to use a ***using namespace directive***, which makes it possible to use all of the types in a namespace without qualification. The example

```
// HelloApp.cs
using Microsoft.CSharp.Introduction;
class HelloApp
{
    static void Main() {
        HelloMessage m = new HelloMessage();
        System.Console.WriteLine(m.Message);
    }
}
```

shows a using namespace directive that refers to the `Microsoft.CSharp.Introduction` namespace. The occurrences of `HelloMessage` are shorthand for `Microsoft.CSharp.Introduction.HelloMessage`.

C# also enables the definition and use of aliases. A ***using alias directive*** defines an alias for a type. Such aliases can be useful in situation in which name collisions occur between two libraries, or when a small number of types from a much larger namespace are being used. The example

```
using MessageSource = Microsoft.CSharp.Introduction.HelloMessage;
```

shows a using alias directive that defines `MessageSource` as an alias for the `HelloMessage` class.

The code we have written can be compiled into a library containing the class `HelloMessage` and an application containing the class `HelloApp`. The details of this compilation step might differ based on the compiler or tool being used. Using the command-line compiler provided in Visual Studio 7.0, the correct invocations are

```
csc /target:library HelloLibrary.cs
```

which produces the class library `HelloLibrary.dll` and

```
csc /reference:HelloLibrary.dll HelloApp.cs
```

which produces the application `HelloApp.exe`.

1.13 Versioning

Versioning is the process of evolving a component over time in a compatible manner.
A new version of a component is ***source compatible*** with a previous version if code that
depends on the previous version can, when recompiled, work with the new version.
In contrast, a new version of a component is ***binary compatible*** if a program that
depended on the old version can, without recompilation, work with the new version.

Most languages do not support binary compatibility at all, and many do little to facilitate
source compatibility. In fact, some languages contain flaws that make it impossible,
in general, to evolve a class over time without breaking at least some client code.

As an example, consider the situation of a base class author who ships a class named
Base. In the first version, Base contains no F method. A component named Derived
derives from Base, and introduces an F. This Derived class, along with the class Base that
it depends on, is released to customers, who deploy to numerous clients and servers.

```csharp
// Author A
namespace A
{
    public class Base    // version 1
    {
    }
}
// Author B
namespace B
{
    class Derived: A.Base
    {
        public virtual void F() {
            System.Console.WriteLine("Derived.F");
        }
    }
}
```

So far, so good. But now the versioning trouble begins. The author of Base produces
a new version, and adds its own F method.

```
// Author A
namespace A
{
   public class Base     // version 2
   {
      public virtual void F() {    // added in version 2
         System.Console.WriteLine("Base.F");
      }
   }
}
```

This new version of `Base` should be both source and binary compatible with the initial version. (If it weren't possible to simply add a method then a base class could never evolve.) Unfortunately, the new `F` in `Base` makes the meaning of `Derived`'s `F` unclear. Did `Derived` mean to override `Base`'s `F`? This seems unlikely, since when `Derived` was compiled, `Base` did not even have an `F`! Further, if `Derived`'s `F` does override `Base`'s `F`, then it must adhere to the contract specified by `Base`—a contract that was unspecified when `Derived` was written? In some cases, this is impossible. For example, the contract of `Base`'s `F` might require that overrides of it always call the base. `Derived`'s `F` could not possibly adhere to such a contract.

C# addresses this versioning problem by requiring developers to clearly state their intent. In the original code example, the code was clear, since `Base` did not even have an `F`. Clearly, `Derived`'s `F` is intended as a new method rather than an override of a base method, since no base method named `F` exists.

```
// Author A
namespace A
{
   public class Base
   {
   }
}
// Author B
namespace B
{
   class Derived: A.Base
   {
      public virtual void F() {
         System.Console.WriteLine("Derived.F");
      }
   }
}
```

If `Base` adds an `F` and ships a new version, then the intent of a binary version of `Derived` is still clear—`Derived`'s `F` is semantically unrelated, and should not be treated as an override.

However, when `Derived` is recompiled, the meaning is unclear—the author of `Derived` may intend its `F` to override `Base`'s `F`, or to hide it. Since the intent is unclear, the compiler produces a warning, and by default makes `Derived`'s `F` hide `Base`'s `F`. This course of action duplicates the semantics for the case in which `Derived` is not recompiled. The warning that is generated alerts `Derived`'s author to the presence of the `F` method in `Base`.

If `Derived`'s `F` is semantically unrelated to `Base`'s `F`, then `Derived`'s author can express this intent—and, in effect, turn off the warning—by using the `new` keyword in the declaration of `F`.

```
// Author A
namespace A
{
   public class Base        // version 2
   {
      public virtual void F() { // added in version 2
         System.Console.WriteLine("Base.F");
      }
   }
}
// Author B
namespace B
{
   class Derived: A.Base   // version 2a: new
   {
      new public virtual void F() {
         System.Console.WriteLine("Derived.F");
      }
   }
}
```

On the other hand, `Derived`'s author might investigate further, and decide that `Derived`'s `F` should override `Base`'s `F`. This intent can be specified by using the `override` keyword, as shown below.

```
// Author A
namespace A
{
   public class Base             // version 2
   {
      public virtual void F() { // added in version 2
         System.Console.WriteLine("Base.F");
      }
   }
}
```

```
// Author B
namespace B
{
   class Derived: A.Base   // version 2b: override
   {
      public override void F() {
         base.F();
         System.Console.WriteLine("Derived.F");
      }
   }
}
```

The author of `Derived` has one other option, and that is to change the name of `F`, thus completely avoiding the name collision. Though this change would break source and binary compatibility for `Derived`, the importance of this compatibility varies depending on the scenario. If `Derived` is not exposed to other programs, then changing the name of `F` is likely a good idea, as it would improve the readability of the program—there would no longer be any confusion about the meaning of `F`.

1.14 Attributes

C# is a procedural language, but like all procedural languages it does have some declarative elements. For example, the accessibility of a method in a class is specified by decorating it `public`, `protected`, `internal`, `protected internal`, or `private`. Through its support for attributes, C# generalizes this capability, so that programmers can invent new kinds of declarative information, specify this declarative information for various program entities, and retrieve this declarative information at run-time. Programs specify this additional declarative information by defining and using attributes.

For instance, a framework might define a `HelpAttribute` attribute that can be placed on program elements such as classes and methods, enabling developers to provide a mapping from program elements to documentation for them. The example

```
using System;
[AttributeUsage(AttributeTargets.All)]
public class HelpAttribute: Attribute
{
   public HelpAttribute(string url) {
      this.url = url;
   }
   public string Topic = null;
   private string url;
   public string Url {
      get { return url; }
   }
}
```

defines an attribute class named `HelpAttribute`, or `Help` for short, that has one positional parameter (`string url`) and one named argument (`string Topic`). Positional parameters are defined by the formal parameters for public constructors of the attribute class, and named parameters are defined by public read-write properties of the attribute class.

The example

```
[Help("http://www.mycompany.com/.../Class1.htm")]
public class Class1
{
   [Help("http://www.mycompany.com/.../Class1.htm", Topic = "F")]
   public void F() {}
}
```

shows several uses of the attribute.

Attribute information for a given program element can be retrieved at run-time by using reflection support. The example

```
using System;
class Test
{
   static void Main() {
      Type type = typeof(Class1);
      object[] arr = type.GetCustomAttributes(typeof(HelpAttribute));
      if (arr.Length == 0)
         Console.WriteLine("Class1 has no Help attribute.");
      else {
         HelpAttribute ha = (HelpAttribute) arr[0];
         Console.WriteLine("Url = {0}, Topic = {1}", ha.Url, ha.Topic);
      }
   }
}
```

checks to see if `Class1` has a `Help` attribute, and writes out the associated `Topic` and `Url` values if the attribute is present.

2. Lexical structure

2.1 Phases of translation

A C# **program** consists of one or more **source files**. A source file is an ordered sequence of Unicode characters. Source files typically have a one-to-one correspondence with files in a file system, but this correspondence is not required.

Conceptually speaking, a program is compiled using two steps:

1. Lexical analysis, which translates a stream of input characters into a stream of tokens.
2. Syntactic analysis, which translates the stream of tokens into executable code.

2.2 Grammar notation

Lexical and syntactic grammars for C# are interspersed throughout this specification. The lexical grammar defines how characters can be combined to form tokens; the syntactic grammar defines how tokens can be combined to form C# programs.

Grammar productions include non-terminal symbols and terminal symbols. In grammar productions, *non-terminal* symbols are shown in italic type, and `terminal` symbols are shown in a fixed-width font. Each non-terminal is defined by a set of productions. The first line of a set of productions is the name of the non-terminal, followed by a colon. Each successive indented line contains the right-hand side for a production that has the non-terminal symbol as the left-hand side. The example:

nonsense:
```
    terminal1
    terminal2
```

defines the *nonsense* non-terminal as having two productions, one with `terminal1` on the right-hand side and one with `terminal2` on the right-hand side.

Alternatives are normally listed on separate lines, though in cases where there are many alternatives, the phrase "one of" precedes a list of the options. This is simply shorthand for listing each of the alternatives on a separate line.

The example:

letter: one of

    A   B   C   a   b   c

is shorthand for:

letter: one of

    A
    B
    C
    a
    b
    c

A subscripted suffix "*opt*", as in *identifier_{opt,}* is used as shorthand to indicate an optional symbol. The example:

whole:
    first-part   second-part_{opt}   last-part

is shorthand for:

whole:
    first-part   last-part
    first-part   second-part   last-part

2.3 Lexical analysis

The lexical analysis phase translates a stream of input characters into a stream of input elements. If more than one input element could possibly match the next sequence of characters, the longest possible input element is used, regardless of whether subsequent characters or tokens could be correct. For example, the text "5++6" always becomes three input elements: "5", "++", and "6", even though the alternative decomposition of "5", "+", "+", "6" might be syntactically more correct.

Each character in the stream of input characters is part of only one input element at a time; once a sequence of characters is formed into a input element, it is not subject to being rescanned for other tokens. For example, within a verbatim string literal token (section 2.4.4.5), characters are not subject to being matched as preprocessing tokens.

Once the character stream has been broken into input elements, whitespace and comments are discarded, and pre-processing directives are processed, leaving only a stream of tokens. Syntactic and semantic processing then occurs only upon that stream of tokens.

2.3.1 Input

input:
  input-elements$_{opt}$

input-elements:
  input-element
  input-elements   input-element

input-element:
  comment
  white-space
  pp-directive
  token

2.3.2 Input characters

input-character:
  any Unicode character

2.3.3 Line terminators

new-line:
  The carriage return character (`U+000D`)
  The line feed character (`U+000A`)
  The carriage return character followed by a line feed character
  The line separator character (`U+2028`)
  The paragraph separator character (`U+2029`)

2.3.4 Comments

Two forms of comments are supported: regular comments and one-line comments.

A ***regular comment*** begins with the characters `/*` and ends with the characters `*/`. Regular comments can occupy a portion of a line, a single line, or multiple lines. The example

```
/* Hello, world program
     This program writes "hello, world" to the console
*/
class Hello
{
   static void Main() {
      Console.WriteLine("hello, world");
   }
}
```

includes a regular comment.

A *one-line comment* begins with the characters // and extends to the end of the line.
The example

```
// Hello, world program
//    This program writes "hello, world" to the console
//
class Hello // any name will do for this class
{
    static void Main() { // this method must be named "Main"
        Console.WriteLine("hello, world");
    }
}
```

shows several one-line comments.

comment:
  regular-comment
  one-line-comment

regular-comment:
  / * *rest-of-regular-comment*

rest-of-regular-comment:
  * *rest-of-regular-comment-star*
  not-star   *rest-of-regular-comment*

rest-of-regular-comment-star:
  /
  * *rest-of-regular-comment-star*
  not-star-or-slash   *rest-of-regular-comment*

not-star:
  Any *input-character* except *

not-star-or-slash:
  Any *input-character* except * and /

one-line-comment:
  / /   *one-line-comment-text*   *new-line*

one-line-comment-text:
  input-character
  one-line-comment-text   *input-character*

2.3.5 White space

white-space:
  new-line
  The tab character (U+0009)
  The vertical tab character (U+000B)
  The form feed character (U+000C)
  The "control-Z" or "substitute" character (U+001A)
  All characters with Unicode class Zs

2.4 Tokens

There are several kinds of tokens: identifiers, keywords, literals, operators, and punctuators. White space and comments are not tokens, though they may act as separators for tokens.

token:
  identifier
  keyword
  literal
  operator-or-punctuator

2.4.1 Unicode character escape sequences

A Unicode character escape sequence represents a Unicode character. Unicode character escape sequences are processed in identifiers, non-verbatim string literals, and character literals. A Unicode character escape is not processed in any other location (for example, to form an operator, punctuator, or keyword).

unicode-character-escape-sequence:
  \u *hex-digit hex-digit hex-digit hex-digit*
  \U *hex-digit hex-digit hex-digit hex-digit hex-digit hex-digit hex-digit hex-digit*

A Unicode escape sequence represents the single Unicode character formed by the hexadecimal number following the "\u" or "\U" characters. Since C# uses a 16-bit encoding of Unicode characters in characters and strings, a Unicode character in the range U+10000 to U+10FFFF is represented using two Unicode "surrogate" characters. Unicode characters with code points above 0x10FFFF are not supported.

Multiple translations are not performed. For instance, the string literal "\u005Cu005C" is equivalent to "\u005C" rather than "\\". (The Unicode value \u005C is the character "\".)

The example

```
class Class1
{
   static void Test(bool \u0066) {
      char c = '\u0066';
      if (\u0066)
         Console.WriteLine(c.ToString());
   }
}
```

shows several uses of \u0066, which is the character escape sequence for the letter "f". The program is equivalent to

```
class Class1
{
   static void Test(bool f) {
      char c = 'f';
      if (f)
         Console.WriteLine(c.ToString());
   }
}
```

2.4.2 Identifiers

These identifier rules exactly correspond to those recommended by the Unicode 3.0 standard, Technical Report 15, Annex 7, except that underscore is allowed as an initial character (as is traditional in the C programming language), Unicode escape characters are permitted in identifiers, and the "@" character is allowed as a prefix to enable keywords to be used as identifiers.

identifier:
    available-identifier
    @ *identifier-or-keyword*

available-identifier:
    An *identifier-or-keyword* that is not a *keyword*

identifier-or-keyword:
    identifier-start-character *identifier-part-characters*$_{opt}$

identifier-start-character:
    letter-character
    _ (the underscore character)

identifier-part-characters:
    identifier-part-character
    identifier-part-characters *identifier-part-character*

identifier-part-character:
  letter-character
  decimal-digit-character
  connecting-character
  combining-character
  formatting-character

letter-character:
  A Unicode character of classes Lu, Ll, Lt, Lm, Lo, or Nl
  A *unicode-character-escape-sequence* representing a character of classes Lu, Ll, Lt, Lm, Lo, or Nl

combining-character:
  A Unicode character of classes Mn or Mc
  A *unicode-character-escape-sequence* representing a character of classes Mn or Mc

decimal-digit-character:
  A Unicode character of the class Nd
  A *unicode-character-escape-sequence* representing a character of the class Nd

connecting-character:
  A Unicode character of the class Pc
  A *unicode-character-escape-sequence* representing a character of the class Pc

formatting-character:
  A Unicode character of the class Cf
  A *unicode-character-escape-sequence* representing a character of the class Cf

Examples of legal identifiers include "identifier1", "_identifier2", and "@if".

The prefix "@" enables the use of keywords as identifiers, which is useful when interfacing with other programming languages. The character @ is not actually part of the identifier, and so might be seen in other languages as a normal identifier, without the prefix. Use of the @ prefix for identifiers that are not keywords is permitted, but strongly discouraged as a matter of style.

The example:

```
class @class
{
    static void @static(bool @bool) {
        if (@bool)
            Console.WriteLine("true");
        else
            Console.WriteLine("false");
    }
}
```

(continued)

(continued)

```
class Class1
{
   static void M {
      @class.@static(true);
   }
}
```

defines a class named "class" with a static method named "static" that takes a parameter named "bool".

Two identifiers are considered the same if they are identical after the following transformations are applied, in order:

- The prefix "@", if used, is removed.
- Each *unicode-character-escape-sequence* is transformed into its corresponding Unicode character

Identifiers beginning with two consecutive underscore characters are reserved for use by the implementation, and are not recommended for use by ordinary programs. For example, an implementation may provide extensions that are triggered by the use of keywords that begin with two underscores.

2.4.3 Keywords

A *keyword* is an identifier-like sequence of characters that is reserved, and cannot be used as an identifier except when prefaced by the @ character.

keyword: one of

abstract	delegate	if	override	this
as	do	implicit	params	throw
base	double	in	private	true
bool	else	int	protectedpublic	try
break	enum	interface	readonly	typeof
byte	event	internal	ref	uint
case	explicit	is	return	ulong
catch	extern	lock	sbyte	unchecked
char	false	long	sealed	unsafe
checked	finally	namespace	short	ushort
class	fixed	new	sizeof	using
const	float	null	stackallocstatic	virtual
continue	for	object	string	void
decimal	foreach	operator	struct	while
default	goto	out	switch	

In some places in the grammar, specific identifiers have special meaning, but are not keywords. For example, within a property declaration, the "get" and "set" identifiers have special meaning (section 10.6.2). An identifier is never a valid token in these locations, so this use does not conflict with a use of these words as identifiers.

2.4.4 Literals

A *literal* is a source code representation of a value.

literal:
    boolean-literal
    integer-literal
    real-literal
    character-literal
    string-literal
    null-literal

2.4.4.1 Boolean literals

There are two boolean literal values: true and false.

boolean-literal:
    true
    false

The type of a *boolean-literal* is bool.

2.4.4.2 Integer literals

Integer literals have two possible forms: decimal and hexadecimal.

integer-literal:
    decimal-integer-literal
    hexadecimal-integer-literal

decimal-integer-literal:
    decimal-digits   *integer-type-suffix$_{opt}$*

decimal-digits:
    decimal-digit
    decimal-digits   *decimal-digit*

decimal-digit: one of
    0 1 2 3 4 5 6 7 8 9

integer-type-suffix: one of
    U u L l UL Ul uL ul LU Lu lU lu

hexadecimal-integer-literal:
    0x   *hex-digits*   *integer-type-suffix$_{opt}$*
    0X   *hex-digits*   *integer-type-suffix$_{opt}$*

hex-digits:
   hex-digit
   hex-digits   hex-digit

hex-digit: one of
   0 1 2 3 4 5 6 7 8 9 A B C D E F a b c d e f

The type of an integer literal is determined as follows:

- If the literal has no suffix, it has the first of these types in which its value can be represented: `int`, `uint`, `long`, `ulong`.
- If the literal is suffixed by `U` or `u`, it has the first of these types in which its value can be represented: `uint`, `ulong`.
- If the literal is suffixed by `L` or `l`, it has the first of these types in which its value can be represented: `long`, `ulong`.
- If the literal is suffixed by `UL`, `Ul`, `uL`, `ul`, `LU`, `Lu`, `lU`, or `lu`, it is of type `ulong`.

If the value represented by an integer literal is outside the range of the `ulong` type, an error occurs.

As a matter of style, it is suggested that "L" be used instead of "l" when writing literals of type `long`, since it is easy to confuse the letter "l" with the digit "1".

To permit the smallest possible `int` and `long` values to be written as decimal integer literals, the following two rules exist:

- When a *decimal-integer-literal* with the value 2147483648 (2^{31}) and no *integer-type-suffix* appears as the token immediately following a unary minus operator token (section 7.6.2), the result is a constant of type `int` with the value −2147483648 (-2^{31}). In all other situations, such a *decimal-integer-literal* is of type `uint`.
- When a *decimal-integer-literal* with the value 9223372036854775808 (2^{63}) and no *integer-type-suffix* or the *integer-type-suffix* `L` or `l` appears as the token immediately following a unary minus operator token (section 7.6.2), the result is a constant of type `long` with the value −9223372036854775808 (-2^{63}). In all other situations, such a *decimal-integer-literal* is of type `ulong`.

2.4.4.3 Real literals

real-literal:
   decimal-digits . decimal-digits exponent-part$_{opt}$ real-type-suffix$_{opt}$
   . decimal-digits exponent-part$_{opt}$ real-type-suffix$_{opt}$
   decimal-digits exponent-part real-type-suffix$_{opt}$
   decimal-digits real-type-suffix

exponent-part:
  e *sign$_{opt}$ decimal-digits*
  E *sign$_{opt}$ decimal-digits*

sign: one of
  + -

real-type-suffix: one of
  F f D d M m

If no real type suffix is specified, the type of the real literal is `double`. Otherwise, the real type suffix determines the type of the real literal, as follows:

- A real literal suffixed by F or f is of type `float`. For example, the literals 1f, 1.5f, 1e10f, and 123.456F are all of type `float`.
- A real literal suffixed by D or d is of type `double`. For example, the literals 1d, 1.5d, 1e10d, and 123.456D are all of type `double`.
- A real literal suffixed by M or m is of type `decimal`. For example, the literals 1m, 1.5m, 1e10m, and 123.456M are all of type `decimal`.

If the specified literal cannot be represented in the indicated type, then a compile-time error occurs.

2.4.4.4 Character literals

A character literal represents a single character, and usually consists of a character in quotes, as in 'a'.

character-literal:
  ' *character* '

character:
  single-character
  simple-escape-sequence
  hexadecimal-escape-sequence
  unicode-character-escape-sequence

single-character:
  Any character except ' (U+0027), \ (U+005C), and *new-line*

simple-escape-sequence: one of
  \' \" \\ \0 \a \b \f \n \r \t \v

hexadecimal-escape-sequence:
  \x *hex-digit hex-digit$_{opt}$ hex-digit$_{opt}$ hex-digit$_{opt}$*

A character that follows a backslash character (\) in a *character* must be one of the following characters: ', ", \, 0, a, b, f, n, r, t, u, U, x, v. Otherwise, a compile-time error occurs.

A hexadecimal escape sequence represents a single Unicode character, with the value formed by the hexadecimal number following "\x".

A simple escape sequence represents a Unicode character encoding, as described in the table below.

Escape sequence	Character name	Unicode encoding
\'	Single quote	0x0027
\"	Double quote	0x0022
\\	Backslash	0x005C
\0	Null	0x0000
\a	Alert	0x0007
\b	Backspace	0x0008
\f	Form feed	0x000C
\n	New line	0x000A
\r	Carriage return	0x000D
\t	Horizontal tab	0x0009
\v	Vertical tab	0x000B

The type of a *character-literal* is `char`.

2.4.4.5 String literals

C# supports two forms of string literals: regular string literals and verbatim string literals. A regular string literal consists of zero or more characters enclosed in double quotes, as in `"hello, world"`, and may include both simple escape sequences (such as `\t` for the tab character) and hexadecimal escape sequences.

A verbatim string literal consists of an @ character followed by a double-quote character, zero or more characters, and a closing double-quote character. A simple example is `@"hello, world"`. In a verbatim string literal, the characters between the delimiters are interpreted verbatim, with the only exception being a *quote-escape-sequence*.
In particular, simple escape sequences and hexadecimal escape sequences are not processed in verbatim string literals. A verbatim string literal may span multiple lines.

string-literal:
    regular-string-literal
    verbatim-string-literal

regular-string-literal:
    "   *regular-string-literal-characters$_{opt}$*   "

regular-string-literal-characters:
    regular-string-literal-character
    regular-string-literal-characters   regular-string-literal-character

regular-string-literal-character:
   single-regular-string-literal-character
   simple-escape-sequence
   hexadecimal-escape-sequence
   unicode-character-escape-sequence

single-regular-string-literal-character:
   Any character except " (U+0022), \ (U+005C), and *new-line*

verbatim-string-literal:
   @"   *verbatim -string-literal-characters*_{opt}   "

verbatim-string-literal-characters:
   verbatim-string-literal-character
   verbatim-string-literal-characters   verbatim-string-literal-character

verbatim-string-literal-character:
   single-verbatim-string-literal-character
   quote-escape-sequence

single-verbatim-string-literal-character:
   any character except "

quote-escape-sequence:
   ""

A character that follows a backslash character (\) in a *regular-string-literal-character* must be one of the following characters: ', ", \, 0, a, b, f, n, r, t, u, U, x, v. Otherwise, a compile-time error occurs.

The example

```
string a = "hello, world";              // hello, world
string b = @"hello, world";             // hello, world
string c = "hello \t world";            // hello     world
string d = @"hello \t world";           // hello \t world
string e = "Joe said \"Hello\" to me";   // Joe said "Hello"
string f = @"Joe said ""Hello"" to me"; // Joe said "Hello"
string g = "\\\\sever\\share\\file.txt"; // \\server\share\file.txt
string h = @"\\server\share\file.txt";   // \\server\share\file.txt
string i = "one\ntwo\nthree";
string j = @"one
two
three";
```

shows a variety of string literals. The last string literal, j, is a verbatim string literal that spans multiple lines. The characters between the quotation marks, including white space such as newline characters, are preserved verbatim.

The type of a *string-literal* is `string`.

Each string literal does not necessarily result in a new string instance. When two or more string literals that are equivalent according to the string equality operator (section 7.9.7) appear in the same program, these string literals refer to the same string instance. For instance, the output of the program

```
class Test
{
    static void Main() {
        object a = "hello";
        object b = "hello";
        Console.WriteLine(a == b);
    }
}
```

is `True` because the two literals refer to the same string instance.

2.4.4.6 The null literal

null-literal:
   null

The type of a *null-literal* is the null type.

2.4.5 Operators and punctuators

There are several kinds of operators and punctuators. Operators are used in expressions to describe operations involving one or more operands. For example, the expression `a + b` uses the + operator to add the two operands `a` and `b`. Punctuators are for grouping and separating. For example, the punctuator `;` is used to separate statements that appear in statement lists.

operator-or-punctuator: one of

{	}	[	]	(	)	.	,	:	;
+	-	*	/	%	&	|	^	!	~
=	<	>	?	++	--	&&	||	<<	>>
==	!=	<=	>=	+=	-=	*=	/=	%=	&=
|=	^=	<<=	>>=	->					

2.5 Pre-processing directives

The term "pre-processing directives" in C# is used for consistency with the C programming language only. In C#, there is no separate pre-processing step; pre-processing directives are processed as part of the lexical analysis phase.

Pre-processing directives always begin with a '#' character, which must be at the beginning of the line, excepting whitespace. Whitespace may optionally occur between the '#' and the following identifier.

pp-directive:
   pp-declaration
   pp-conditional-compilation
   pp-line-number
   pp-diagnostic-line
   pp-region

For *pp-declaration*, *pp-conditional-compilation*, and *pp-line-number* directives, the rest of the line is lexically analyzed according the usual rules, and comments and white-space are ignored. It is illegal for an input element (such as a regular comment) to be unterminated at the end of the line.

For *pp-diagnostic-line* and *pp-region* directives, the rest of the line is not lexically analyzed.

2.5.1 Pre-processing identifiers

Pre-processing identifiers employ a grammar similar to the grammar used for regular C# identifiers:

pp-identifier:
   An *identifier-or-keyword* that is not `true` or `false`

The symbols `true` and `false` are not legal pre-processing identifiers, and so cannot be defined with `#define` or undefined with `#undef`.

2.5.2 Pre-processing expressions

The operators `!`, `==`, `!=`, `&&` and `||` are permitted in pre-processing expressions. Parentheses can be used for grouping in pre-processing expressions. Pre-processing expressions are evaluated at compile-time according to the same rules as boolean expressions are evaluated at run-time. An identifier that is "defined" (section 2.5.3) evaluates as `true`, otherwise as `false`.

pp-expression:
   pp-equality-expression

pp-primary-expression:
   `true`
   `false`
   pp-identifier
   `(` *pp-expression* `)`

pp-unary-expression:
   pp-primary-expression
   ! *pp-unary-expression*

pp-equality-expression:
   pp-equality-expression == *pp-logical-and-expression*
   pp-equality-expression != *pp-logical-and-expression*

pp-logical-and-expression:
   pp-unary-expression
   pp-logical-and-expression && *pp-unary-expression*

pp-logical-or-expression:
   pp-logical-and-expression
   pp-logical-or-expression || *pp-logical-and-expression*

2.5.3 Pre-processing declarations

Names can be defined and undefined for use in pre-processing. A #define defines an identifier within the scope of a file. A #undef "undefines" an identifier within the scope of a file—if the identifier was defined earlier then it becomes undefined. If an identifier is defined then it is semantically equivalent to true; if an identifier is undefined then it is semantically equivalent to false.

Note that defining a pre-processing identifier with #define has no impact on any uses of that identifier outside of pre-processing directives.

pp-declaration:
   # define *pp-identifier new-line*
   # undef *pp-identifier new-line*

The example:

```
#define A
#undef B
class C
{
#if A
   void F() {}
#else
   void G() {}
#endif
#if B
   void H() {}
#else
   void I() {}
#endif
}
```

becomes:

```
class C
{
   void F() {}
   void I() {}
}
```

A *pp-declaration* is restricted to occur before any tokens in the input file. In other words, #define and #undef must precede any "real code" in the file, or a compile-time error occurs. Thus, it is possible to intersperse #if and #define as in the example below:

```
#define A
#if A
   #define B
#endif
namespace N
{
   #if B
   class Class1 {}
   #endif
}
```

The following example is illegal because a #define follows real code:

```
#define A
namespace N
{
   #define B
   #if B
   class Class1 {}
   #endif
}
```

A #undef may "undefine" a name that is not defined. The example below defines a name and then undefines it twice; the second #undef has no effect but is still legal.

```
#define A
#undef A
#undef A
```

2.5.4 #if, #elif, #else, #endif

pp-conditional-compilation:
    # if *pp-expression new-line*
    # elif *pp-expression new-line*
    # else *new-line group*_{opt}
    # endif *new-line*

A set of *pp-conditional-compilation* directives are used to conditionally include or exclude portions of program text. The *pp-conditional-compilation* directives must occur in order, as follows: exactly one #if directive, zero or more #elif directives, zero or one #else directive, and exactly one #endif directive. Sets of *pp-conditional-compilation* directives can nest, as long as one complete set occurs entirely between two directives of the containing set.

When a set of *pp-conditional-compilation* directives is processed, it causes some of the text between directives to be included, or subject to lexical analysis, and some to be excluded, and not subject to any further processing. The text to be included or excluded is the text that lies strictly between the *pp-conditional-compilation* directives. The affected text is included or excluded before being subject to lexical analysis; if excluded, it is not scanned for input elements such as comments, literals, or other tokens.

Text is included or excluded according to the results of evaluating the expression(s) in the directives as follows:

- If the *pp-expression* on the #if directive evaluates to true, then the text between the #if and the next *pp-conditional-compilation* directive in the set is included, and all other text between the #if and the #endif directive is excluded.

- Otherwise, if any #elif directives are present, then the *pp-expression*s associated with them are evaluated in order. If any evaluates to true, then the text between the first #elif directive that evaluates to true and the next *pp-conditional-compilation* directive in the set is included, and all other text between the #if and the #endif directives is excluded.

- Otherwise, if an #else directive is present, then the text between the #else directive and the #endif directive is included, and all other text between the #if and the #endif directives is excluded.

- Otherwise, all of the text between the #if and the #endif directives is excluded.

The example:

```
#define Debug
class Class1
{
#if Debug
    void Trace(string s) {}
#endif
}
```

becomes:

```
class Class1
{
    void Trace(string s) {}
}
```

If sections can nest. Example:

```
#define Debug      // Debugging on
#undef Trace       // Tracing off
class PurchaseTransaction
{
   void Commit() {
      #if Debug
         CheckConsistency();
         #if Trace
            WriteToLog(this.ToString());
         #endif
      #endif
      CommitHelper();
   }
}
```

Text that is not included is not subject to lexical analysis. For example, the following is legal despite the unterminated comment in the "#else" section:

```
#define Debug      // Debugging on
class PurchaseTransaction
{
   void Commit() {
      #if Debug
         CheckConsistency();
      #else
         /* Do something else
      #endif
   }
}
```

Pre-processing directives are not processed if they appear inside other input elements. For example, the following program:

```
class Hello
{
   static void Main() {
      System.Console.WriteLine(@"hello,
#if Debug
      world
#else
      Nebraska
#endif
      ");
   }
}
```

produces the following output

```
hello,
#if Debug
        world
#else
        Nebraska
#endif
```

2.5.5 #error and #warning

The #error and #warning directives enable code to report error and warning conditions to the compiler for integration with standard compile-time errors and warnings.

pp-diagnostic-line:
    # error *pp-message*
    # warning *pp-message*

pp-message:
    pp-message-characters new-line

pp-message-characters:
    pp-mesage-character
    pp-message-characters pp-message-character

pp-message-character:
    Any character except *new-line*

The example

```
#warning Code review needed before check-in
#define DEBUG
#if DEBUG && RETAIL
    #error A build can't be both debug and retail!
#endif
class Class1
{...}
```

always produces a warning ("Code review needed before check-in"), and produces an error if the pre-processing identifiers DEBUG and RETAIL are both defined.

2.5.6 #region and #endregion

pp-region:
    # region *pp-message*
    # endregion *pp-message*

The #region and #endregion directives bracket a "region" of code. No semantic meaning is attached to a region; regions are intended for use by the programmer or automated tools to mark a piece of code. The message attached to the #region and #endregion has no semantic meaning; it merely serves to identify the region. Each source file must have an equal number of #region and #endregion directives, and each #region must be matched with a #endregion later in the file.

#region and #endregion must nest properly with respect to conditional compilation directives. More precisely, it is illegal for a *pp-conditional-compilation* directive to occur between a #region directive and it's matching #endregion directive, unless all of the *pp-conditional-compilation* directives of the set occur between #region and #endregion.

2.5.7 #line

The #line feature enables a developer to alter the line number and source file names that are used by the compiler in output such as warnings and errors. If no line directives are present then the line number and file name are determined automatically by the compiler. The #line directive is most commonly used in meta-programming tools that generate C# source code from some other text input. After a #line directive, the compiler treats the line *after* the directive as having the given line number (and file name, if specified).

pp-line-number:
    # line *integer-literal*
    # line *integer-literal file-name*

file-name:
    " *file-name-characters* "

file-name-characters:
    file-name-character
    file-name-characters file-name-character

file-name-character:
    Any character except " (U+0022), and *new-line*

Note that a *file-name* differs from an ordinary string literal in that escape characters are not processed; the '\' character simply designates an ordinary back-slash character within a *file-name*.

3. Basic concepts

3.1 Program Startup

Program startup occurs when the execution environment calls a designated method, which is referred to as the program's ***entry point***. This entry point method is always named `Main`, and can have one of the following signatures:

```
static void Main() {…}
static void Main(string[] args) {…}
static int Main() {…}
static int Main(string[] args) {…}
```

As shown, the entry point may optionally return an `int` value. This return value is used in program termination (section 3.2).

The entry point may optionally have one formal parameter, and this formal parameter may have any name. If such a parameter is declared, it must obey the following constraints:

- The value of this parameter must not be `null`.
- Let `args` be the name of the parameter. If the length of the array designated by `args` is greater than zero, the array members `args[0]` through `args[args.Length-1]`, inclusive, must refer to strings, called ***program parameters***, which are given implementation-defined values by the host environment prior to program startup. The intent is to supply to the program information determined prior to program startup from elsewhere in the hosted environment. If the host environment is not capable of supplying strings with letters in both uppercase and lowercase, the implementation shall ensure that the strings are received in lowercase.

Since C# supports method overloading, a class or struct may contain multiple definitions of some method, provided each has a different signature. However, within a single program, no class or struct shall contain more than one method called `Main` whose definition qualifies it to be used as a program entry point. Other overloaded versions of `Main` are permitted, provided they have more than one parameter, or their only parameter is other than type `string[]`.

A program can be made up of multiple classes or structs, two or more of which contain a method called `Main` whose definition qualifies it to be used as a program entry point. In such cases, one of these `Main` methods must be chosen as the entry point so that program startup can occur. This choice of an entry point is beyond the scope of this specification—no mechanism for specifying or determining an entry point is provided.

In C#, every method must be defined as a member of a class or struct. Ordinarily, the declared accessibility (section 3.5.1) of a method is determined by the access modifiers (section 10.2.3) specified in its declaration, and similarly the declared accessibility of a type is determined by the access modifiers specified in its declaration. In order for a given method of a given type to be callable, both the type and the member must be accessible. However, the program entry point is a special case. Specifically, the execution environment can access the program's entry point regardless of its declared accessibility and regardless of the declared accessibility of its enclosing type declarations.

In all other respects, entry point methods behave like those that are not entry points.

3.2 Program Termination

Program termination returns control to the execution environment.

If the return type of the program's **entry point** method is int, the value returned serves as the program's **termination status code**. The purpose of this code is to allow communication of success or failure to the execution environment.

If the return type of the entry point method is void, reaching the right brace (}) which terminates that method, or executing a return statement that has no expression, results in a termination status code of 0.

Prior to a program's termination, finalizers for all of its objects that have not yet been finalized are called, unless such finalization has been suppressed. (The means by which a finalizer can be suppressed is outside the scope of this specification.)

3.3 Declarations

Declarations in a C# program define the constituent elements of the program. C# programs are organized using namespaces (section 9), which can contain type declarations and nested namespace declarations. Type declarations (section 9.5) are used to define classes (section 10), structs (section 11), interfaces (section 13), enums (section 14), and delegates (section 15). The kinds of members permitted in a type declaration depends on the form of the type declaration. For instance, class declarations can contain declarations for instance constructors (section 10.10), destructors (section 10.12), static constructors (section 10.11), constants (section 10.3), fields (section 10.4), methods (section 10.5), properties (section 10.6), events (section 10.7), indexers (section 10.8), operators (section 10.9), and nested types.

A declaration defines a name in the **declaration space** to which the declaration belongs. Except for overloaded constructor, method, indexer, and operator names, it is an error to have two or more declarations that introduce members with the same name in a declaration space. It is never possible for a declaration space to contain different kinds of members with the same name. For example, a declaration space can never contain a field and a method by the same name.

There are several different types of declaration spaces, as described in the following.

- Within all source files of a program, *namespace-member-declaration*s with no enclosing *namespaoe-deolaration* are members of a single combined declaration space called the **global declaration space**.

- Within all source files of a program, *namespace-member-declaration*s within *namespace-declaration*s that have the same fully qualified namespace name are members of a single combined declaration space.

- Each class, struct, or interface declaration creates a new declaration space. Names are introduced into this declaration space through *class-member-declaration*s, *struct-member-declaration*s, or *interface-member-declaration*s. Except for overloaded constructor declarations and static constructor declarations, a class or struct member declaration cannot introduce a member by the same name as the class or struct. A class, struct, or interface permits the declaration of overloaded methods and indexers. A class or struct furthermore permits the declaration of overloaded constructors and operators. For instance, a class, struct, or interface may contain multiple method declarations with the same name, provided these method declarations differ in their signature (section 3.6). Note that base classes do not contribute to the declaration space of a class, and base interfaces do not contribute to the declaration space of an interface. Thus, a derived class or interface is allowed to declare a member with the same name as an inherited member. Such a member is said to **hide** the inherited member.

- Each enumeration declaration creates a new declaration space. Names are introduced into this declaration space through *enum-member-declaration*s.

- Each *block* or *switch-block* creates a separate declaration space for local variables. Names are introduced into this declaration space through *local-variable-declaration*s. If a block is the body of a constructor or method declaration, the parameters declared in the *formal-parameter-list* are members of the block's **local variable declaration space**. The local variable declaration space of a block includes any nested blocks. Thus, within a nested block it is not possible to declare a local variable with the same name as a local variable in an enclosing block.

- Each *block* or *switch-block* creates a separate declaration space for labels. Names are introduced into this declaration space through *labeled-statement*s, and the names are referenced through *goto-statement*s. The **label declaration space** of a block includes any nested blocks. Thus, within a nested block it is not possible to declare a label with the same name as a label in an enclosing block.

The textual order in which names are declared is generally of no significance. In particular, textual order is not significant for the declaration and use of namespaces, types, constants, methods, properties, events, indexers, operators, constructors, destructors, and static constructors. Declaration order is significant in the following ways:

- Declaration order for field declarations and local variable declarations determines the order in which their initializers (if any) are executed.
- Local variables must be defined before they are used (section 3.7).
- Declaration order for enum member declarations (section 14.2) is significant when *constant-expression* values are omitted.

The declaration space of a namespace is "open ended", and two namespace declarations with the same fully qualified name contribute to the same declaration space. For example

```
namespace Megacorp.Data
{
    class Customer
    {
        ...
    }
}
namespace Megacorp.Data
{
    class Order
    {
        ...
    }
}
```

The two namespace declarations above contribute to the same declaration space, in this case declaring two classes with the fully qualified names `Megacorp.Data.Customer` and `Megacorp.Data.Order`. Because the two declarations contribute to the same declaration space, it would have been an error if each contained a declaration of a class with the same name.

The declaration space of a block includes any nested blocks. Thus, in the following example, the `F` and `G` methods are in error because the name `i` is declared in the outer block and cannot be redeclared in the inner block. However, the `H` and `I` methods are valid since the two `i`'s are declared in separate non-nested blocks.

```
class A
{
   void F() {
      int i = 0;
      if (true) {
         int i = 1;
      }
   }
void G() {
      if (true) {
         int i = 0;
      }
      int i = 1;
   }
void H() {
      if (true) {
         int i = 0;
      }
      if (true) {
         int i = 1;
      }
   }
void I() {
      for (int i = 0; i < 10; i++)
         H();
      for (int i = 0; i < 10; i++)
         H();
   }
}
```

3.4 Members

Namespaces and types have *members*. The members of an entity are generally available through the use of a qualified name that starts with a reference to the entity, followed by a "." token, followed by the name of the member.

Members of a type are either declared in the type or *inherited* from the base class of the type. When a type inherits from a base class, all members of the base class, except constructors and destructors, become members of the derived type. The declared accessibility of a base class member does not control whether the member is inherited—inheritance extends to any member that isn't a constructor or destructor. However, an inherited member may not be accessible in a derived type, either because of its declared accessibility (section 3.5.1) or because it is hidden by a declaration in the type itself (section 3.7.1.2).

3.4.1 Namespace members

Namespaces and types that have no enclosing namespace are members of the *global namespace*. This corresponds directly to the names declared in the global declaration space.

Namespaces and types declared within a namespace are members of that namespace. This corresponds directly to the names declared in the declaration space of the namespace.

Namespaces have no access restrictions. It is not possible to declare private, protected, or internal namespaces, and namespace names are always publicly accessible.

3.4.2 Struct members

The members of a struct are the members declared in the struct and the members inherited from class `object`.

The members of a simple type correspond directly to the members of the struct type aliased by the simple type:

- The members of `sbyte` are the members of the `System.SByte` struct.
- The members of `byte` are the members of the `System.Byte` struct.
- The members of `short` are the members of the `System.Int16` struct.
- The members of `ushort` are the members of the `System.UInt16` struct.
- The members of `int` are the members of the `System.Int32` struct.
- The members of `uint` are the members of the `System.UInt32` struct.
- The members of `long` are the members of the `System.Int64` struct.
- The members of `ulong` are the members of the `System.UInt64` struct.
- The members of `char` are the members of the `System.Char` struct.
- The members of `float` are the members of the `System.Single` struct.
- The members of `double` are the members of the `System.Double` struct.
- The members of `decimal` are the members of the `System.Decimal` struct.
- The members of `bool` are the members of the `System.Boolean` struct.

3.4.3 Enumeration members

The members of an enumeration are the constants declared in the enumeration and the members inherited from class `object`.

3.4.4 Class members

The members of a class are the members declared in the class and the members inherited from the base class (except for class `object` which has no base class). The members inherited from the base class include the constants, fields, methods, properties, events, indexers, operators, and types of the base class, but not the constructors, destructors, and static constructors of the base class. Base class members are inherited without regard to their accessibility.

A class declaration may contain declarations of constants, fields, methods, properties, events, indexers, operators, constructors, destructors, static constructors, and types.

The members of `object` and `string` correspond directly to the members of the class types they alias:

- The members of `object` are the members of the `System.Object` class.
- The members of `string` are the members of the `System.String` class.

3.4.5 Interface members

The members of an interface are the members declared in the interface and in all base interfaces of the interface, and the members inherited from class `object`.

3.4.6 Array members

The members of an array are the members inherited from class `System.Array`.

3.4.7 Delegate members

The members of a delegate are the members inherited from class `System.Delegate`.

3.5 Member access

Declarations of members allow control over member access. The accessibility of a member is established by the declared accessibility (section 3.5.1) of the member combined with the accessibility of the immediately containing type, if any.

When access to a particular member is allowed, the member is said to be **accessible**. Conversely, when access to a particular member is disallowed, the member is said to be **inaccessible**. Access to a member is permitted when the textual location in which the access takes place is included in the accessibility domain (section 3.5.2) of the member.

3.5.1 Declared accessibility

The *declared accessibility* of a member can be one of the following:

- Public, which is selected by including a `public` modifier in the member declaration. The intuitive meaning of `public` is "access not limited".

- Protected internal (meaning protected or internal), which is selected by including both a `protected` and an `internal` modifier in the member declaration. The intuitive meaning of `protected internal` is "access limited to this program or types derived from the containing class".

- Protected, which is selected by including a `protected` modifier in the member declaration. The intuitive meaning of `protected` is "access limited to the containing class or types derived from the containing class".

- Internal, which is selected by including an `internal` modifier in the member declaration. The intuitive meaning of `internal` is "access limited to this program".

- Private, which is selected by including a `private` modifier in the member declaration. The intuitive meaning of `private` is "access limited to the containing type".

Depending on the context in which a member declaration takes place, only certain types of declared accessibility are permitted. Furthermore, when a member declaration does not include any access modifiers, the context in which the declaration takes place determines the default declared accessibility.

- Namespaces implicitly have `public` declared accessibility. No access modifiers are allowed on namespace declarations.

- Types declared in compilation units or namespaces can have `public` or `internal` declared accessibility and default to `internal` declared accessibility.

- Class members can have any of the five types of declared accessibility and default to `private` declared accessibility. (Note that a type declared as a member of a class can have any of the five types of declared accessibility, whereas a type declared as a member of a namespace can have only `public` or `internal` declared accessibility.)

- Struct members can have `public`, `internal`, or `private` declared accessibility and default to `private` declared accessibility. Struct members cannot have `protected` or `protected internal` declared accessibility.

- Interface members implicitly have `public` declared accessibility. No access modifiers are allowed on interface member declarations.

- Enumeration members implicitly have `public` declared accessibility. No access modifiers are allowed on enumeration member declarations.

3.5.2 Accessibility domains

The *accessibility domain* of a member is the (possibly disjoint) sections of program text in which access to the member is permitted. For purposes of defining the accessibility domain of a member, a member is said to be top-level if it is not declared within a type, and a member is said to be nested if it is declared within another type. Furthermore, the program text of a program is defined as all program text contained in all source files of the program, and the program text of a type is defined as all program text contained between the opening and closing "{" and "}" tokens in the *class-body*, *struct-body*, *interface-body*, or *enum-body* of the type (including, possibly, types that are nested within the type).

The accessibility domain of a predefined type (such as `object`, `int`, or `double`) is unlimited.

The accessibility domain of a top-level type `T` declared in a program `P` is defined as follows:

- If the declared accessibility of `T` is `public`, the accessibility domain of `T` is the program text of `P` and any program that references `P`.
- If the declared accessibility of `T` is `internal`, the accessibility domain of `T` is the program text of `P`.

From these definitions it follows that the accessibility domain of a top-level type is always at least the program text of the program in which the type is declared.

The accessibility domain of a nested member `M` declared in a type `T` within a program `P` is defined as follows (noting that M may itself possibly be a type):

- If the declared accessibility of `M` is `public`, the accessibility domain of `M` is the accessibility domain of `T`.
- If the declared accessibility of `M` is `protected internal`, the accessibility domain of `M` is the intersection of the accessibility domain of `T` with the program text of `P` and the program text of any type derived from `T` declared outside `P`.
- If the declared accessibility of `M` is `protected`, the accessibility domain of `M` is the intersection of the accessibility domain of `T` with the program text of `T` and any type derived from `T`.
- If the declared accessibility of `M` is `internal`, the accessibility domain of `M` is the intersection of the accessibility domain of `T` with the program text of `P`.
- If the declared accessibility of `M` is `private`, the accessibility domain of `M` is the program text of `T`.

From these definitions it follows that the accessibility domain of a nested member is always at least the program text of the type in which the member is declared. Furthermore, it follows that the accessibility domain of a member is never more inclusive than the accessibility domain of the type in which the member is declared.

In intuitive terms, when a type or member M is accessed, the following steps are evaluated to ensure that the access is permitted:

- First, if M is declared within a type (as opposed to a compilation unit or a namespace), an error occurs if that type is not accessible.
- Then, if M is public, the access is permitted.
- Otherwise, if M is protected internal, the access is permitted if it occurs within the program in which M is declared, or if it occurs within a class derived from the class in which M is declared and takes place through the derived class type (section 3.5.3).
- Otherwise, if M is protected, the access is permitted if it occurs within the class in which M is declared, or if it occurs within a class derived from the class in which M is declared and takes place through the derived class type (section 3.5.3).
- Otherwise, if M is internal, the access is permitted if it occurs within the program in which M is declared.
- Otherwise, if M is private, the access is permitted if it occurs within the type in which M is declared.
- Otherwise, the type or member is inaccessible, and an error occurs.

In the example

```
public class A
{
   public static int X;
   internal static int Y;
   private static int Z;
}
internal class B
{
   public static int X;
   internal static int Y;
   private static int Z;
   public class C
   {
      public static int X;
      internal static int Y;
      private static int Z;
   }
   private class D
   {
      public static int X;
      internal static int Y;
      private static int Z;
   }
}
```

the classes and members have the following accessibility domains:

- The accessibility domain of A and A.X is unlimited.
- The accessibility domain of A.Y, B, B.X, B.Y, B.C, B.C.X, and B.C.Y is the program text of the containing program.
- The accessibility domain of A.Z is the program text of A.
- The accessibility domain of B.Z and B.D is the program text of B, including the program text of B.C and B.D.
- The accessibility domain of B.C.Z is the program text of B.C.
- The accessibility domain of B.D.X, B.D.Y, and B.D.Z is the program text of B.D.

As the example illustrates, the accessibility domain of a member is never larger than that of a containing type. For example, even though all X members have public declared accessibility, all but A.X have accessibility domains that are constrained by a containing type.

As described in section 3.4, all members of a base class, except for constructors and destructors, are inherited by derived types. This includes even private members of a base class. However, the accessibility domain of a private member includes only the program text of the type in which the member is declared. In the example

```
class A
{
   int x;
   static void F(B b) {
      b.x = 1;    // Ok
   }
}
class B: A
{
   static void F(B b) {
      b.x = 1;    // Error, x not accessible
   }
}
```

the B class inherits the private member x from the A class. Because the member is private, it is only accessible within the *class-body* of A. Thus, the access to b.x succeeds in the A.F method, but fails in the B.F method.

3.5.3 Protected access

When a `protected` member is accessed outside the program text of the class in which it is declared, and when a `protected internal` member is accessed outside the program text of the program in which it is declared, the access is required to take place *through* the derived class type in which the access occurs. Let B be a base class that declares a protected member M, and let D be a class that derives from B. Within the *class-body* of D, access to M can take one of the following forms:

- An unqualified *type-name* or *primary-expression* of the form M.
- A *type-name* of the form T.M, provided T is D or a class derived from D.
- A *primary-expression* of the form E.M, provided the type of E is D or a class derived from D.
- A *primary-expression* of the form base.M.

In addition to these forms of access, a derived class can access a protected constructor of a base class in a *constructor-initializer* (section 10.10.1).

In the example

```
public class A
{
    protected int x;
    static void F(A a, B b) {
        a.x = 1;    // Ok
        b.x = 1;    // Ok
    }
}
public class B: A
{
    static void F(A a, B b) {
        a.x = 1;    // Error, must access through instance of B
        b.x = 1;    // Ok
    }
}
```

within A, it is possible to access x through instances of both A and B, since in either case the access takes place *through* an instance of A or a class derived from A. However, within B, it is not possible to access x through an instance of A, since A does not derive from B.

3.5.4 Accessibility constraints

Several constructs In the C# language require a type to be *at least as accessible as* a member or another type. A type T is said to be at least as accessible as a member or type M if the accessibility domain of T is a superset of the accessibility domain of M. In other words, T is at least as accessible as M if T is accessible in all contexts where M is accessible.

The following accessibility constraints exist:

- The direct base class of a class type must be at least as accessible as the class type itself.
- The explicit base interfaces of an interface type must be at least as accessible as the interface type itself.
- The return type and parameter types of a delegate type must be at least as accessible as the delegate type itself.
- The type of a constant must be at least as accessible as the constant itself.
- The type of a field must be at least as accessible as the field itself.
- The return type and parameter types of a method must be at least as accessible as the method itself.
- The type of a property must be at least as accessible as the property itself.
- The type of an event must be at least as accessible as the event itself.
- The type and parameter types of an indexer must be at least as accessible as the indexer itself.
- The return type and parameter types of an operator must be at least as accessible as the operator itself.
- The parameter types of a constructor must be at least as accessible as the constructor itself.

In the example

```
class A {…}
public class B: A {…}
```

the B class is in error because A is not at least as accessible as B.

Likewise, in the example

```
class A {…}
public class B
{
    A F() {…}
    internal A G() {…}
    public A H() {…}
}
```

the H method in B is in error because the return type A is not at least as accessible as the method.

3.6 Signatures and overloading

Methods, constructors, indexers, and operators are characterized by their *signatures*:

- The signature of a method consists of the name of the method and the type and kind (value, reference, or output) of each of its formal parameters. The signature of a method specifically does not include the return type, nor does it include the `params` modifier that may be specified for the last parameter.

- The signature of a constructor consists of the type and kind (value, reference, or output) of each of its formal parameters. The signature of a constructor specifically does not include the `params` modifier that may be specified for the last parameter.

- The signature of an indexer consists of the type of each of its formal parameters. The signature of an indexer specifically does not include the element type.

- The signature of an operator consists of the name of the operator and the type of each of its formal parameters. The signature of an operator specifically does not include the result type.

Signatures are the enabling mechanism for *overloading* of members in classes, structs, and interfaces:

- Overloading of methods permits a class, struct, or interface to declare multiple methods with the same name, provided the signatures of the methods are all unique.

- Overloading of constructors permits a class or struct to declare multiple constructors, provided the signatures of the constructors are all unique.

- Overloading of indexers permits a class, struct, or interface to declare multiple indexers, provided the signatures of the indexers are all unique.

- Overloading of operators permits a class or struct to declare multiple operators with the same name, provided the signatures of the operators are all unique.

The following example shows a set of overloaded method declarations along with their signatures.

```
interface ITest
{
    void F();                      // F()
    void F(int x);                 // F(int)
    void F(ref int x);             // F(ref int)
    void F(out int x);             // F(out int)
    void F(int x, int y);          // F(int, int)
    int F(string s);               // F(string)
    int F(int x);                  // F(int)
    void F(string[] a);            // F(string[])
    void F(params string[] a);     // F(string[])
}
```

Note that the `ref` and `out` parameter modifiers (section 10.5.1) are part of a signature. Thus, `F(int)`, `F(ref int)`, and `F(out int)` are all unique signatures. Also note that the return type and the `params` modifier are not part of a signature, and that it is not possible to overload solely based on return type or solely based on the inclusion or exclusion of the `params` modifier. Because of these restrictions, compiling the above example would produce errors for the methods with the duplicate signatures `F(int)` and `F(string[])`.

3.7 Scopes

The **scope** of a name is the region of program text within which it is possible to refer to the entity declared by the name without qualification of the name. Scopes can be **nested**, and an inner scope may redeclare the meaning of a name from an outer scope. The name from the outer scope is then said to be **hidden** in the region of program text covered by the inner scope, and access to the outer name is only possible by qualifying the name.

- The scope of a namespace member declared by a *namespace-member-declaration* with no enclosing *namespace-declaration* is the entire program text of each compilation unit.

- The scope of a namespace member declared by a *namespace-member-declaration* within a *namespace-declaration* whose fully qualified name is N is the *namespace-body* of every *namespace-declaration* whose fully qualified name is N or starts with the same sequence of identifiers as N.

- The scope of a name defined or imported by a *using-directive* extends over the *namespace-member-declarations* of the *compilation-unit* or *namespace-body* in which the *using-directive* occurs. A *using-directive* may make zero or more namespace or type names available within a particular *compilation-unit* or *namespace-body*, but does not contribute any new members to the underlying declaration space. In other words, a *using-directive* is not transitive but rather affects only the *compilation-unit* or *namespace-body* in which it occurs.

- The scope of a member declared by a *class-member-declaration* is the *class-body* in which the declaration occurs. In addition, the scope of a class member extends to the *class-body* of those derived classes that are included in the accessibility domain (section 3.5.2) of the member.

- The scope of a member declared by a *struct-member-declaration* is the *struct-body* in which the declaration occurs.

- The scope of a member declared by an *enum-member-declaration* is the *enum-body* in which the declaration occurs.

- The scope of a parameter declared in a *constructor-declaration* is the *constructor-initializer* and *block* of that *constructor-declaration*.

- The scope of a parameter declared in a *method-declaration* is the *method-body* of that *method-declaration*.

- The scope of a parameter declared in an *indexer-declaration* is the *accessor-declarations* of that *indexer-declaration*.

- The scope of a parameter declared in an *operator-declaration* is the *block* of that *operator-declaration*.

- The scope of a local variable declared in a *local-variable-declaration* is the block in which the declaration occurs. It is an error to refer to a local variable in a textual position that precedes the *variable-declarator* of the local variable.

- The scope of a local variable declared in a *for-initializer* of a `for` statement is the *for-initializer*, the *for-condition*, the *for-iterator*, and the contained *statement* of the `for` statement.

- The scope of a label declared in a *labeled-statement* is the *block* in which the declaration occurs.

Within the scope of a namespace, class, struct, or enumeration member it is possible to refer to the member in a textual position that precedes the declaration of the member. For example

```
class A
{
   void F() {
      i = 1;
   }
   int i = 0;
}
```

Here, it is valid for F to refer to i before it is declared.

Within the scope of a local variable, it is an error to refer to the local variable in a textual position that precedes the *variable-declarator* of the local variable. For example

```
class A
{
    int i = 0;
    void F() {
        i = 1;                      // Error, use precedes declaration
        int i;
        i = 2;
    }
    void G() {
        int j = (j = 1);       // Legal
    }
    void H() {
        int a = 1, b = ++a;  // Legal
    }
}
```

In the F method above, the first assignment to i specifically does not refer to the field declared in the outer scope. Rather, it refers to the local variable and it is in error because it textually precedes the declaration of the variable. In the G method, the use of j in the initializer for the declaration of j is legal because the use does not precede the *variable-declarator*. In the H method, a subsequent *variable-declarator* legally refers to a local variable declared in an earlier *variable-declarator* within the same *local-variable-declaration*.

The scoping rules for local variables are designed to guarantee that the meaning of a name used in an expression context is always the same within a block. If the scope of a local variable was to extend only from its declaration to the end of the block, then in the example above, the first assignment would assign to the instance variable and the second assignment would assign to the local variable, possibly leading to errors if the statements of the block were later to be rearranged.

The meaning of a name within a block may differ based on the context in which the name is used. In the example

```
class Test
{
    static void Main() {
        string A = "hello, world";
        string s = A;                       // expression context
        Type t = typeof(A);                 // type context
        Console.WriteLine(s);               // writes "hello, world"
        Console.WriteLine(t.ToString());     // writes "Type: A"
    }
}
```

the name A is used in an expression context to refer to the local variable A and in a type context to refer to the class A.

3.7.1 Name hiding

The scope of an entity typically encompasses more program text than the declaration space of the entity. In particular, the scope of an entity may include declarations that introduce new declaration spaces containing entities of the same name. Such declarations cause the original entity to become **hidden**. Conversely, an entity is said to be **visible** when it is not hidden.

Name hiding occurs when scopes overlap through nesting and when scopes overlap through inheritance. The characteristics of the two types of hiding are described in the following sections.

3.7.1.1 Hiding through nesting

Name hiding through nesting can occur as a result of nesting namespaces or types within namespaces, as a result of nesting types within classes or structs, and as a result of parameter and local variable declarations. Name hiding through nesting of scopes always occurs "silently", i.e., no errors or warnings are reported when outer names are hidden by inner names.

In the example

```
class A
{
    int i = 0;
    void F() {
        int i = 1;
    }
    void G() {
        i = 1;
    }
}
```

within the F method, the instance variable i is hidden by the local variable i, but within the G method, i still refers to the instance variable.

When a name in an inner scope hides a name in an outer scope, it hides all overloaded occurrences of that name. In the example

```
class Outer
{
    static void F(int i) {}
    static void F(string s) {}
    class Inner
    {
```

```
    void G() {
        F(1);           // Invokes Outer.Inner.F
        F("Hello");     // Error
    }
    static void F(long l) {}
  }
}
```

the call `F(1)` invokes the `F` declared in `Inner` because all outer occurrences of `F` are hidden by the inner declaration. For the same reason, the call `F("Hello")` is in error.

3.7.1.2 Hiding through inheritance

Name hiding through inheritance occurs when classes or structs redeclare names that were inherited from base classes. This type of name hiding takes one of the following forms:

- A constant, field, property, event, or type introduced in a class or struct hides all base class members with the same name.
- A method introduced in a class or struct hides all non-method base class members with the same name, and all base class methods with the same signature (method name and parameter count, modifiers, and types).
- An indexer introduced in a class or struct hides all base class indexers with the same signature (parameter count and types).

The rules governing operator declarations (section 10.9) make it impossible for a derived class to declare an operator with the same signature as an operator in a base class. Thus, operators never hide one another.

Contrary to hiding a name from an outer scope, hiding an accessible name from an inherited scope causes a warning to be reported. In the example

```
class Base
{
    public void F() {}
}
class Derived: Base
{
    public void F() {}      // Warning, hiding an inherited name
}
```

the declaration of F in Derived causes a warning to be reported. Hiding an inherited name is specifically not an error, since that would preclude separate evolution of base classes. For example, the above situation might have come about because a later version of Base introduced an F method that wasn't present in an earlier version of the class. Had the above situation been an error, then *any* change made to a base class in a separately versioned class library could potentially cause derived classes to become invalid.

The warning caused by hiding an inherited name can be eliminated through use of the new modifier:

```
class Base
{
    public void F() {}
}
class Derived: Base
{
    new public void F() {}
}
```

The new modifier indicates that the F in Derived is "new", and that it is indeed intended to hide the inherited member.

A declaration of a new member hides an inherited member only within the scope of the new member.

```
class Base
{
    public static void F() {}
}
class Derived: Base
{
    new private static void F() {}  // Hides Base.F in Derived only
}
class MoreDerived: Derived
{
    static void G() { F(); }        // Invokes Base.F
}
```

In the example above, the declaration of F in Derived hides the F that was inherited from Base, but since the new F in Derived has private access, its scope does not extend to MoreDerived. Thus, the call F() in MoreDerived.G is valid and will invoke Base.F.

3.8 Namespace and type names

Several contexts in a C# program require a *namespace-name* or a *type-name* to be specified. Either form of name is written as one or more identifiers separated by "." tokens.

namespace-name:
   namespace-or-type-name

type-name:
   namespace-or-type-name

namespace-or-type-name:
   identifier
   namespace-or-type-name . *identifier*

A *type-name* is a *namespace-or-type-name* that refers to a type. Following resolution as described below, the *namespace-or-type-name* of a *type-name* must refer to a type, or otherwise an error occurs.

A *namespace-name* is a *namespace-or-type-name* that refers to a namespace. Following resolution as described below, the *namespace-or-type-name* of a *namespace-name* must refer to a namespace, or otherwise an error occurs.

The meaning of a *namespace-or-type-name* is determined as follows:

- If the *namespace-or-type-name* consists of a single identifier:
  - If the *namespace-or-type-name* appears within the body of a class or struct declaration, then starting with that class or struct declaration and continuing with each enclosing class or struct declaration (if any), if a member with the given name exists, is accessible, and denotes a type, then the *namespace-or-type-name* refers to that member. Note that non-type members (constructors, constants, fields, methods, properties, indexers, and operators) are ignored when determining the meaning of a *namespace-or-type-name*.
  - Otherwise, starting with the namespace declaration in which the *namespace-or-type-name* occurs (if any), continuing with each enclosing namespace declaration (if any), and ending with the global namespace, the following steps are evaluated until an entity is located:
    - If the namespace contains a namespace member with the given name, then the *namespace-or-type-name* refers to that member and, depending on the member, is classified as a namespace or a type.
    - Otherwise, if the namespace declaration contains a *using-alias-directive* that associates the given name with an imported namespace or type, then the *namespace-or-type-name* refers to that namespace or type.

- Otherwise, if the namespaces imported by the *using-namespace-directive*s of the namespace declaration contain exactly one type with the given name, then the *namespace-or-type-name* refers to that type.
- Otherwise, if the namespaces imported by the *using-namespace-directive*s of the namespace declaration contain more than one type with the given name, then the *namespace-or-type-name* is ambiguous and an error occurs.
  - Otherwise, the *namespace-or-type-name* is undefined and an error occurs.
- Otherwise, the *namespace-or-type-name* is of the form N.I, where N is a *namespace-or-type-name* consisting of all identifiers but the rightmost one, and I is the rightmost identifier. N is first resolved as a *namespace-or-type-name*. If the resolution of N is not successful, an error occurs. Otherwise, N.I is resolved as follows:
  - If N is a namespace and I is the name of an accessible member of that namespace, then N.I refers to that member and, depending on the member, is classified as a namespace or a type.
  - If N is a class or struct type and I is the name of an accessible type in N, then N.I refers to that type.
  - Otherwise, N.I is an *invalid namespace-or-type-name*, and an error occurs.

3.8.1 Fully qualified names

Every namespace and type has a ***fully qualified name*** which uniquely identifies the namespace or type amongst all others. The fully qualified name of a namespace or type N is determined as follows:

- If N is a member of the global namespace, its fully qualified name is N.
- Otherwise, its fully qualified name is S.N, where S is the fully qualified name of the namespace or type in which N is declared.

In other words, the fully qualified name of N is the complete hierarchical path of identifiers that lead to N, starting from the global namespace. Because every member of a namespace or type must have a unique name, it follows that the fully qualified name of a namespace or type is always unique.

The example below shows several namespace and type declarations along with their associated fully qualified names.

```
class A {}          // A
namespace X         // X
{
    class B         // X.B
    {
        class C {}  // X.B.C
    }
    namespace Y     // X.Y
    {
        class D {}  // X.Y.D
    }
}
namespace X.Y       // X.Y
{
    class E {}      // X.Y.E
}
```

4. Types

The types of the C# language are divided into two categories: Value types and reference types.

type:
   value-type
   reference-type

A third category of types, pointers, is available only in unsafe code. This is discussed further in section A.2.

Value types differ from reference types in that variables of the value types directly contain their data, whereas variables of the reference types store **references** to their data, the latter known as **objects**. With reference types, it is possible for two variables to reference the same object, and thus possible for operations on one variable to affect the object referenced by the other variable. With value types, the variables each have their own copy of the data, and it is not possible for operations on one to affect the other.

C#'s type system is unified such that *a value of any type can be treated as an object*. Every type in C# directly or indirectly derives from the `object` class type, and `object` is the ultimate base class of all types. Values of reference types are treated as objects simply by viewing the values as type `object`. Values of value types are treated as objects by performing boxing and unboxing operations (section 4.3).

4.1 Value types

A value type is either a struct type or an enumeration type. C# provides a set of predefined struct types called the **simple types**. The simple types are identified through reserved words, and are further subdivided into numeric types, integral types, and floating-point types.

value-type:
   struct-type
   enum-type

struct-type:
   type-name
   simple-type

simple-type:
   numeric-type
   `bool`

numeric-type:
    integral-type
    floating-point-type
    `decimal`

integral-type:
    `sbyte`
    `byte`
    `short`
    `ushort`
    `int`
    `uint`
    `long`
    `ulong`
    `char`

floating-point-type:
    `float`
    `double`

enum-type:
    type-name

All value types implicitly inherit from class `object`. It is not possible for any type to derive from a value type, and value types are thus implicitly sealed.

A variable of a value type always contains a value of that type. Unlike reference types, it is not possible for a value of a value type to be `null` or to reference an object of a more derived type.

Assignment to a variable of a value type creates a *copy* of the value being assigned. This differs from assignment to a variable of a reference type, which copies the reference but not the object identified by the reference.

4.1.1 Default constructors

All value types implicitly declare a public parameterless constructor called the ***default constructor***. The default constructor returns a zero-initialized instance known as the ***default value*** for the value type:

- For all *simple-types*, the default value is the value produced by a bit pattern of all zeros:

    - For `sbyte`, `byte`, `short`, `ushort`, `int`, `uint`, `long`, and `ulong`, the default value is `0`.

    - For `char`, the default value is `'\x0000'`.

    - For `float`, the default value is `0.0f`.

    - For `double`, the default value is `0.0d`.

    - For `decimal`, the default value is `0.0m`.

    - For `bool`, the default value is `false`.

- For an *enum-type* E, the default value is 0.
- For a *struct-type*, the default value is the value produced by setting all value type fields to their default value and all reference type fields to null.

Like any other constructor, the default constructor of a value type is invoked using the new operator. In the example below, the i and j variables are both initialized to zero.

```
class A
{
   void F() {
      int i = 0;
      int j = new int();
   }
}
```

Because every value type implicitly has a public parameterless constructor, it is not possible for a struct type to contain an explicit declaration of a parameterless constructor. A struct type is however permitted to declare parameterized constructors. For example

```
struct Point
{
   int x, y;
   public Point(int x, int y) {
      this.x = x;
      this.y = y;
   }
}
```

Given the above declaration, the statements

```
Point p1 = new Point();
Point p2 = new Point(0, 0);
```

both create a Point with x and y initialized to zero.

4.1.2 Struct types

A struct type is a value type that can declare constructors, constants, fields, methods, properties, indexers, operators, and nested types. Struct types are described in section11.

4.1.3 Simple types

C# provides a set of predefined struct types called the simple types. The simple types are identified through reserved words, but these reserved words are simply aliases for predefined struct types in the System namespace, as described in the table below.

Reserved word	Aliased type
sbyte	System.SByte
byte	System.Byte
short	System.Int16
ushort	System.UInt16
int	System.Int32
uint	System.UInt32
long	System.Int64
ulong	System.UInt64
char	System.Char
float	System.Single
double	System.Double
bool	System.Boolean
decimal	System.Decimal

Because a simple type aliases a struct type, every simple type has members. For example, int has the members declared in System.Int32 and the members inherited from System.Object, and the following statements are permitted:

```
int i = int.MaxValue;       // System.Int32.MaxValue constant
string s = i.ToString();    // System.Int32.ToString() instance method
string t = 123.ToString();  // System.Int32.ToString() instance method
```

The simple types differ from other struct types in that they permit certain additional operations:

- Most simple types permit values to be created by writing *literals* (section 2.4.4). For example, 123 is a literal of type int and 'a' is a literal of type char. C# makes no provision for literals of other struct types, and values of other struct types are ultimately always created through constructors of those struct types.

- When the operands of an expression are all simple type constants, it is possible for the compiler to evaluate the expression at compile-time. Such an expression is known as a *constant-expression* (section 7.15). Expressions involving operators defined by other struct types always imply run time evaluation.

- Through const declarations it is possible to declare constants of the simple types (section 10.3). It is not possible to have constants of other struct types, but a similar effect is provided by static readonly fields.
- Conversions involving simple types can participate in evaluation of conversion operators defined by other struct types, but a user-defined conversion operator can never participate in evaluation of another user-defined operator (section 6.4.2).

4.1.4 Integral types

C# supports nine integral types: sbyte, byte, short, ushort, int, uint, long, ulong, and char. The integral types have the following sizes and ranges of values:

- The sbyte type represents signed 8-bit integers with values between −128 and 127.
- The byte type represents unsigned 8-bit integers with values between 0 and 255.
- The short type represents signed 16-bit integers with values between −32768 and 32767.
- The ushort type represents unsigned 16-bit integers with values between 0 and 65535.
- The int type represents signed 32-bit integers with values between −2147483648 and 2147483647.
- The uint type represents unsigned 32-bit integers with values between 0 and 4294967295.
- The long type represents signed 64-bit integers with values between −9223372036854775808 and 9223372036854775807.
- The ulong type represents unsigned 64-bit integers with values between 0 and 18446744073709551615.
- The char type represents unsigned 16-bit integers with values between 0 to 65535. The set of possible values for the char type corresponds to the Unicode character set.

The integral-type unary and binary operators always operate with signed 32-bit precision, unsigned 32-bit precision, signed 64-bit precision, or unsigned 64-bit precision:

- For the unary + and ~ operators, the operand is converted to type T, where T is the first of int, uint, long, and ulong that can fully represent all possible values of the operand. The operation is then performed using the precision of type T, and the type of the result is T.
- For the unary—operator, the operand is converted to type T, where T is the first of int and long that can fully represent all possible values of the operand. The operation is then performed using the precision of type T, and the type of the result is T. The unary—operator cannot be applied to operands of type ulong.

- For the binary +, -, *, /, %, &, ^, |, ==, !=, >, <, >=, and <= operators, the operands are converted to type T, where T is the first of int, uint, long, and ulong that can fully represent all possible values of each operand. The operation is then performed using the precision of type T, and the type of the result is T (or bool for the relational operators). It is not possible for one operand to be of type long and the other to be of type ulong with the binary operators.

- For the binary << and >> operators, the left operand is converted to type T, where T is the first of int, uint, long, and ulong that can fully represent all possible values of the operand. The operation is then performed using the precision of type T, and the type of the result is T.

The char type is classified as an integral type, but it differs from the other integral types in two ways:

- There are no implicit conversions from other types to the char type. In particular, even though the sbyte, byte, and ushort types have ranges of values that are fully representable using the char type, implicit conversions from sbyte, byte, or ushort to char do not exist.

- Constants of the char type must be written as *character-literals*. Character constants can only be written as *integer-literals* in combination with a cast. For example, (char)10 is the same as '\x000A'.

The checked and unchecked operators and statements are used to control overflow checking for integral-type arithmetic operations and conversions (section 7.5.12). In a checked context, an overflow produces a compile-time error or causes an OverflowException to be thrown. In an unchecked context, overflows are ignored and any high-order bits that do not fit in the destination type are discarded.

4.1.5 Floating point types

C# supports two floating point types: float and double. The float and double types are represented using the 32-bit single-precision and 64-bit double-precision IEEE 754 formats, which provide the following sets of values:

- Positive zero and negative zero. In most situations, positive zero and negative zero behave identically as the simple value zero, but certain operations distinguish between the two.

- Positive infinity and negative infinity. Infinities are produced by such operations as dividing a non-zero number by zero. For example 1.0 / 0.0 yields positive infinity, and -1.0 / 0.0 yields negative infinity.

- The ***Not-a-Number*** value, often abbreviated NaN. NaN's are produced by invalid floating-point operations, such as dividing zero by zero.

- The finite set of non-zero values of the form $s \times m \times 2^e$, where s is 1 or -1, and m and e are determined by the particular floating-point type: For float, $0 < m < 2^{24}$ and $-149 \leq e \leq 104$, and for double, $0 < m < 2^{53}$ and $-1075 \leq e \leq 970$.

The `float` type can represent values ranging from approximately 1.5×10^{-45} to 3.4×10^{38} with a precision of 7 digits.

The `double` type can represent values ranging from approximately 5.0×10^{-324} to 1.7×10^{308} with a precision of 15–16 digits.

If one of the operands of a binary operator is of a floating-point type, then the other operand must be of an integral type or a floating-point type, and the operation is evaluated as follows:

- If one of the operands of is of an integral type, then that operand is converted to the floating-point type of the other operand.
- Then, if either of the operands is of type `double`, the other operand is converted to `double`, the operation is performed using at least `double` range and precision, and the type of the result is `double` (or `bool` for the relational operators).
- Otherwise, the operation is performed using at least `float` range and precision, and the type of the result is `float` (or `bool` for the relational operators).

The floating-point operators, including the assignment operators, never produce exceptions. Instead, in exceptional situations, floating-point operations produce zero, infinity, or NaN, as described below:

- If the result of a floating-point operation is too small for the destination format, the result of the operation becomes positive zero or negative zero.
- If the result of a floating-point operation is too large for the destination format, the result of the operation becomes positive infinity or negative infinity.
- If a floating-point operation is invalid, the result of the operation becomes NaN.
- If one or both operands of a floating-point operation is NaN, the result of the operation becomes NaN.

Floating-point operations may be performed with higher precision than the result type of the operation. For example, some hardware architectures support an "extended" or "long double" floating-point type with greater range and precision than the `double` type, and implicitly perform all floating-point operations using this higher precision type. Only at excessive cost in performance can such hardware architectures be made to perform floating-point operations with *less* precision, and rather than require an implementation to forfeit both performance and precision, C# allows a higher precision type to be used for all floating-point operations. Other than delivering more precise results, this rarely has any measurable effects. However, in expressions of the form x * y / z, where the multiplication produces a result that is outside the `double` range, but the subsequent division brings the temporary result back into the `double` range, the fact that the expression is evaluated in a higher range format may cause a finite result to be produced instead of an infinity.

4.1.6 The decimal type

The `decimal` type is a 128-bit data type suitable for financial and monetary calculations. The `decimal` type can represent values ranging from 1.0×10^{-28} to approximately 7.9×10^{28} with 28–29 significant digits.

The finite set of values of type `decimal` are of the form $s \times m \times 10^e$, where s is 1 or –1, $0 \leq m < 2^{96}$, and $-28 \leq e \leq 0$. The decimal type does not support signed zeros, infinities, or NaN's.

A `decimal` is represented as a 96-bit integer scaled by a power of ten. For `decimal`s with an absolute value less than `1.0m`, the value is exact to the 28th decimal place, but no further. For `decimal`s with an absolute value greater than or equal to `1.0m`, the value is exact to 28 or 29 digits. Contrary to the `float` and `double` data types, decimal fractional numbers such as 0.1 can be represented exactly in the `decimal` representation. In the `float` and `double` representations, such numbers are often infinite fractions, making those representations more prone to round-off errors.

If one of the operands of a binary operator is of type `decimal`, then the other operand must be of an integral type or of type `decimal`. If an integral type operand is present, it is converted to `decimal` before the operation is performed.

Operations on values of type `decimal` are exact to 28 or 29 digits, but to no more than 28 decimal places. Results are rounded to the nearest representable value, and, when a result is equally close to two representable values, to the value that has an even number in the least significant digit position.

If a decimal arithmetic operation produces a value that is too small for the decimal format after rounding, the result of the operation becomes zero. If a `decimal` arithmetic operation produces a result that is too large for the `decimal` format, an `OverflowException` is thrown.

The `decimal` type has greater precision but smaller range than the floating-point types. Thus, conversions from the floating-point types to `decimal` might produce overflow exceptions, and conversions from `decimal` to the floating-point types might cause loss of precision. For these reasons, no implicit conversions exist between the floating-point types and `decimal`, and without explicit casts, it is not possible to mix floating-point and `decimal` operands in the same expression.

4.1.7 The bool type

The `bool` type represents boolean logical quantities. The possible values of type `bool` are `true` and `false`.

No standard conversions exist between `bool` and other types. In particular, the `bool` type is distinct and separate from the integral types, and a `bool` value cannot be used in place of an integral value, nor vice versa.

In the C and C++ languages, a zero integral value or a null pointer can be converted to the boolean value `false`, and a non-zero integral value or a non-null pointer can be converted to the boolean value `true`. In C#, such conversions are accomplished by explicitly comparing an integral value to zero or explicitly comparing an object reference to `null`.

4.1.8 Enumeration types

An enumeration type is a distinct type with named constants. Every enumeration type has an underlying type, which may be `byte`, `sbyte`, `short`, `ushort`, `int`, `uint`, `long` or `ulong`. Enumeration types are defined through enumeration declarations (section 14.1).

4.2 Reference types

A reference type is a class type, an interface type, an array type, or a delegate type.

reference-type:
    class-type
    interface-type
    array-type
    delegate-type

class-type:
    type-name
    `object`
    `string`

interface-type:
    type-name

array-type:
    non-array-type   rank-specifiers

non-array-type:
    type

rank-specifiers:
    rank-specifier
    rank-specifiers   rank-specifier

rank-specifier:
    [*dim-separators$_{opt}$*   ]

dim-separators:
    ,
    dim-separators   ,

delegate-type:
    type-name

A reference type value is a reference to an *instance* of the type, the latter known as an *object*. The special value `null` is compatible with all reference types and indicates the absence of an instance.

4.2.1 Class types

A class type defines a data structure that contains data members (constants, fields, and events), function members (methods, properties, indexers, operators, constructors, and destructors), and nested types. Class types support inheritance, a mechanism whereby derived classes can extend and specialize base classes. Instances of class types are created using *object-creation-expressions* (section 7.5.10.1).

Class types are described in section 10.

4.2.2 The object type

The `object` class type is the ultimate base class of all other types. Every type in C# directly or indirectly derives from the `object` class type.

The `object` keyword is simply an alias for the predefined `System.Object` class. Writing the keyword `object` is exactly the same as writing `System.Object`, and vice versa.

4.2.3 The string type

The `string` type is a sealed class type that inherits directly from `object`. Instances of the `string` class represent Unicode character strings.

Values of the `string` type can be written as string literals (section 2.4.4).

The `string` keyword is simply an alias for the predefined `System.String` class. Writing the keyword `string` is exactly the same as writing `System.String`, and vice versa.

4.2.4 Interface types

An interface defines a contract. A class or struct that implements an interface must adhere to its contract. An interface may inherit from multiple base interfaces, and a class or struct may implement multiple interfaces.

Interface types are described in section 13.

4.2.5 Array types

An array is a data structure that contains a number of variables which are accessed through computed indices. The variables contained in an array, also called the elements of the array, are all of the same type, and this type is called the element type of the array.

Array types are described in section 12.

4.2.6 Delegate types

A delegate is a data structure that refers to a static method or to an object instance and an instance method of that object.

The closest equivalent of a delegate in C or C++ is a function pointer, but whereas a function pointer can only reference static functions, a delegate can reference both static and instance methods. In the latter case, the delegate stores not only a reference to the method's entry point, but also a reference to the object instance for which to invoke the method.

Delegate types are described in section 15.

4.3 Boxing and unboxing

Boxing and unboxing is a central concept in C#'s type system. It provides a binding link between *value-type*s and *reference-type*s by permitting any value of a *value-type* to be converted to and from type `object`. Boxing and unboxing enables a unified view of the type system wherein a value of any type can ultimately be treated as an object.

4.3.1 Boxing conversions

A boxing conversion permits any *value-type* to be implicitly converted to the type `object` or to any *interface-type* implemented by the *value-type*. Boxing a value of a *value-type* consists of allocating an object instance and copying the *value-type* value into that instance.

The actual process of boxing a value of a *value-type* is best explained by imagining the existence of a **boxing class** for that type. For any *value-type* T, the boxing class would be declared as follows:

```
class T_Box
{
   T value;
   T_Box(T t) {
      value = t;
   }
}
```

Boxing of a value v of type T now consists of executing the expression new T_Box(v), and returning the resulting instance as a value of type object. Thus, the statements

```
int i = 123;
object box = i;
```

conceptually correspond to

```
int i = 123;
object box = new int_Box(i);
```

Boxing classes like T_Box and int_Box above don't actually exist and the dynamic type of a boxed value isn't actually a class type. Instead, a boxed value of type T has the dynamic type T, and a dynamic type check using the is operator can simply reference type T. For example,

```
int i = 123;
object box = i;
if (box is int) {
    Console.Write("Box contains an int");
}
```

will output the string "Box contains an int" on the console.

A boxing conversion implies *making a copy* of the value being boxed. This is different from a conversion of a *reference-type* to type object, in which the value continues to reference the same instance and simply is regarded as the less derived type object. For example, given the declaration

```
struct Point
{
    public int x, y;
    public Point(int x, int y) {
        this.x = x;
        this.y = y;
    }
}
```

the following statements

```
Point p = new Point(10, 10);
object box = p;
p.x = 20;
Console.Write(((Point)box).x);
```

will output the value 10 on the console because the implicit boxing operation that occurs in the assignment of p to box causes the value of p to be copied. Had Point instead been declared a class, the value 20 would be output because p and box would reference the same instance.

4.3.2 Unboxing conversions

An unboxing conversion permits an explicit conversion from type `object` to any *value-type* or from any *interface-type* to any *value-type* that implements the *interface-type*. An unboxing operation consists of first checking that the object instance is a boxed value of the given *value-type*, and then copying the value out of the instance.

Referring to the imaginary boxing class described in the previous section, an unboxing conversion of an object `box` to a *value-type* T consists of executing the expression `((T_Box)box).value`. Thus, the statements

```
object box = 123;
int i = (int)box;
```

conceptually correspond to

```
object box = new int_Box(123);
int i = ((int_Box)box).value;
```

For an unboxing conversion to a given *value-type* to succeed at run-time, the value of the source argument must be a reference to an object that was previously created by boxing a value of that *value-type*. If the source argument is `null` or a reference to an incompatible object, an `InvalidCastException` is thrown.

5. Variables

Variables represent storage locations. Every variable has a type that determines what values can be stored in the variable. C# is a type-safe language, and the C# compiler guarantees that values stored in variables are always of the appropriate type. The value of a variable can be changed through assignment or through use of the ++ and -- operators.

A variable must be ***definitely assigned*** (section 5.3) before its value can be obtained.

As described in the following sections, variables are either ***initially assigned*** or ***initially unassigned***. An initially assigned variable has a well-defined initial value and is always considered definitely assigned. An initially unassigned variable has no initial value. For an initially unassigned variable to be considered definitely assigned at a certain location, an assignment to the variable must occur in every possible execution path leading to that location.

5.1 Variable categories

C# defines seven categories of variables: static variables, instance variables, array elements, value parameters, reference parameters, output parameters, and local variables. The sections that follow describe each of these categories.

In the example

```
class A
{
    public static int x;
    int y;
    void F(int[] v, int a, ref int b, out int c) {
        int i = 1;
        c = a + b++;
    }
}
```

x is a static variable, y is an instance variable, v[0] is an array element, a is a value parameter, b is a reference parameter, c is an output parameter, and i is a local variable.

5.1.1 Static variables

A field declared with the `static` modifier is called a ***static variable***. A static variable comes into existence when the type in which it is declared is loaded (section 10.11), and ceases to exist when the program terminates.

The initial value of a static variable is the default value (section 5.2) of the variable's type.

For purposes of definite assignment checking, a static variable is considered initially assigned.

5.1.2 Instance variables

A field declared without the `static` modifier is called an ***instance variable***.

5.1.2.1 Instance variables in classes

An instance variable of a class comes into existence when a new instance of that class is created, and ceases to exist when there are no references to that instance and the instance's destructor (if any) has executed.

The initial value of an instance variable of a class is the default value (section 5.2) of the variable's type.

For purposes of definite assignment checking, an instance variable of a class is considered initially assigned.

5.1.2.2 Instance variables in structs

An instance variable of a struct has exactly the same lifetime as the struct variable to which it belongs. In other words, when a variable of a struct type comes into existence or ceases to exist, so too do the instance variables of the struct.

The initial assignment state of an instance variable of a struct in the same as that of the containing struct variable. In other words, when a struct variable is considered initially assigned, so too are its instance variables, and when a struct variable is considered initially unassigned, its instance variables are likewise unassigned.

5.1.3 Array elements

The elements of an array come into existence when an array instance is created, and cease to exist when there are no references to that array instance.

The initial value of each of the elements of an array is the default value (section 5.2) of the type of the array elements.

For purposes of definite assignment checking, an array element is considered initially assigned.

5.1.4 Value parameters

A parameter declared without a `ref` or `out` modifier is a ***value parameter***.

A value parameter comes into existence upon invocation of the function member (method, constructor, accessor, or operator) to which the parameter belongs, and is initialized with the value of the argument given in the invocation. A value parameter ceases to exist upon return of the function member.

For purposes of definite assignment checking, a value parameter is considered initially assigned.

5.1.5 Reference parameters

A parameter declared with a `ref` modifier is a ***reference parameter***.

A reference parameter does not create a new storage location. Instead, a reference parameter represents the same storage location as the variable given as the argument in the function member invocation. Thus, the value of a reference parameter is always the same as the underlying variable.

The following definite assignment rules apply to reference parameters. Note the different rules for output parameters described in section 5.1.6.

- A variable must be definitely assigned (section 5.3) before it can be passed as a reference parameter in a function member invocation.
- Within a function member, a reference parameter is considered initially assigned.

Within an instance method or instance accessor of a struct type, the `this` keyword behaves exactly as a reference parameter of the struct type (section 7.5.7).

5.1.6 Output parameters

A parameter declared with an `out` modifier is an ***output parameter***.

An output parameter does not create a new storage location. Instead, an output parameter represents the same storage location as the variable given as the argument in the function member invocation. Thus, the value of an output parameter is always the same as the underlying variable.

The following definite assignment rules apply to output parameters. Note the different rules for reference parameters described in section 5.1.5.

- A variable need not be definitely assigned before it can be passed as an output parameter in a function member invocation.
- Following a function member invocation, each variable that was passed as an output parameter is considered assigned in that execution path.

- Within a function member, an output parameter is considered initially unassigned.
- Every output parameter of a function member must be definitely assigned (section 5.3) before the function member returns.

Within a constructor of a struct type, the `this` keyword behaves exactly as an output parameter of the struct type (section 7.5.7).

5.1.7 Local variables

A *local variable* is declared by a *local-variable-declaration*, which may occur in a *block*, a *for-statement*, a *switch-statement*, or a *using-statement*. A local variable comes into existence when control enters the *block*, *for-statement*, *switch-statement*, or *using-statement* that immediately contains the local variable declaration. A local variable ceases to exist when control leaves its immediately containing *block*, *for-statement*, *switch-statement*, or *using-statement*.A local variable is not automatically initialized and thus has no default value. For purposes of definite assignment checking, a local variable is considered initially unassigned. A *local-variable-declaration* may include a *variable-initializer*, in which case the variable is considered definitely assigned in its entire scope, except within the expression provided in the *variable-initializer*.

Within the scope of a local variable, it is an error to refer to the local variable in a textual position that precedes its *variable-declarator*.

5.2 Default values

The following categories of variables are automatically initialized to their default values:

- Static variables.
- Instance variables of class instances.
- Array elements.

The default value of a variable depends on the type of the variable and is determined as follows:

- For a variable of a *value-type*, the default value is the same as the value computed by the *value-type*'s default constructor (section 4.1.1).
- For a variable of a *reference-type*, the default value is `null`.

5.3 Definite assignment

At a given location in the executable code of a function member, a variable is said to be **definitely assigned** if the compiler can prove, by static flow analysis, that the variable has been automatically initialized or has been the target of at least one assignment. The rules of definite assignment are:

- An initially assigned variable (section 5.3.1) is always considered definitely assigned.
- An initially unassigned variable (section 5.3.2) is considered definitely assigned at a given location if all possible execution paths leading to that location contain at least one of the following:
  - A simple assignment (section 7.13.1) in which the variable is the left operand.
  - An invocation expression (section 7.5.5) or object creation expression (section 7.5.10.1) that passes the variable as an output parameter.
  - For a local variable, a local variable declaration (section 8.5) that includes a variable initializer.

The definite assignment state of instance variables of a *struct-type* variable are tracked individually as well as collectively. In additional to the rules above, the following rules apply to *struct-type* variables and their instance variables:

- An instance variable is considered definitely assigned if its containing *struct-type* variable is considered definitely assigned.
- A *struct-type* variable is considered definitely assigned if each of its instance variables are considered definitely assigned.

Definite assignment is a requirement in the following contexts:

- A variable must be definitely assigned at each location where its value is obtained. This ensures that undefined values never occur. The occurrence of a variable in an expression is considered to obtain the value of the variable, except when
  - the variable is the left operand of a simple assignment,
  - the variable is passed as an output parameter, or
  - the variable is a *struct-type* variable and occurs as the left operand of a member access.
- A variable must be definitely assigned at each location where it is passed as a reference parameter. This ensures that the function member being invoked can consider the reference parameter initially assigned.

- All output parameters of a function member must be definitely assigned at each location where the function member returns (through a `return` statement or through execution reaching the end of the function member body). This ensures that function members do no return undefined values in output parameters, thus enabling the compiler to consider a function member invocation that takes a variable as an output parameter equivalent to an assignment to the variable.

- The `this` variable of a *struct-type* constructor must be definitely assigned at each location where the constructor returns.

The following example demonstrates how the different blocks of a `try` statement affect definite assignment.

```
class A
{
    static void F() {
        int i, j;
        try {
            // neither i nor j definitely assigned
            i = 1;
            // i definitely assigned
            j = 2;
            // i and j definitely assigned
        }
        catch {
            // neither i nor j definitely assigned
            i = 3;
            // i definitely assigned
        }
        finally {
            // neither i nor j definitely assigned
            i = 4;
            // i definitely assigned
            j = 5;
            // i and j definitely assigned
        }
        // i and j definitely assigned
    }
}
```

The static flow analysis performed to determine the definite assignment state of a variable takes into account the special behavior of the &&, ||, and ?: operators. In each of the methods in the example

```
class A
{
   static void F(int x, int y) {
      int i;
      if (x >= 0 && (i = y) >= 0) {
         // i definitely assigned
      }
      else {
         // i not definitely assigned
      }
      // i not definitely assigned
   }
   static void G(int x, int y) {
      int i;
      if (x >= 0 || (i = y) >= 0) {
         // i not definitely assigned
      }
      else {
         // i definitely assigned
      }
      // i not definitely assigned
   }
}
```

the variable i is considered definitely assigned in one of the embedded statements of an if statement but not in the other. In the if statement in the F method, the variable i is definitely assigned in the first embedded statement because execution of the expression (i = y) always precedes execution of this embedded statement. In contrast, the variable i is not definitely assigned in the second embedded statement since the variable i may be unassigned. Specifically, the variable i is unassigned if the value of the variable x is negative. Similarly, in the G method, the variable i is definitely assigned in the second embedded statement but not in the first embedded statement.

5.3.1 Initially assigned variables

The following categories of variables are classified as initially assigned:

- Static variables.
- Instance variables of class instances.
- Instance variables of initially assigned struct variables.
- Array elements.
- Value parameters.
- Reference parameters.

5.3.2 Initially unassigned variables

The following categories of variables are classified as initially unassigned:

- Instance variables of initially unassigned struct variables.
- Output parameters, including the `this` variable of struct constructors.
- Local variables.

5.4 Variable references

A *variable-reference* is an *expression* that is classified as a variable. A *variable-reference* denotes a storage location that can be accessed both to fetch the current value and to store a new value. In C and C++, a *variable-reference* is known as an *lvalue*.

variable-reference:
    expression

The following constructs require an *expression* to be a *variable-reference*:

- The left hand side of an *assignment* (which may also be a property access or an indexer access).
- An argument passed as a `ref` or `out` parameter in a method or constructor invocation.

6. Conversions

6.1 Implicit conversions

The following conversions are classified as implicit conversions:

- Identity conversions
- Implicit numeric conversions
- Implicit enumeration conversions.
- Implicit reference conversions
- Boxing conversions
- Implicit constant expression conversions
- User-defined implicit conversions

Implicit conversions can occur in a variety of situations, including function member invocations (section 7.4.3), cast expressions (section 7.6.8), and assignments (section 7.13).

The pre-defined implicit conversions always succeed and never cause exceptions to be thrown. Properly designed user-defined implicit conversions should exhibit these characteristics as well.

6.1.1 Identity conversion

An identity conversion converts from any type to the same type. This conversion exists only such that an entity that already has a required type can be said to be convertible to that type.

6.1.2 Implicit numeric conversions

The implicit numeric conversions are:

- From `sbyte` to `short`, `int`, `long`, `float`, `double`, or `decimal`.
- From `byte` to `short`, `ushort`, `int`, `uint`, `long`, `ulong`, `float`, `double`, or `decimal`.
- From `short` to `int`, `long`, `float`, `double`, or `decimal`.
- From `ushort` to `int`, `uint`, `long`, `ulong`, `float`, `double`, or `decimal`.
- From `int` to `long`, `float`, `double`, or `decimal`.
- From `uint` to `long`, `ulong`, `float`, `double`, or `decimal`.
- From `long` to `float`, `double`, or `decimal`.
- From `ulong` to `float`, `double`, or `decimal`.
- From `char` to `ushort`, `int`, `uint`, `long`, `ulong`, `float`, `double`, or `decimal`.
- From `float` to `double`.

Conversions from `int`, `uint`, or `long` to `float` and from `long` to `double` may cause a loss of precision, but will never cause a loss of magnitude. The other implicit numeric conversions never lose any information.

There are no implicit conversions to the `char` type. This in particular means that values of the other integral types do not automatically convert to the `char` type.

6.1.3 Implicit enumeration conversions

An implicit enumeration conversion permits the *decimal-integer-literal* 0 to be converted to any *enum-type*.

6.1.4 Implicit reference conversions

The implicit reference conversions are:

- From any *reference-type* to `object`.
- From any *class-type* S to any *class-type* T, provided S is derived from T.
- From any *class-type* S to any *interface-type* T, provided S implements T.
- From any *interface-type* S to any *interface-type* T, provided S is derived from T.
- From an *array-type* S with an element type S_E to an *array-type* T with an element type T_E, provided all of the following are true:
  - S and T differ only in element type. In other words, S and T have the same number of dimensions.
  - Both S_E and T_E are *reference-types*.
  - An implicit reference conversion exists from S_E to T_E.
- From any *array-type* to `System.Array`.
- From any *delegate-type* to `System.Delegate`.
- From any *array-type* or *delegate-type* to `System.ICloneable`.
- From the null type to any *reference-type*.

The implicit reference conversions are those conversions between *reference-type*s that can be proven to always succeed, and therefore require no checks at run-time.

Reference conversions, implicit or explicit, never change the referential identity of the object being converted. In other words, while a reference conversion may change the type of a value, it never changes the value itself.

6.1.5 Boxing conversions

A boxing conversion permits any *value-type* to be implicitly converted to the type `object` or to any *interface-type* implemented by the *value-type*. Boxing a value of a *value-type* consists of allocating an object instance and copying the *value-type* value into that instance.

Boxing conversions are further described in section 4.3.1.

6.1.6 Implicit constant expression conversions

An implicit constant expression conversion permits the following conversions:

- A *constant-expression* (section 7.15) of type `int` can be converted to type `sbyte`, `byte`, `short`, `ushort`, `uint`, or `ulong`, provided the value of the *constant-expression* is within the range of the destination type.

- A *constant-expression* of type `long` can be converted to type `ulong`, provided the value of the *constant-expression* is not negative.

6.1.7 User-defined implicit conversions

A user-defined implicit conversion consists of an optional standard implicit conversion, followed by execution of a user-defined implicit conversion operator, followed by another optional standard implicit conversion. The exact rules for evaluating user-defined conversions are described in section 6.4.3.

6.2 Explicit conversions

The following conversions are classified as explicit conversions:

- All implicit conversions.
- Explicit numeric conversions.
- Explicit enumeration conversions.
- Explicit reference conversions.
- Explicit interface conversions.
- Unboxing conversions.
- User-defined explicit conversions.

Explicit conversions can occur in cast expressions (section 7.6.8).

The explicit conversions are conversions that cannot be proved to always succeed, conversions that are known to possibly lose information, and conversions across domains of types sufficiently different to merit explicit notation.

The set explicit conversions includes all implicit conversions. This in particular means that redundant cast expressions are allowed.

6.2.1 Explicit numeric conversions

The explicit numeric conversions are the conversions from a *numeric-type* to another *numeric-type* for which an implicit numeric conversion (section 6.1.2) does not already exist:

- From `sbyte` to `byte`, `ushort`, `uint`, `ulong`, or `char`.
- From `byte` to `sbyte` and `char`.
- From `short` to `sbyte`, `byte`, `ushort`, `uint`, `ulong`, or `char`.
- From `ushort` to `sbyte`, `byte`, `short`, or `char`.
- From `int` to `sbyte`, `byte`, `short`, `ushort`, `uint`, `ulong`, or `char`.
- From `uint` to `sbyte`, `byte`, `short`, `ushort`, `int`, or `char`.
- From `long` to `sbyte`, `byte`, `short`, `ushort`, `int`, `uint`, `ulong`, or `char`.
- From `ulong` to `sbyte`, `byte`, `short`, `ushort`, `int`, `uint`, `long`, or `char`.
- From `char` to `sbyte`, `byte`, or `short`.
- From `float` to `sbyte`, `byte`, `short`, `ushort`, `int`, `uint`, `long`, `ulong`, `char`, or `decimal`.
- From `double` to `sbyte`, `byte`, `short`, `ushort`, `int`, `uint`, `long`, `ulong`, `char`, `float`, or `decimal`.
- From `decimal` to `sbyte`, `byte`, `short`, `ushort`, `int`, `uint`, `long`, `ulong`, `char`, `float`, or `double`.

Because the explicit conversions include all implicit and explicit numeric conversions, it is always possible to convert from any *numeric-type* to any other *numeric-type* using a cast expression (section 7.6.8).

The explicit numeric conversions possibly lose information or possibly cause exceptions to be thrown. An explicit numeric conversion is processed as follows:

- For a conversion from an integral type to another integral type, the processing depends on the overflow checking context (section 7.5.12) in which the conversion takes place:
  - In a `checked` context, the conversion succeeds if the source argument is within the range of the destination type, but throws an `OverflowException` if the source argument is outside the range of the destination type.
  - In an `unchecked` context, the conversion always succeeds, and simply consists of discarding the most significant bits of the source value.
- For a conversion from `float`, `double`, or `decimal` to an integral type, the source value is rounded towards zero to the nearest integral value, and this integral value becomes the result of the conversion. If the resulting integral value is outside the range of the destination type, an `OverflowException` is thrown.

- For a conversion from `double` to `float`, the `double` value is rounded to the nearest `float` value. If the `double` value is too small to represent as a `float`, the result becomes positive zero or negative zero. If the `double` value is too large to represent as a `float`, the result becomes positive infinity or negative infinity. If the `double` value is NaN, the result is also NaN.

- For a conversion from `float` or `double` to `decimal`, the source value is converted to `decimal` representation and rounded to the nearest number after the 28th decimal place if required (section 4.1.6). If the source value is too small to represent as a `decimal`, the result becomes zero. If the source value is NaN, infinity, or too large to represent as a `decimal`, an `InvalidCastException` is thrown.

- For a conversion from `decimal` to `float` or `double`, the `decimal` value is rounded to the nearest `double` or `float` value. While this conversion may lose precision, it never causes an exception to be thrown.

6.2.2 Explicit enumeration conversions

The explicit enumeration conversions are:

- From `sbyte`, `byte`, `short`, `ushort`, `int`, `uint`, `long`, `ulong`, `char`, `float`, `double`, or `decimal` to any *enum-type*.
- From any *enum-type* to `sbyte`, `byte`, `short`, `ushort`, `int`, `uint`, `long`, `ulong`, `char`, `float`, `double`, or `decimal`.
- From any *enum-type* to any other *enum-type*.

An explicit enumeration conversion between two types is processed by treating any participating *enum-type* as the underlying type of that *enum-type*, and then performing an implicit or explicit numeric conversion between the resulting types. For example, given an *enum-type* E with and underlying type of `int`, a conversion from E to `byte` is processed as an explicit numeric conversion (section 6.2.1) from `int` to `byte`, and a conversion from `byte` to E is processed as an implicit numeric conversion (section 6.1.2) from `byte` to `int`.

6.2.3 Explicit reference conversions

The explicit reference conversions are:

- From `object` to any *reference-type*.
- From any *class-type* S to any *class-type* T, provided S is a base class of T.
- From any *class-type* S to any *interface-type* T, provided S is not sealed and provided S does not implement T.
- From any *interface-type* S to any *class-type* T, provided T is not sealed or provided T implements S.
- From any *interface-type* S to any *interface-type* T, provided S is not derived from T.

- From an *array-type* S with an element type S_E to an *array-type* T with an element type T_E, provided all of the following are true:
  - S and T differ only in element type. In other words, S and T have the same number of dimensions.
  - Both S_E and T_E are *reference-types*.
  - An explicit reference conversion exists from S_E to T_E.
- From `System.Array` to any *array-type*.
- From `System.Delegate` to any *delegate-type*.
- From `System.ICloneable` to any *array-type* or *delegate-type*.

The explicit reference conversions are those conversions between reference-types that require run-time checks to ensure they are correct.

For an explicit reference conversion to succeed at run-time, the value of the source argument must be `null` or the *actual* type of the object referenced by the source argument must be a type that can be converted to the destination type by an implicit reference conversion (section 6.1.4). If an explicit reference conversion fails, an `InvalidCastException` is thrown.

Reference conversions, implicit or explicit, never change the referential identity of the object being converted. In other words, while a reference conversion may change the type of a value, it never changes the value itself.

6.2.4 Unboxing conversions

An unboxing conversion permits an explicit conversion from type `object` to any *value-type* or from any *interface-type* to any *value-type* that implements the *interface-type*. An unboxing operation consists of first checking that the object instance is a boxed value of the given *value-type*, and then copying the value out of the instance.

Unboxing conversions are further described in section 4.3.2.

6.2.5 User-defined explicit conversions

A user-defined explicit conversion consists of an optional standard explicit conversion, followed by execution of a user-defined implicit or explicit conversion operator, followed by another optional standard explicit conversion. The exact rules for evaluating user-defined conversions are described in section 6.4.4.

6.3 Standard conversions

The standard conversions are those pre-defined conversions that can occur as part of a user-defined conversion.

6.3.1 Standard implicit conversions

The following implicit conversions are classified as standard implicit conversions:

- Identity conversions (section 6.1.1)
- Implicit numeric conversions (section 6.1.2)
- Implicit reference conversions (section 6.1.4)
- Boxing conversions (section 6.1.5)
- Implicit constant expression conversions (section 6.1.6)

The standard implicit conversions specifically exclude user-defined implicit conversions.

6.3.2 Standard explicit conversions

The standard explicit conversions are all standard implicit conversions plus the subset of the explicit conversions for which an opposite standard implicit conversion exists. In other words, if a standard implicit conversion exists from a type A to a type B, then a standard explicit conversion exists from type A to type B and from type B to type A.

6.4 User-defined conversions

C# allows the pre-defined implicit and explicit conversions to be augmented by *user-defined conversions*. User-defined conversions are introduced by declaring conversion operators (section 10.9.3) in class and struct types.

6.4.1 Permitted user-defined conversions

C# permits only certain user-defined conversions to be declared. In particular, it is not possible to redefine an already existing implicit or explicit conversion. A class or struct is permitted to declare a conversion from a source type S to a target type T only if all of the following are true:

- S and T are different types.
- Either S or T is the class or struct type in which the operator declaration takes place.
- Neither S nor T is object or an *interface-type*.
- T is not a base class of S, and S is not a base class of T.

The restrictions that apply to user-defined conversions are discussed further in section 10.9.3.

6.4.2 Evaluation of user-defined conversions

A user-defined conversion converts a value from its type, called the **source type**, to another type, called the **target type**. Evaluation of a user-defined conversion centers on finding the **most specific** user-defined conversion operator for the particular source and target types. This determination is broken into several steps:

- Finding the set of classes and structs from which user-defined conversion operators will be considered. This set consists of the source type and its base classes and the target type and its base classes (with the implicit assumptions that only classes and structs can declare user-defined operators, and that non-class types have no base classes).

- From that set of types, determining which user-defined conversion operators are applicable. For a conversion operator to be applicable, it must be possible to perform a standard conversion (section 6.3) from the source type to the argument type of the operator, and it must be possible to perform a standard conversion from the result type of the operator to the target type.

- From the set of applicable user-defined operators, determining which operator is unambiguously the most specific. In general terms, the most specific operator is the operator whose argument type is "closest" to the source type and whose result type is "closest" to the target type. The exact rules for establishing the most specific user-defined conversion operator are defined in the following sections.

Once a most specific user-defined conversion operator has been identified, the actual execution of the user-defined conversion involves up to three steps:

- First, if required, performing a standard conversion from the source type to the argument type of the user-defined conversion operator.

- Next, invoking the user-defined conversion operator to perform the conversion.

- Finally, if required, performing a standard conversion from the result type of the user-defined conversion operator to the target type.

Evaluation of a user-defined conversion never involves more than one user-defined conversion operator. In other words, a conversion from type S to type T will never first execute a user-defined conversion from S to X and then execute a user-defined conversion from X to T.

Exact definitions of evaluation of user-defined implicit or explicit conversions are given in the following sections. The definitions make use of the following terms:

- If a standard implicit conversion (section 6.3.1) exists from a type A to a type B, and if neither A nor B are *interface-type*s, then A is said to be **encompassed by** B, and B is said to **encompass** A.

- The ***most encompassing type*** in a set of types is the one type that encompasses all other types in the set. If no single type encompasses all other types, then the set has no most encompassing type. In more intuitive terms, the most encompassing type is the "largest" type in the set—the one type to which each of the other types can be implicitly converted.

- The ***most encompassed type*** in a set of types is the one type that is encompassed by all other types in the set. If no single type is encompassed by all other types, then the set has no most encompassed type. In more intuitive terms, the most encompassed type is the "smallest" type in the set—the one type that can be implicitly converted to each of the other types.

6.4.3 User-defined implicit conversions

A user-defined implicit conversion from type S to type T is processed as follows:

- Find the set of types, D, from which user-defined conversion operators will be considered. This set consists of S (if S is a class or struct), the base classes of S (if S is a class), T (if T is a class or struct), and the base classes of T (if T is a class).

- Find the set of applicable user-defined conversion operators, U. This set consists of the user-defined implicit conversion operators declared by the classes or structs in D that convert from a type encompassing S to a type encompassed by T. If U is empty, the conversion is undefined and an error occurs.

- Find the most specific source type, S_x, of the operators in U:
  - If any of the operators in U convert from S, then S_x is S.
  - Otherwise, S_x is the most encompassed type in the combined set of source types of the operators in U. If no most encompassed type can be found, then the conversion is ambiguous and an error occurs.

- Find the most specific target type, T_x, of the operators in U:
  - If any of the operators in U convert to T, then T_x is T.
  - Otherwise, T_x is the most encompassing type in the combined set of target types of the operators in U. If no most encompassing type can be found, then the conversion is ambiguous and an error occurs.

- If U contains exactly one user-defined conversion operator that converts from S_x to T_x, then this is the most specific conversion operator. If no such operator exists, or if more than one such operator exists, then the conversion is ambiguous and an error occurs. Otherwise, the user-defined conversion is applied:
  - If S is not S_x, then a standard implicit conversion from S to S_x is performed.
  - The most specific user-defined conversion operator is invoked to convert from S_x to T_x.
  - If T_x is not T, then a standard implicit conversion from T_x to T is performed.

6.4.4 User-defined explicit conversions

A user-defined explicit conversion from type S to type T is processed as follows:

- Find the set of types, D, from which user-defined conversion operators will be considered. This set consists of S (if S is a class or struct), the base classes of S (if S is a class), T (if T is a class or struct), and the base classes of T (if T is a class).
- Find the set of applicable user-defined conversion operators, U. This set consists of the user-defined implicit or explicit conversion operators declared by the classes or structs in D that convert from a type encompassing or encompassed by S to a type encompassing or encompassed by T. If U is empty, the conversion is undefined and an error occurs.
- Find the most specific source type, S_x, of the operators in U:
  - If any of the operators in U convert from S, then S_x is S.
  - Otherwise, if any of the operators in U convert from types that encompass S, then S_x is the most encompassed type in the combined set of source types of those operators. If no most encompassed type can be found, then the conversion is ambiguous and an error occurs.
  - Otherwise, S_x is the most encompassing type in the combined set of source types of the operators in U. If no most encompassing type can be found, then the conversion is ambiguous and an error occurs.
- Find the most specific target type, T_x, of the operators in U:
  - If any of the operators in U convert to T, then T_x is T.
  - Otherwise, if any of the operators in U convert to types that are encompassed by T, then T_x is the most encompassing type in the combined set of source types of those operators. If no most encompassing type can be found, then the conversion is ambiguous and an error occurs.
  - Otherwise, T_x is the most encompassed type in the combined set of target types of the operators in U. If no most encompassed type can be found, then the conversion is ambiguous and an error occurs.
- If U contains exactly one user-defined conversion operator that converts from S_x to T_x, then this is the most specific conversion operator. If no such operator exists, or if more than one such operator exists, then the conversion is ambiguous and an error occurs. Otherwise, the user-defined conversion is applied:
  - If S is not S_x, then a standard explicit conversion from S to S_x is performed.
  - The most specific user-defined conversion operator is invoked to convert from S_x to T_x.
  - If T_x is not T, then a standard explicit conversion from T_x to T is performed.

7. Expressions

An expression is a sequence of operators and operands that specifies a computation. This chapter defines the syntax, order of evaluation, and meaning of expressions.

7.1 Expression classifications

An expression is classified as one of the following:

- A value. Every value has an associated type.
- A variable. Every variable has an associated type, namely the declared type of the variable.
- A namespace. An expression with this classification can only appear as the left hand side of a *member-access* (section 7.5.4). In any other context, an expression classified as a namespace causes an error.
- A type. An expression with this classification can only appear as the left hand side of a *member-access* (section 7.5.4), or as an operand for the `as` operator (section 7.9.10), the `is` operator (section 7.9.9), or the `typeof` operator (section 7.5.11). In any other context, an expression classified as a type causes an error.
- A method group, which is a set of overloaded methods resulting from a member lookup (section 7.3). A method group may have associated instance expression. When an instance method is invoked, the result of evaluating the instance expression becomes the instance represented by `this` (section 7.5.7). A method group is only permitted in an *invocation-expression* (section 7.5.5) or a *delegate-creation-expression* (section 7.5.10.3). In any other context, an expression classified as a method group causes an error.
- A property access. Every property access has an associated type, namely the type of the property. A property access may furthermore have an associated instance expression. When an accessor (the `get` or `set` block) of an instance property access is invoked, the result of evaluating the instance expression becomes the instance represented by `this` (section 7.5.7).
- An event access. Every event access has an associated type, namely the type of the event. An event access may furthermore have an associated instance expression. An event access may appear as the left hand operand of the `+=` and `-=` operators (section 7.13.3). In any other context, an expression classified as an event access causes an error.

- An indexer access. Every indexer access has an associated type, namely the element type of the indexer. Furthermore, an indexer access has an associated instance expression and an associated argument list. When an accessor (the `get` or `set` block) of an indexer access is invoked, the result of evaluating the instance expression becomes the instance represented by `this` (section 7.5.7), and the result of evaluating the argument list becomes the parameter list of the invocation.

- Nothing. This occurs when the expression is an invocation of a method with a return type of `void`. An expression classified as nothing is only valid in the context of a *statement-expression* (section 8.6).

The final result of an expression is never a namespace, type, method group, or event access. Rather, as noted above, these categories of expressions are intermediate constructs that are only permitted in certain contexts.

A property access or indexer access is always reclassified as a value by performing an invocation of the *get-accessor* or the *set-accessor*. The particular accessor is determined by the context of the property or indexer access: If the access is the target of an assignment, the *set-accessor* is invoked to assign a new value (section 7.13.1). Otherwise, the *get-accessor* is invoked to obtain the current value (section 7.1.1).

7.1.1 Values of expressions

Most of the constructs that involve an expression ultimately require the expression to denote a *value*. In such cases, if the actual expression denotes a namespace, a type, a method group, or nothing, an error occurs. However, if the expression denotes a property access, an indexer access, or a variable, the value of the property, indexer, or variable is implicitly substituted:

- The value of a variable is simply the value currently stored in the storage location identified by the variable. A variable must be considered definitely assigned (section 5.3) before its value can be obtained, or otherwise a compile-time error occurs.

- The value of a property access expression is obtained by invoking the *get-accessor* of the property. If the property has no *get-accessor*, an error occurs. Otherwise, a function member invocation (section 7.4.3) is performed, and the result of the invocation becomes the value of the property access expression.

- The value of an indexer access expression is obtained by invoking the *get-accessor* of the indexer. If the indexer has no *get-accessor*, an error occurs. Otherwise, a function member invocation (section 7.4.3) is performed with the argument list associated with the indexer access expression, and the result of the invocation becomes the value of the indexer access expression.

7.2 Operators

Expressions are constructed from *operands* and *operators*. The operators of an expression indicate which operations to apply to the operands. Examples of operators include +, -, *, /, and new. Examples of operands include literals, fields, local variables, and expressions.

There are three types of operators:

- Unary operators. The unary operators take one operand and use either prefix notation (such as -x) or postfix notation (such as x++).
- Binary operators. The binary operators take two operands and all use infix notation (such as x + y).
- Ternary operator. Only one ternary operator, ?:, exists. The ternary operator takes three operands and uses infix notation (c? x: y).

The order of evaluation of operators in an expression is determined by the *precedence* and *associativity* of the operators (section 7.2.1).

Certain operators can be *overloaded*. Operator overloading permits user-defined operator implementations to be specified for operations where one or both of the operands are of a user-defined class or struct type (section 7.2.2).

7.2.1 Operator precedence and associativity

When an expression contains multiple operators, the *precedence* of the operators control the order in which the individual operators are evaluated. For example, the expression x + y * z is evaluated as x + (y * z) because the * operator has higher precedence than the + operator. The precedence of an operator is established by the definition of its associated grammar production. For example, an *additive-expression* consists of a sequence of *multiplicative-expression*s separated by + or - operators, thus giving the + and - operators lower precedence than the *, /, and % operators.

The following table summarizes all operators in order of precedence from highest to lowest:

Section	Category	Operators
7.5	Primary	(x) x.y f(x) a[x] x++ x-- new typeof sizeof checked unchecked
7.6	Unary	+ - ! ~ ++x --x (T)x
7.7	Multiplicative	* / %
7.7	Additive	+ -
7.8	Shift	<< >>

(continued)

(continued)

Section	Category	Operators
7.9	Relational	`<  >  <=  >=  is  as`
7.9	Equality	`==  !=`
7.10	Logical AND	`&`
7.10	Logical XOR	`^`
7.10	Logical OR	`|`
7.11	Conditional AND	`&&`
7.11	Conditional OR	`||`
7.12	Conditional	`?:`
7.13	Assignment	`=  *=  /=  %=  +=  -=  <<=  >>=  &=  ^=  |=`

When an operand occurs between two operators with the same precedence, the **associativity** of the operators controls the order in which the operations are performed:

- Except for the assignment operators, all binary operators are **left-associative**, meaning that operations are performed from left to right. For example, x + y + z is evaluated as (x + y) + z.

- The assignment operators and the conditional operator (?:) are **right-associative**, meaning that operations are performed from right to left. For example, x = y = z is evaluated as x = (y = z).

Precedence and associativity can be controlled using parentheses. For example, x + y * z first multiplies y by z and then adds the result to x, but (x + y) * z first adds x and y and then multiplies the result by z.

7.2.2 Operator overloading

All unary and binary operators have predefined implementations that are automatically available in any expression. In addition to the predefined implementations, user-defined implementations can be introduced by including `operator` declarations in classes and structs (section 10.9). User-defined operator implementations always take precedence over predefined operator implementations: Only when no applicable user-defined operator implementations exist will the predefined operator implementations be considered.

The **overloadable unary operators** are:

```
+   -   !   ~   ++   --   true   false
```

The **overloadable binary operators** are:

```
+   -   *   /   %   &   |   ^   <<   >>   ==   !=   >   <   >=   <=
```

Only the operators listed above can be overloaded. In particular, it is not possible to overload member access, method invocation, or the =, &&, ||, ?:, new, typeof, sizeof, and is operators.

When a binary operator is overloaded, the corresponding assignment operator is also implicitly overloaded. For example, an overload of operator * is also an overload of operator *=. This is described further in section 7.13. Note that the assignment operator itself (=) cannot be overloaded. An assignment always performs a simple bit-wise copy of a value into a variable.

Cast operations, such as (T)x, are overloaded by providing user-defined conversions (section 6.4).

Element access, such as a[x], is not considered an overloadable operator. Instead, user-defined indexing is supported through indexers (section 10.8).

In expressions, operators are referenced using operator notation, and in declarations, operators are referenced using functional notation. The following table shows the relationship between operator and functional notations for unary and binary operators. In the first entry, *op* denotes any overloadable unary operator. In the second entry, *op* denotes the unary ++ and -- operators. In the third entry, *op* denotes any overloadable binary operator.

Operator notation	Functional notation
op x	operator *op*(x)
x *op*	operator *op*(x)
x *op* y	operator *op*(x, y)

User-defined operator declarations always require at least one of the parameters to be of the class or struct type that contains the operator declaration. Thus, it is not possible for a user-defined operator to have the same signature as a predefined operator.

User-defined operator declarations cannot modify the syntax, precedence, or associativity of an operator. For example, the * operator is always a binary operator, always has the precedence level specified in section 7.2.1, and is always left-associative.

While it is possible for a user-defined operator to perform any computation it pleases, implementations that produce results other than those that are intuitively expected are strongly discouraged. For example, an implementation of operator == should compare the two operands for equality and return an appropriate result.

The descriptions of individual operators in section 7.5 through section 7.13 specify the predefined implementations of the operators and any additional rules that apply to each operator. The descriptions make use of the terms **unary operator overload resolution**, **binary operator overload resolution**, and **numeric promotion**, definitions of which are found in the following sections.

7.2.3 Unary operator overload resolution

An operation of the form *op* x or x *op*, where *op* is an overloadable unary operator, and x is an expression of type X, is processed as follows:

- The set of candidate user-defined operators provided by X for the operation operator *op*(x) is determined using the rules of section 7.2.5.

- If the set of candidate user-defined operators is not empty, then this becomes the set of candidate operators for the operation. Otherwise, the predefined unary operator *op* implementations become the set of candidate operators for the operation. The predefined implementations of a given operator are specified in the description of the operator (section 7.5 and section 7.6).

- The overload resolution rules of section 7.4.2 are applied to the set of candidate operators to select the best operator with respect to the argument list (x), and this operator becomes the result of the overload resolution process. If overload resolution fails to select a single best operator, an error occurs.

7.2.4 Binary operator overload resolution

An operation of the form x *op* y, where *op* is an overloadable binary operator, x is an expression of type X, and y is an expression of type Y, is processed as follows:

- The set of candidate user-defined operators provided by X and Y for the operation operator *op*(x, y) is determined. The set consists of the union of the candidate operators provided by X and the candidate operators provided by Y, each determined using the rules of section 7.2.5. If X and Y are the same type, or if X and Y are derived from a common base type, then shared candidate operators only occur in the combined set once.

- If the set of candidate user-defined operators is not empty, then this becomes the set of candidate operators for the operation. Otherwise, the predefined binary operator *op* implementations become the set of candidate operators for the operation. The predefined implementations of a given operator are specified in the description of the operator (section 7.7 through section 7.13).

- The overload resolution rules of section 7.4.2 are applied to the set of candidate operators to select the best operator with respect to the argument list (x, y), and this operator becomes the result of the overload resolution process. If overload resolution fails to select a single best operator, an error occurs.

7.2.5 Candidate user-defined operators

Given a type T and an operation operator *op*(A), where *op* is an overloadable operator and A is an argument list, the set of candidate user-defined operators provided by T for operator *op*(A) is determined as follows:

- For all operator *op* declarations in T, if at least one operator is applicable (section 7.4.2.1) with respect to the argument list A, then the set of candidate operators consists of all applicable operator *op* declarations in T.
- Otherwise, if T is object, the set of candidate operators is empty.
- Otherwise, the set of candidate operators provided by T is the set of candidate operators provided by the direct base class of T.

7.2.6 Numeric promotions

Numeric promotion consists of automatically performing certain implicit conversions of the operands of the predefined unary and binary numeric operators. Numeric promotion is not a distinct mechanism, but rather an effect of applying overload resolution to the predefined operators. Numeric promotion specifically does not affect evaluation of user-defined operators, although user-defined operators can be implemented to exhibit similar effects.

As an example of numeric promotion, consider the predefined implementations of the binary * operator:

```
int operator *(int x, int y);
uint operator *(uint x, uint y);
long operator *(long x, long y);
ulong operator *(ulong x, ulong y);
float operator *(float x, float y);
double operator *(double x, double y);
decimal operator *(decimal x, decimal y);
```

When overload resolution rules (section 7.4.2) are applied to this set of operators, the effect is to select the first of the operators for which implicit conversions exist from the operand types. For example, for the operation b * s, where b is a byte and s is a short, overload resolution selects operator *(int, int) as the best operator. Thus, the effect is that b and s are converted to int, and the type of the result is int. Likewise, for the operation i * d, where i is an int and d is a double, overload resolution selects operator *(double, double) as the best operator.

7.2.6.1 Unary numeric promotions

Unary numeric promotion occurs for the operands of the predefined +, -, and ~ unary operators. Unary numeric promotion simply consists of converting operands of type sbyte, byte, short, ushort, or char to type int. Additionally, for the unary - operator, unary numeric promotion converts operands of type uint to type long.

7.2.6.2 Binary numeric promotions

Binary numeric promotion occurs for the operands of the predefined +, -, *, /, %, &, |, ^, ==, !=, >, <, >=, and <= binary operators. Binary numeric promotion implicitly converts both operands to a common type which, in case of the non-relational operators, also becomes the result type of the operation. Binary numeric promotion consists of applying the following rules, in the order they appear here:

- If either operand is of type `decimal`, the other operand is converted to type `decimal`, or an error occurs if the other operand is of type `float` or `double`.
- Otherwise, if either operand is of type `double`, the other operand is converted to type `double`.
- Otherwise, if either operand is of type `float`, the other operand is converted to type `float`.
- Otherwise, if either operand is of type `ulong`, the other operand is converted to type `ulong`, or an error occurs if the other operand is of type `sbyte`, `short`, `int`, or `long`.
- Otherwise, if either operand is of type `long`, the other operand is converted to type `long`.
- Otherwise, if either operand is of type `uint` and the other operand is of type `sbyte`, `short`, or `int`, both operands are converted to type `long`.
- Otherwise, if either operand is of type `uint`, the other operand is converted to type `uint`.
- Otherwise, both operands are converted to type `int`.

Note that the first rule disallows any operations that mix the `decimal` type with the `double` and `float` types. The rule follows from the fact that there are no implicit conversions between the `decimal` type and the `double` and `float` types.

Also note that it is not possible for an operand to be of type `ulong` when the other operand is of a signed integral type. The reason is that no integral type exists that can represent the full range of `ulong` as well as the signed integral types.

In both of the above cases, a cast expression can be used to explicitly convert one operand to a type that is compatible with the other operand.

In the example

```
decimal AddPercent(decimal x, double percent) {
    return x * (1.0 + percent / 100.0);
}
```

a compile-time error occurs because a `decimal` cannot be multiplied by a `double`. The error is resolved by explicitly converting the second operand to `decimal`:

```
decimal AddPercent(decimal x, double percent) {
    return x * (decimal)(1.0 + percent / 100.0);
}
```

7.3 Member lookup

A member lookup is the process whereby the meaning of a name in the context of a type is determined. A member lookup may occur as part of evaluating a *simple-name* (section 7.5.2) or a *member-access* (section 7.5.4) in an expression.

A member lookup of a name N in a type T is processed as follows:

- First, the set of all accessible (section 3.5) members named N declared in T and the base types (section 7.3.1) of T is constructed. Declarations that include an override modifier are excluded from the set. If no members named N exist and are accessible, then the lookup produces no match, and the following steps are not evaluated.
- Next, members that are hidden by other members are removed from the set. For every member S.M in the set, where S in the type in which the member M is declared, the following rules are applied:
  - If M is a constant, field, property, event, type, or enumeration member, then all members declared in a base type of S are removed from the set.
  - If M is a method, then all non-method members declared in a base type of S are removed from the set, and all methods with the same signature as M declared in a base type of S are removed from the set.
- Finally, having removed hidden members, the result of the lookup is determined:
  - If the set consists of a single non-method member, then this member is the result of the lookup.
  - Otherwise, if the set contains only methods, then this group of methods is the result of the lookup.
  - Otherwise, the lookup is ambiguous, and a compile-time error occurs (this situation can only occur for a member lookup in an interface that has multiple direct base interfaces).

For member lookups in types other than interfaces, and member lookups in interfaces that are strictly single-inheritance (each interface in the inheritance chain has exactly zero or one direct base interface), the effect of the lookup rules is simply that derived members hide base members with the same name or signature. Such single-inheritance lookups are never ambiguous. The ambiguities that can possibly arise from member lookups in multiple-inheritance interfaces are described in section 13.2.5.

7.3.1 Base types

For purposes of member lookup, a type T is considered to have the following base types:

- If T is object, then T has no base type.
- If T is a *value-type*, the base type of T is the class type object.
- If T is a *class-type*, the base types of T are the base classes of T, including the class type object.

- If T is an *interface-type*, the base types of T are the base interfaces of T and the class type object.
- If T is an *array-type*, the base types of T are the class types System.Array and object.
- If T is a *delegate-type*, the base types of T are the class types System.Delegate and object.

7.4 Function members

Function members are members that contain executable statements. Function members are always members of types and cannot be members of namespaces. C# defines the following five categories of function members:

- Constructors
- Methods
- Properties
- Indexers
- User-defined operators

The statements contained in function members are executed through function member invocations. The actual syntax for writing a function member invocation depends on the particular function member category. However, all function member invocations are expressions, allow arguments to be passed to the function member, and allow the function member to compute and return a result.

The argument list (section 7.4.1) of a function member invocation provides actual values or variable references for the parameters of the function member.

Invocations of constructors, methods, indexers, and operators employ overload resolution to determine which of a candidate set of function members to invoke. This process is described in section 7.4.2.

Once a particular function member has been identified at compile-time, possibly through overload resolution, the actual run-time process of invoking the function member is described in section 7.4.3.

The following table summarizes the processing that takes place in constructs involving the five categories of function members. In the table, e, x, y, and value indicate expressions classified as variables or values, T indicates an expression classified as a type, F is the simple name of a method, and P is the simple name of a property.

Construct	Example	Description
Constructor invocation	new T(x, y)	Overload resolution is applied to select the best constructor in the class or struct T. The constructor is invoked with the argument list (x, y).
Method invocation	F(x, y)	Overload resolution is applied to select the best method F in the containing class or struct. The method is invoked with the argument list (x, y). If the method is not static, the instance expression is this.
	T.F(x, y)	Overload resolution is applied to select the best method F in the class or struct T. An error occurs if the method is not static. The method is invoked with the argument list (x, y).
	e.F(x, y)	Overload resolution is applied to select the best method F in the class, struct, or interface given by the type of e. An error occurs if the method is static. The method is invoked with the instance expression e and the argument list (x, y).
Property access	P	The get accessor of the property P in the containing class or struct is invoked. An error occurs if P is write-only. If P is not static, the instance expression is this.
	P = value	The set accessor of the property P in the containing class or struct is invoked with the argument list (value). An error occurs if P is read-only. If P is not static, the instance expression is this.
	T.P	The get accessor of the property P in the class or struct T is invoked. An error occurs if P is not static or if P is write-only.
	T.P = value	The set accessor of the property P in the class or struct T is invoked with the argument list (value). An error occurs if P is not static or if P is read-only.
	e.P	The get accessor of the property P in the class, struct, or interface given by the type of e is invoked with the instance expression e. An error occurs if P is static or if P is write-only.
	e.P = value	The set accessor of the property P in the class, struct, or interface given by the type of e is invoked with the instance expression e and the argument list (value). An error occurs if P is static or if P is read-only.

(continued)

(continued)

Construct	Example	Description
Indexer access	`e[x, y]`	Overload resolution is applied to select the best indexer in the class, struct, or interface given by the type of e. The `get` accessor of the indexer is invoked with the instance expression e and the argument list `(x, y)`. An error occurs if the indexer is write-only.
	`e[x, y] = value`	Overload resolution is applied to select the best indexer in the class, struct, or interface given by the type of e. The `set` accessor of the indexer is invoked with the instance expression e and the argument list `(x, y, value)`. An error occurs if the indexer is read-only.
Operator invocation	`-x`	Overload resolution is applied to select the best unary operator in the class or struct given by the type of x. The selected operator is invoked with the argument list `(x)`.
	`x + y`	Overload resolution is applied to select the best binary operator in the classes or structs given by the types of x and y. The selected operator is invoked with the argument list `(x, y)`.

7.4.1 Argument lists

Every function member invocation includes an argument list which provides actual values or variable references for the parameters of the function member. The syntax for specifying the argument list of a function member invocation depends on the function member category:

- For constructors, methods, and delegates, the arguments are specified as an *argument-list*, as described below.
- For properties, the argument list is empty when invoking the `get` accessor, and consists of the expression specified as the right operand of the assignment operator when invoking the `set` accessor.
- For indexers, the argument list consists of the expressions specified between the square brackets in the indexer access. When invoking the `set` accessor, the argument list additionally includes the expression specified as the right operand of the assignment operator.
- For user-defined operators, the argument list consists of the single operand of the unary operator or the two operands of the binary operator.

The arguments of properties, indexers, and user-defined operators are always passed as value parameters (section 10.5.1.1). Reference and output parameters are not supported for these categories of function members.

The arguments of a constructor, method, or delegate invocation are specified as an *argument-list*:

argument-list:
  argument
  argument-list , *argument*

argument:
  expression
  `ref` *variable-reference*
  `out` *variable-reference*

An *argument-list* consists of zero or more *argument*s, separated by commas. Each argument can take one of the following forms:

- An *expression*, indicating that the argument is passed as a value parameter (section 10.5.1.1).

- The keyword `ref` followed by a *variable-reference* (section 5.4), indicating that the argument is passed as a reference parameter (section 10.5.1.2). A variable must be definitely assigned (section 5.3) before it can be passed as a reference parameter.

- The keyword `out` followed by a *variable-reference* (section 5.4), indicating that the argument is passed as an output parameter (section 10.5.1.3). A variable is considered definitely assigned (section 5.3) following a function member invocation in which the variable is passed as an output parameter.

During the run-time processing of a function member invocation (section 7.4.3), the expressions or variable references of an argument list are evaluated in order, from left to right, as follows:

- For a value parameter, the argument expression is evaluated and an implicit conversion (section 6.1) to the corresponding parameter type is performed. The resulting value becomes the initial value of the value parameter in the function member invocation.

- For a reference or output parameter, the variable reference is evaluated and the resulting storage location becomes the storage location represented by the parameter in the function member invocation. If the variable reference given as a reference or output parameter is an array element of a *reference-type*, a run-time check is performed to ensure that element type of the array is identical to the type of the parameter. If this check fails, an `ArrayTypeMismatchException` is thrown.

Methods, indexers, and constructors may declare their last parameter to be a parameter array (section 10.5.1.4). Such function members are invoked either in their normal form or in their expanded form depending on which is applicable (section 7.4.2.1):

- When a function member with a parameter array is invoked in its normal form, the argument given for the parameter array must be a single expression of a type that is implicitly convertible (section 6.1) to the parameter array type. In this case, the parameter array acts precisely like a value parameter.

- When a function member with a parameter array is invoked in its expanded form, the invocation must specify zero or more arguments for the parameter array, where each argument is an expression of a type that is implicitly convertible (section 6.1) to the element type of the parameter array. In this case, the invocation creates an instance of the parameter array type with a length corresponding to the number of arguments, initializes the elements of the array instance with the given argument values, and uses the newly created array instance as the actual argument.

The expressions of an argument list are always evaluated in the order they are written. Thus, the example

```
class Test
{
    static void F(int x, int y, int z) {
        Console.WriteLine("x = {0}, y = {1}, z = {2}", x, y, z);
    }
    static void Main() {
        int i = 0;
        F(i++, i++, i++);
    }
}
```

produces the output

```
x = 0, y = 1, z = 2
```

The array co-variance rules (section 12.5) permit a value of an array type A[] to be a reference to an instance of an array type B[], provided an implicit reference conversion exists from B to A. Because of these rules, when an array element of a *reference-type* is passed as a reference or output parameter, a run-time check is required to ensure that the actual element type of the array is *identical* to that of the parameter. In the example

```
class Test
{
    static void F(ref object x) {…}
    static void Main() {
        object[] a = new object[10];
        object[] b = new string[10];
        F(ref a[0]);      // Ok
        F(ref b[1]);      // ArrayTypeMismatchException
    }
}
```

the second invocation of F causes an `ArrayTypeMismatchException` to be thrown because the actual element type of b is `string` and not `object`.

When a function member with a parameter array is invoked in its expanded form, the invocation is processed exactly as if an array creation expression with an array initializer (section 7.5.10.2) was inserted around the expanded parameters. For example, given the declaration

```
void F(int x, int y, params object[] args);
```

the following invocations of the expanded form of the method

```
F(10, 20);
F(10, 20, 30, 40);
F(10, 20, 1, "hello", 3.0);
```

correspond exactly to

```
F(10, 20, new object[] {});
F(10, 20, new object[] {30, 40});
F(10, 20, new object[] {1, "hello", 3.0});
```

Note in particular that an empty array is created when there are zero arguments given for the parameter array.

7.4.2 Overload resolution

Overload resolution is a mechanism for selecting the best function member to invoke given an argument list and a set of candidate function members. Overload resolution selects the function member to invoke in the following distinct contexts within C#:

- Invocation of a method named in an *invocation-expression* (section 7.5.5).
- Invocation of a constructor named in an *object-creation-expression* (section 7.5.10.1).
- Invocation of an indexer accessor through an *element-access* (section 7.5.6).
- Invocation of a predefined or user-defined operator referenced in an expression (section 7.2.3 and section 7.2.4).

Each of these contexts defines the set of candidate function members and the list of arguments in its own unique way. However, once the candidate function members and the argument list have been identified, the selection of the best function member is the same in all cases:

- First, the set of candidate function members is reduced to those function members that are applicable with respect to the given argument list (section 7.4.2.1). If this reduced set is empty, an error occurs.

- Then, given the set of applicable candidate function members, the best function member in that set is located. If the set contains only one function member, then that function member is the best function member. Otherwise, the best function member is the one function member that is better than all other function members with respect to the given argument list, provided that each function member is compared to all other function members using the rules in section 7.4.2.2. If there is not exactly one function member that is better than all other function members, then the function member invocation is ambiguous and an error occurs.

The following sections define the exact meanings of the terms *applicable function member* and *better function member*.

7.4.2.1 Applicable function member

A function member is said to be an *applicable function member* with respect to an argument list A when all of the following are true:

- The number of arguments in A is identical to the number of parameters in the function member declaration.
- For each argument in A, the parameter passing mode of the argument is identical to the parameter passing mode of the corresponding parameter, and
  - for a value parameter or a parameter array, an implicit conversion (section 6.1) exists from the type of the argument to the type of the corresponding parameter, or
  - for a `ref` or `out` parameter, the type of the argument is identical to the type of the corresponding parameter.

For a function member that includes a parameter array, if the function member is applicable by the above rules, it is said to be applicable in its *normal form*. If a function member that includes a parameter array is not applicable in its normal form, the function member may instead be applicable in its *expanded form*:

- The expanded form is constructed by replacing the parameter array in the function member declaration with zero or more value parameters of the element type of the parameter array such that the number of arguments in the argument list A matches the total number of parameters. If A has fewer arguments than the number of fixed parameters in the function member declaration, the expanded form of the function member cannot be constructed and is thus not applicable.
- If the class, struct, or interface in which the function member is declared already contains another function member with the same signature as the expanded form, the expanded form is not applicable.

- Otherwise, the expanded form is applicable if for each argument in A the parameter passing mode of the argument is identical to the parameter passing mode of the corresponding parameter, and
  - for a fixed value parameter or a value parameter created by the expansion, an implicit conversion (section 6.1) exists from the type of the argument to the type of the corresponding parameter, or
  - for a `ref` or `out` parameter, the type of the argument is identical to the type of the corresponding parameter.

7.4.2.2 Better function member

Given an argument list A with a set of argument types A_1, A_2, ..., A_N and two applicable function members M_p and M_q with parameter types P_1, P_2, ..., P_N and Q_1, Q_2, ..., Q_N, M_p is defined to be a ***better function member*** than M_q if

- for each argument, the implicit conversion from A_x to P_x is not worse than the implicit conversion from A_x to Q_x, and
- for at least one argument, the conversion from A_x to P_x is better than the conversion from A_x to Q_x.

When performing this evaluation, if M_p or M_q is applicable in its expanded form, then P_x or Q_x refers to a parameter in the expanded form of the parameter list.

7.4.2.3 Better conversion

Given an implicit conversion C_1 that converts from a type S to a type T_1, and an implicit conversion C_2 that converts from a type S to a type T_2, the ***better conversion*** of the two conversions is determined as follows:

- If T_1 and T_2 are the same type, neither conversion is better.
- If S is T_1, C_1 is the better conversion.
- If S is T_2, C_2 is the better conversion.
- If an Implicit conversion from T_1 to T_2 exists, and no implicit conversion from T_2 to T_1 exists, C_1 is the better conversion.
- If an implicit conversion from T_2 to T_1 exists, and no implicit conversion from T_1 to T_2 exists, C_2 is the better conversion.
- If T_1 is `sbyte` and T_2 is `byte`, `ushort`, `uint`, or `ulong`, C_1 is the better conversion.
- If T_2 is `sbyte` and T_1 is `byte`, `ushort`, `uint`, or `ulong`, C_2 is the better conversion.
- If T_1 is `short` and T_2 is `ushort`, `uint`, or `ulong`, C_1 is the better conversion.
- If T_2 is `short` and T_1 is `ushort`, `uint`, or `ulong`, C_2 is the better conversion.

- If T_1 is int and T_2 is uint, or ulong, C_1 is the better conversion.
- If T_2 is int and T_1 is uint, or ulong, C_2 is the better conversion.
- If T_1 is long and T_2 is ulong, C_1 is the better conversion.
- If T_2 is long and T_1 is ulong, C_2 is the better conversion.
- Otherwise, neither conversion is better.

If an implicit conversion C_1 is defined by these rules to be a better conversion than an implicit conversion C_2, then it is also the case that C_2 is a **_worse conversion_** than C_1.

7.4.3 Function member invocation

This section describes the process that takes place at run-time to invoke a particular function member. It is assumed that a compile-time process has already determined the particular member to invoke, possibly by applying overload resolution to a set of candidate function members.

For purposes of describing the invocation process, function members are divided into two categories:

- Static function members. These are static methods, constructors, static property accessors, and user-defined operators. Static function members are always non-virtual.

- Instance function members. These are instance methods, instance property accessors, and indexer accessors. Instance function members are either non-virtual or virtual, and are always invoked on a particular instance. The instance is computed by an instance expression, and it becomes accessible within the function member as this (section 7.5.7).

The run-time processing of a function member invocation consists of the following steps, where M is the function member and, if M is an instance member, E is the instance expression:

- If M is a static function member:
  - The argument list is evaluated as described in section 7.4.1.
  - M is invoked.

- If M is an instance function member declared in a *value-type*:
  - E is evaluated. If this evaluation causes an exception, then no further steps are executed.
  - If E is not classified as a variable, then a temporary local variable of E's type is created and the value of E is assigned to that variable. E is then reclassified as a reference to that temporary local variable. The temporary variable is accessible as this within M, but not in any other way. Thus, only when E is a true variable is it possible for the caller to observe the changes that M makes to this.
  - The argument list is evaluated as described in section 7.4.1.
  - M is invoked. The variable referenced by E becomes the variable referenced by this.
- If M is an instance function member declared in a *reference-type*:
  - E is evaluated. If this evaluation causes an exception, then no further steps are executed.
  - The argument list is evaluated as described in section 7.4.1.
  - If the type of E is a *value-type*, a boxing conversion (section 4.3.1) is performed to convert E to type object, and E is considered to be of type object in the following steps.
  - The value of E is checked to be valid. If the value of E is null, a NullReferenceException is thrown and no further steps are executed.
  - The function member implementation to invoke is determined: If M is a non-virtual function member, then M is the function member implementation to invoke. Otherwise, M is a virtual function member and the function member implementation to invoke is determined through virtual function member lookup (section 7.4.4) or interface function member lookup (section 7.4.5).
  - The function member implementation determined in the step above is invoked. The object referenced by E becomes the object referenced by this.

7.4.3.1 Invocations on boxed instances

A function member implemented in a *value-type* can be invoked through a boxed instance of that *value-type* in the following situations:

- When the function member is an override of a method inherited from type object and is invoked through an instance expression of type object.
- When the function member is an implementation of an interface function member and is invoked through an instance expression of an *interface-type*.
- When the function member is invoked through a delegate.

In these situations, the boxed instance is considered to contain a variable of the *value-type*, and this variable becomes the variable referenced by this within the function member invocation. This in particular means that when a function member is invoked on a boxed instance, it is possible for the function member to modify the value contained in the boxed instance.

7.4.4 Virtual function member lookup

7.4.5 Interface function member lookup

7.5 Primary expressions

primary-expression:
    literal
    simple-name
    parenthesized-expression
    member-access
    invocation-expression
    element-access
    this-access
    base-access
    post-increment-expression
    post-decrement-expression
    new-expression
    typeof-expression
    sizeof-expression
    checked-expression
    unchecked-expression

7.5.1 Literals

A *primary-expression* that consists of a *literal* (section 2.4.4) is classified as a value.

7.5.2 Simple names

A *simple-name* consists of a single identifier.

simple-name:
    identifier

A *simple-name* is evaluated and classified as follows:

- If the *simple-name* appears within a *block* and if the *block* contains a local variable or parameter with the given name, then the *simple-name* refers to that local variable or parameter and is classified as a variable.

- Otherwise, for each type T, starting with the immediately enclosing class, struct, or enumeration declaration and continuing with each enclosing outer class or struct declaration (if any), if a member lookup of the *simple-name* in T produces a match:
  - If T is the immediately enclosing class or struct type and the lookup identifies one or more methods, the result is a method group with an associated instance expression of this.
  - If T is the immediately enclosing class or struct type, if the lookup identifies an instance member, and if the reference occurs within the *block* of a constructor, an instance method, or an instance accessor, the result is exactly the same as a member access (section 7.5.4) of the form this.E, where E is the *simple-name*.
  - Otherwise, the result is exactly the same as a member access (section 7.5.4) of the form T.E, where E is the *simple-name*. In this case, it is an error for the *simple-name* to refer to an instance member.
- Otherwise, starting with the namespace declaration in which the *simple-name* occurs (if any), continuing with each enclosing namespace declaration (if any), and ending with the global namespace, the following steps are evaluated until an entity is located:
  - If the namespace contains a namespace member with the given name, then the *simple-name* refers to that member and, depending on the member, is classified as a namespace or a type.
  - Otherwise, if the namespace declaration contains a *using-alias-directive* that associates the given name with an imported namespace or type, then the *simple-name* refers to that namespace or type.
  - Otherwise, if the namespaces imported by the *using-namespace-directive*s of the namespace declaration contain exactly one type with the given name, then the *simple-name* refers to that type.
  - Otherwise, if the namespaces imported by the *using-namespace-directive*s of the namespace declaration contain more than one type with the given name, then the *simple-name* is ambiguous and an error occurs.
- Otherwise, the name given by the *simple-name* is undefined and an error occurs.

7.5.2.1 Invariant meaning in blocks

For each occurrence of a given identifier as a *simple-name* in an expression, every other occurrence of the same identifier as a *simple-name* in an expression within the immediately enclosing *block* (section 8.2) or *switch-block* (section 8.7.2) must refer to the same entity. This rule ensures that the meaning of an name in the context of an expression is always the same within a block.

The example

```
class Test
{
   double x;
   void F(bool b) {
      x = 1.0;
      if (b) {
         int x = 1;
      }
   }
}
```

is in error because x refers to different entities within the outer block (the extent of which includes the nested block in the if statement). In contrast, the example

```
class Test
{
   double x;
   void F(bool b) {
      if (b) {
         x = 1.0;
      }
      else {
         int x = 1;
      }
   }
}
```

is permitted because the name x is never used in the outer block.

Note that the rule of invariant meaning applies only to simple names. It is perfectly valid for the same identifier to have one meaning as a simple name and another meaning as right operand of a member access (section 7.5.4). For example:

```
struct Point
{
   int x, y;
   public Point(int x, int y) {
      this.x = x;
      this.y = y;
   }
}
```

The example above illustrates a common pattern of using the names of fields as parameter names in a constructor. In the example, the simple names x and y refer to the parameters, but that does not prevent the member access expressions this.x and this.y from accessing the fields.

7.5.3 Parenthesized expressions

A *parenthesized-expression* consists of an *expression* enclosed in parentheses.

parenthesized-expression:
  (*expression*   )

A *parenthesized-expression* is evaluated by evaluating the *expression* within the parentheses. If the *expression* within the parentheses denotes a namespace, type, or method group, an error occurs. Otherwise, the result of the *parenthesized-expression* is the result of the evaluation of the contained *expression*.

7.5.4 Member access

A *member-access* consists of a *primary-expression* or a *predefined-type*, followed by a "." token, followed by an *identifier*.

member-access:
  primary-expression   .   *identifier*
  predefined-type   .   *identifier*

predefined-type: one of
```
bool     byte     char     decimal   doublefloat   int     long
object   sbyte    short    string    uint    ulong   ushort
```

A *member-access* of the form E.I, where E is a *primary-expression* or a *predefined-type* and I is an *identifier*, is evaluated and classified as follows:

- If E is a namespace and I is the name of an accessible member of that namespace, then the result is that member and, depending on the member, is classified as a namespace or a type.

- If E is a *predefined-type* or a *primary-expression* classified as a type, and a member lookup (section 7.3) of I in E produces a match, then E.I is evaluated and classified as follows:

  - If I identifies a type, then the result is that type.

  - If I identifies one or more methods, then the result is a method group with no associated instance expression.

  - If I identifies a static property, then the result is a property access with no associated instance expression.

- If I identifies a `static` field:
  - If the field is `readonly` and the reference occurs outside the static constructor of the class or struct in which the field is declared, then the result is a value, namely the value of the static field I in E.
  - Otherwise, the result is a variable, namely the static field I in E.
- If I identifies a `static` event:
  - If the reference occurs within the class or struct in which the event is declared, then E.I is processed exactly as if I was a static field or property.
  - Otherwise, the result is an event access with no associated instance expression.
- If I identifies a constant, then the result is a value, namely the value of that constant.
- If I identifies an enumeration member, then the result is a value, namely the value of that enumeration member.
- Otherwise, E.I is an invalid member reference, and an error occurs.

- If E is a property access, indexer access, variable, or value, the type of which is T, and a member lookup (section 7.3) of I in T produces a match, then E.I is evaluated and classified as follows:
  - First, if E is a property or indexer access, then the value of the property or indexer access is obtained (section 7.1.1) and E is reclassified as a value.
  - If I identifies one or more methods, then the result is a method group with an associated instance expression of E.
  - If I identifies an instance property, then the result is a property access with an associated instance expression of E.
  - If T is a *class-type* and I identifies an instance field of that *class-type*:
    - If the value of E is `null`, then a `NullReferenceException` is thrown.
    - Otherwise, if the field is `readonly` and the reference occurs outside an instance constructor of the class in which the field is declared, then the result is a value, namely the value of the field I in the object referenced by E.
    - Otherwise, the result is a variable, namely the field I in the object referenced by E.
  - If T is a *struct-type* and I identifies an instance field of that *struct-type*:
    - If E is a value, or if the field is `readonly` and the reference occurs outside an instance constructor of the struct in which the field is declared, then the result is a value, namely the value of the field I in the struct instance given by E.
    - Otherwise, the result is a variable, namely the field I in the struct instance given by E.

- If I identifies an instance event:
  - If the reference occurs within the class or struct in which the event is declared, then E.I is processed exactly as if I was an instance field or property.
  - Otherwise, the result is an event access with an associated instance expression of E.
- Otherwise, E.I is an invalid member reference, and an error occurs.

7.5.4.1 Identical simple names and type names

In a member access of the form E.I, if E is a single identifier, and if the meaning of E as a *simple-name* (section 7.5.2) is a constant, field, property, local variable, or parameter with the same type as the meaning of E as a *type-name* (section 3.8), then both possible meanings of E are permitted. The two possible meanings of E.I are never ambiguous, since I must necessarily be a member of the type E in both cases. In other words, the rule simply permits access to the static members of E where an error would have otherwise occurred. For example:

```
struct Color
{
    public static readonly Color White = new Color(…);
    public static readonly Color Black = new Color(…);
    public Color Complement() {…}
}
class A
{
    public Color Color;                // Field Color of type Color
    void F() {
        Color = Color.Black;           // References Color.Black static member
        Color = Color.Complement();    // Invokes Complement() on Color field
    }
    static void G() {
        Color c = Color.White;         // References Color.White static member
    }
}
```

Within the A class, those occurrences of the Color identifier that reference the Color type are underlined, and those that reference the Color field are not underlined.

7.5.5 Invocation expressions

An *invocation-expression* is used to invoke a method.

invocation-expression:
   primary-expression (*argument-list*opt)

The *primary-expression* of an *invocation-expression* must be a method group or a value of a *delegate-type*. If the *primary-expression* is a method group, the *invocation-expression* is a method invocation (section 7.5.5.1). If the *primary-expression* is a value of a *delegate-type*, the *invocation-expression* is a delegate invocation (section 7.5.5.2). If the *primary-expression* is neither a method group nor a value of a *delegate-type*, an error occurs.

The optional *argument-list* (section 7.4.1) provides values or variable references for the parameters of the method.

The result of evaluating an *invocation-expression* is classified as follows:

- If the *invocation-expression* invokes a method or delegate that returns void, the result is nothing. An expression that is classified as nothing cannot be an operand of any operator, and is permitted only in the context of a *statement-expression* (section 8.6).

- Otherwise, the result is a value of the type returned by the method or delegate.

7.5.5.1 Method invocations

For a method invocation, the *primary-expression* of the *invocation-expression* must be a method group. The method group identifies the one method to invoke or the set of overloaded methods from which to choose a specific method to invoke. In the latter case, determination of the specific method to invoke is based on the context provided by the types of the arguments in the *argument-list*.

The compile-time processing of a method invocation of the form M(A), where M is a method group and A is an optional *argument-list*, consists of the following steps:

- The set of candidate methods for the method invocation is constructed. Starting with the set of methods associated with M, which were found by a previous member lookup (section 7.3), the set is reduced to those methods that are applicable with respect to the argument list A. The set reduction consists of applying the following rules to each method T.N in the set, where T is the type in which the method N is declared:

  - If N is not applicable with respect to A (section 7.4.2.1), then N is removed from the set.

  - If N is applicable with respect to A (section 7.4.2.1), then all methods declared in a base type of T are removed from the set.

- If the resulting set of candidate methods is empty, then no applicable methods exist, and an error occurs. If the candidate methods are not all declared in the same type, the method invocation is ambiguous, and an error occurs (this latter situation can only occur for an invocation of a method in an interface that has multiple direct base interfaces, as described in section 13.2.5).

- The best method of the set of candidate methods is identified using the overload resolution rules of section 7.4.2. If a single best method cannot be identified, the method invocation is ambiguous, and an error occurs.
- Given a best method, the invocation of the method is validated in the context of the method group: If the best method is a static method, the method group must have resulted from a *simple-name* or a *member-access* through a type. If the best method is an instance method, the method group must have resulted from a *simple-name*, a *member-access* through a variable or value, or a *base-access*. If neither of these requirements are true, a compile-time error occurs.

Once a method has been selected and validated at compile-time by the above steps, the actual run-time invocation is processed according to the rules of function member invocation described in section 7.4.3.

The intuitive effect of the resolution rules described above is as follows: To locate the particular method invoked by a method invocation, start with the type indicated by the method invocation and proceed up the inheritance chain until at least one applicable, accessible, non-override method declaration is found. Then perform overload resolution on the set of applicable, accessible, non-override methods declared in that type and invoke the method thus selected.

7.5.5.2 Delegate invocations

For a delegate invocation, the *primary-expression* of the *invocation-expression* must be a value of a *delegate-type*. Furthermore, considering the *delegate-type* to be a function member with the same parameter list as the *delegate-type*, the *delegate-type* must be applicable (section 7.4.2.1) with respect to the *argument-list* of the *invocation-expression*.

The run-time processing of a delegate invocation of the form D(A), where D is a *primary-expression* of a *delegate-type* and A is an optional *argument-list*, consists of the following steps:

- D is evaluated. If this evaluation causes an exception, no further steps are executed.
- The value of D is checked to be valid. If the value of D is null, a NullReferenceException is thrown and no further steps are executed.
- Otherwise, D is reference to a delegate instance. A function member invocation (section 7.4.3) is performed on the method referenced by the delegate. If the method is an instance method, the instance of the invocation becomes the instance referenced by the delegate.

7.5.6 Element access

An *element-access* consists of a *primary-expression*, followed by a "[" token, followed by an *expression-list*, followed by a "]" token. The *expression-list* consists of one or more *expression*s, separated by commas.

element-access:
   primary-expression [*expression-list*]
expression-list:
   expression
   expression-list , *expression*

If the *primary-expression* of an *element-access* is a value of an *array-type*, the *element-access* is an array access (section 7.5.6.1). Otherwise, the *primary-expression* must be a variable or value of a class, struct, or interface type that has one or more indexer members, and the *element-access* is then an indexer access (section 7.5.6.2).

7.5.6.1 Array access

For an array access, the *primary-expression* of the *element-access* must be a value of an *array-type*. The number of expressions in the *expression-list* must be the same as the rank of the *array-type*, and each expression must be of type int, uint, long, ulong, or of a type that can be implicitly converted to one or more of these types.

The result of evaluating an array access is a variable of the element type of the array, namely the array element selected by the value(s) of the expression(s) in the *expression-list*.

The run-time processing of an array access of the form P[A], where P is a *primary-expression* of an *array-type* and A is an *expression-list*, consists of the following steps:

- P is evaluated. If this evaluation causes an exception, no further steps are executed.

- The index expressions of the *expression-list* are evaluated in order, from left to right. Following evaluation of each index expression, an implicit conversion (section 6.1) to one of the following types is performed: int, uint, long, ulong. The first type in this list for which an implicit conversion exists is chosen. For instance, if the index expression is of type short then an implicit conversion to int is performed, since implicit conversions from short to int and from short to long are possible. If evaluation of an index expression or the subsequent implicit conversion causes an exception, then no further index expressions are evaluated and no further steps are executed.

- The value of P is checked to be valid. If the value of P is null, a NullReferenceException is thrown and no further steps are executed.

- The value of each expression in the *expression-list* is checked against the actual bounds of each dimension of the array instance referenced by P. If one or more values are out of range, an `IndexOutOfRangeException` is thrown and no further steps are executed.
- The location of the array element given by the index expression(s) is computed, and this location becomes the result of the array access.

7.5.6.2 Indexer access

For an indexer access, the *primary-expression* of the *element-access* must be a variable or value of a class, struct, or interface type, and this type must implement one or more indexers that are applicable with respect to the *expression-list* of the *element-access*.

The compile-time processing of an indexer access of the form P[A], where P is a *primary-expression* of a class, struct, or interface type T, and A is an *expression-list*, consists of the following steps:

- The set of indexers provided by T is constructed. The set consists of all indexers declared in T or a base type of T that are not `override` declarations and are accessible in the current context (section 3.5).
- The set is reduced to those indexers that are applicable and not hidden by other indexers. The following rules are applied to each indexer S.I in the set, where S is the type in which the indexer I is declared:
  - If I is not applicable with respect to A (section 7.4.2.1), then I is removed from the set.
  - If I is applicable with respect to A (section 7.4.2.1), then all indexers declared in a base type of S are removed from the set.
- If the resulting set of candidate indexers is empty, then no applicable indexers exist, and an error occurs. If the candidate indexers are not all declared in the same type, the indexer access is ambiguous, and an error occurs (this latter situation can only occur for an indexer access on an instance of an interface that has multiple direct base interfaces).
- The best indexer of the set of candidate indexers is identified using the overload resolution rules of section 7.4.2. If a single best indexer cannot be identified, the indexer access is ambiguous, and an error occurs.
- The result of processing the indexer access is an expression classified as an indexer access. The indexer access expression references the indexer determined in the step above, and has an associated instance expression of P and an associated argument list of A.

Depending on the context in which it is used, an indexer access causes invocation of either the *get-accessor* or the *set-accessor* of the indexer. If the indexer access is the target of an assignment, the *set-accessor* is invoked to assign a new value (section 7.13.1). In all other cases, the *get-accessor* is invoked to obtain the current value (section 7.1.1).

7.5.6.3 String indexing

The `string` class implements an indexer that allows the individual characters of a string to be accessed. The indexer of the `string` class has the following declaration:

```
public char this[int index] { get; }
```

In other words, a read-only indexer that takes a single argument of type `int` and returns an element of type `char`. Values passed for the `index` argument must be greater than or equal to zero and less than the length of the string.

7.5.7 This access

A *this-access* consists of the reserved word `this`.

this-access:
   `this`

A *this-access* is permitted only in the *block* of a constructor, an instance method, or an instance accessor. It has one of the following meanings:

- When `this` is used in a *primary-expression* within a constructor of a class, it is classified as a value. The type of the value is the class within which the reference occurs, and the value is a reference to the object being constructed.

- When `this` is used in a *primary-expression* within an instance method or instance accessor of a class, it is classified as a value. The type of the value is the class within which the reference occurs, and the value is a reference to the object for which the method or accessor was invoked.

- When `this` is used in a *primary-expression* within a constructor of a struct, it is classified as a variable. The type of the variable is the struct within which the reference occurs, and the variable represents the struct being constructed. The `this` variable of a constructor of a struct behaves exactly the same as an `out` parameter of the struct type—this in particular means that the variable must be definitely assigned in every execution path of the constructor.

- When `this` is used in a *primary-expression* within an instance method or instance accessor of a struct, it is classified as a variable. The type of the variable is the struct within which the reference occurs, and the variable represents the struct for which the method or accessor was invoked. The `this` variable of an instance method of a struct behaves exactly the same as a `ref` parameter of the struct type.

Use of `this` in a *primary-expression* in a context other than the ones listed above is an error. In particular, it is not possible to refer to `this` in a static method, a static property accessor, or in a *variable-initializer* of a field declaration.

7.5.8 Base access

A *base-access* consists of the reserved word `base` followed by either a "." token and an identifier or an *expression-list* enclosed in square brackets:

base-access:
> `base` . *identifier*
> `base` [*expression-list*]

A *base-access* is used to access base class members that are hidden by similarly named members in the current class or struct. A *base-access* is permitted only in the *block* of a constructor, an instance method, or an instance accessor. When `base.I` occurs in a class or struct, `I` must denote a member of the base class of that class or struct. Likewise, when `base[E]` occurs in a class, an applicable indexer must exist in the base class.

At compile-time, *base-access* expressions of the form `base.I` and `base[E]` are evaluated exactly as if they were written `((B)this).I` and `((B)this)[E]`, where B is the base class of the class or struct in which the construct occurs. Thus, `base.I` and `base[E]` correspond to `this.I` and `this[E]`, except `this` is viewed as an instance of the base class.

When a *base-access* references a function member (a method, property, or indexer), the function member is considered non-virtual for purposes of function member invocation (section 7.4.3). Thus, within an `override` of a `virtual` function member, a *base-access* can be used to invoke the inherited implementation of the function member. If the function member referenced by a *base-access* is abstract, an error occurs.

7.5.9 Postfix increment and decrement operators

post-increment-expression:
> *primary-expression* ++

post-decrement-expression:
> *primary-expression* --

The operand of a postfix increment or decrement operation must be an expression classified as a variable, a property access, or an indexer access. The result of the operation is a value of the same type as the operand.

If the operand of a postfix increment or decrement operation is a property or indexer access, the property or indexer must have both a `get` and a `set` accessor. If this is not the case, a compile-time error occurs.

Unary operator overload resolution (section 7.2.3) is applied to select a specific operator implementation. Predefined ++ and -- operators exist for the following types: `sbyte`, `byte`, `short`, `ushort`, `int`, `uint`, `long`, `ulong`, `char`, `float`, `double`, `decimal`, and any enum type. The predefined ++ operators return the value produced by adding 1 to the operand, and the predefined -- operators return the value produced by subtracting 1 from the operand.

The run-time processing of a postfix increment or decrement operation of the form x++ or x-- consists of the following steps:

- If x is classified as a variable:
- x is evaluated to produce the variable.
  - The value of x is saved.
  - The selected operator is invoked with the saved value of x as its argument.
  - The value returned by the operator is stored in the location given by the evaluation of x.
  - The saved value of x becomes the result of the operation.
- If x is classified as a property or indexer access:
  - The instance expression (if x is not static) and the argument list (if x is an indexer access) associated with x are evaluated, and the results are used in the subsequent get and set accessor invocations.
  - The get accessor of x is invoked and the returned value is saved.
  - The selected operator is invoked with the saved value of x as its argument.
  - The set accessor of x is invoked with the value returned by the operator as its value argument.
  - The saved value of x becomes the result of the operation.

The ++ and -- operators also support prefix notation, as described in section 7.6.7. The result of x++ or x-- is the value of x *before* the operation, whereas the result of ++x or --x is the value of x *after* the operation. In either case, x itself has the same value after the operation.

An operator ++ or operator -- implementation can be invoked using either postfix or prefix notation. It is not possible to have separate operator implementations for the two notations.

7.5.10 new operator

The new operator is used to create new instances of types.

new-expression:
  object-creation-expression
  array-creation-expression
  delegate-creation-expression

There are three forms of new expressions:

- Object creation expressions are used to create a new instances of class types and value types.
- Array creation expressions are used to create new instances of array types.
- Delegate creation expressions are used to create new instances of delegate types.

The new operator implies creation of an instance of a type, but does not necessarily imply dynamic allocation of memory. In particular, instances of value types require no additional memory beyond the variables in which they reside, and no dynamic allocations occur when new is used to create instances of value types.

7.5.10.1 Object creation expressions

An *object-creation-expression* is used to create a new instance of a *class-type* or a *value-type*.

object-creation-expression:
   new *type* (*argument-list*$_{opt}$) .

The *type* of an *object-creation-expression* must be a *class-type* or a *value-type*. The *type* cannot be an abstract *class-type*.

The optional *argument-list* (section 7.4.1) is permitted only if the *type* is a *class-type* or a *struct-type*.

The compile-time processing of an *object-creation-expression* of the form new T(A), where T is a *class-type* or a *value-type* and A is an optional *argument-list*, consists of the following steps:

- If T is a *value-type* and A is not present:
  - The *object-creation-expression* is a default constructor invocation. The result of the *object-creation-expression* is a value of type T, namely the default value for T as defined in section 4.1.1.
- Otherwise, if T is a *class-type* or a *struct-type*:
  - If T is an abstract *class-type*, an error occurs.
  - The constructor to invoke is determined using the overload resolution rules of section 7.4.2. The set of candidate constructors consists of all accessible constructors declared in T. If the set of candidate constructors is empty, or if a single best constructor cannot be identified, an error occurs.
  - The result of the *object-creation-expression* is a value of type T, namely the value produced by invoking the constructor determined in the step above.
- Otherwise, the *object-creation-expression* is invalid, and an error occurs.

The run-time processing of an *object-creation-expression* of the form `new T(A)`, where `T` is *class-type* or a *struct-type* and `A` is an optional *argument-list*, consists of the following steps:

- If `T` is a *class-type*:
  - A new instance of class `T` is allocated. If there is not enough memory available to allocate the new instance, an `OutOfMemoryException` is thrown and no further steps are executed.
  - All fields of the new instance are initialized to their default values (section 5.2).
  - The constructor is invoked according to the rules of function member invocation (section 7.4.3). A reference to the newly allocated instance is automatically passed to the constructor and the instance can be accessed from within the constructor as `this`.
- If `T` is a *struct-type*:
  - An instance of type `T` is created by allocating a temporary local variable. Since a constructor of a *struct-type* is required to definitely assign a value to each field of the instance being created, no initialization of the temporary variable is necessary.
  - The constructor is invoked according to the rules of function member invocation (section 7.4.3). A reference to the newly allocated instance is automatically passed to the constructor and the instance can be accessed from within the constructor as `this`.

7.5.10.2 Array creation expressions

An *array-creation-expression* is used to create a new instance of an *array-type*.

array-creation-expression:
```
new  non-array-type  [  expression-list  ]  rank-specifiersopt  array-initializeropt
new  array-type  array-initializer
```

An array creation expression of first form allocates an array instance of the type that results from deleting each of the individual expressions from the expression list. For example, the array creation expression `new int[10, 20]` produces an array instance of type `int[,]`, and the array creation expression `new int[10][,]` produces an array of type `int[][,]`. Each expression in the expression list must be of type `int`, `uint`, `long`, or `ulong`, or of a type that can be implicitly converted to one or more of these types. The value of each expression determines the length of the corresponding dimension in the newly allocated array instance.

If an array creation expression of the first form includes an array initializer, each expression in the expression list must be a constant and the rank and dimension lengths specified by the expression list must match those of the array initializer.

In an array creation expression of the second form, the rank of the specified array type must match that of the array initializer. The individual dimension lengths are inferred from the number of elements in each of the corresponding nesting levels of the array initializer. Thus, the expression

```
new int[,] {{0, 1}, {2, 3}, {4, 5}};
```

exactly corresponds to

```
new int[3, 2] {{0, 1}, {2, 3}, {4, 5}};
```

Array initializers are further described in section 12.6.

The result of evaluating an array creation expression is classified as a value, namely a reference to the newly allocated array instance. The run-time processing of an array creation expression consists of the following steps:

- The dimension length expressions of the *expression-list* are evaluated in order, from left to right. Following evaluation of each expression, an implicit conversion (section 6.1) to type `int` is performed. If evaluation of an expression or the subsequent implicit conversion causes an exception, then no further expressions are evaluated and no further steps are executed.

- The computed values for the dimension lengths are validated. If one or more of the values are less than zero, an `IndexOutOfRangeException` is thrown and no further steps are executed.

- An array instance with the given dimension lengths is allocated. If there is not enough memory available to allocate the new instance, an `OutOfMemoryException` is thrown and no further steps are executed.

- All elements of the new array instance are initialized to their default values (section 5.2).

- If the array creation expression contains an array initializer, then each expression in the array initializer is evaluated and assigned to its corresponding array element. The evaluations and assignments are performed in the order the expressions are written in the array initializer—in other words, elements are initialized in increasing index order, with the rightmost dimension increasing first. If evaluation of a given expression or the subsequent assignment to the corresponding array element causes an exception, then no further elements are initialized (and the remaining elements will thus have their default values).

An array creation expression permits instantiation of an array with elements of an array type, but the elements of such an array must be manually initialized. For example, the statement

```
int[][] a = new int[100][];
```

creates a single-dimensional array with 100 elements of type `int[]`. The initial value of each element is `null`. It is not possible for the same array creation expression to also instantiate the sub-arrays, and the statement

```
int[][] a = new int[100][5];     // Error
```

is an error. Instantiation of the sub-arrays must instead be performed manually, as in

```
int[][] a = new int[100][];
for (int i = 0; i < 100; i++) a[i] = new int[5];
```

When an array of arrays has a "rectangular" shape, that is when the sub-arrays are all of the same length, it is more efficient to use a multi-dimensional array. In the example above, instantiation of the array of arrays creates 101 objects—one outer array and 100 sub-arrays. In contrast,

```
int[,] = new int[100, 5];
```

creates only a single object, a two-dimensional array, and accomplishes the allocation in a single statement.

7.5.10.3 Delegate creation expressions

A *delegate-creation-expression* is used to create a new instance of a *delegate-type*.

delegate-creation-expression:
   new *delegate-type* (*expression*)

The argument of a delegate creation expression must be a method group or a value of a *delegate-type*. If the argument is a method group, it identifies the method and, for an instance method, the object for which to create a delegate. If the argument is a value of a *delegate-type*, it identifies a delegate instance of which to create a copy.

The compile-time processing of a *delegate-creation-expression* of the form new D(E), where D is a *delegate-type* and E is an *expression*, consists of the following steps:

- If E is a method group:
  - If the method group resulted from a *base-access*, an error occurs.
  - The set of methods identified by E must include exactly one method with precisely the same signature and return type as those of D, and this becomes the method to which the newly created delegate refers. If no matching method exists, or if more than one matching methods exists, an error occurs. If the selected method is an instance method, the instance expression associated with E determines the target object of the delegate.

- As in a method invocation, the selected method must be compatible with the context of the method group: If the method is a static method, the method group must have resulted from a *simple-name* or a *member-access* through a type. If the method is an instance method, the method group must have resulted from a *simple-name* or a *member-access* through a variable or value. If the selected method does not match the context of the method group, an error occurs.

- The result is a value of type D, namely a newly created delegate that refers to the selected method and target object.

- Otherwise, if E is a value of a *delegate-type*:

  - The *delegate-type* of E must have the exact same signature and return type as D, or otherwise an error occurs.

  - The result is a value of type D, namely a newly created delegate that refers to the same method and target object as E.

- Otherwise, the delegate creation expression is invalid, and an error occurs.

The run-time processing of a *delegate-creation-expression* of the form new D(E), where D is a *delegate-type* and E is an *expression*, consists of the following steps:

- If E is a method group:

  - If the method selected at compile-time is a static method, the target object of the delegate is null. Otherwise, the selected method is an instance method, and the target object of the delegate is determined from the instance expression associated with E:

    - The instance expression is evaluated. If this evaluation causes an exception, no further steps are executed.

    - If the instance expression is of a *reference-type*, the value computed by the instance expression becomes the target object. If the target object is null, a NullReferenceException is thrown and no further steps are executed.

    - If the instance expression is of a *value-type*, a boxing operation (section 4.3.1) is performed to convert the value to an object, and this object becomes the target object.

  - A new instance of the delegate type D is allocated. If there is not enough memory available to allocate the new instance, an OutOfMemoryException is thrown and no further steps are executed.

  - The new delegate instance is initialized with a reference to the method that was determined at compile-time and a reference to the target object computed above.

- If E is a value of a *delegate-type*:

- E is evaluated. If this evaluation causes an exception, no further steps are executed.
  - If the value of E is `null`, a `NullReferenceException` is thrown and no further steps are executed.
  - A new instance of the delegate type D is allocated. If there is not enough memory available to allocate the new instance, an `OutOfMemoryException` is thrown and no further steps are executed.
  - The new delegate instance is initialized with references to the same method and object as the delegate instance given by E.

The method and object to which a delegate refers are determined when the delegate is instantiated and then remain constant for the entire lifetime of the delegate. In other words, it is not possible to change the target method or object of a delegate once it has been created.

It is not possible to create a delegate that refers to a constructor, property, indexer, or user-defined operator.

As described above, when a delegate is created from a method group, the signature and return type of the delegate determine which of the overloaded methods to select. In the example

```
delegate double DoubleFunc(double x);
class A
{
   DoubleFunc f = new DoubleFunc(Square);
   static float Square(float x) {
      return x * x;
   }
   static double Square(double x) {
      return x * x;
   }
}
```

the `A.f` field is initialized with a delegate that refers to the second `Square` method because that method exactly matches the signature and return type of `DoubleFunc`. Had the second `Square` method not been present, a compile-time error would have occurred.

7.5.11 typeof operator

The `typeof` operator is used to obtain the `System.Type` object for a type.

typeof-expression:
    typeof (*type*)

The result of a *typeof-expression* is the `System.Type` object for the indicated type.

The example

```
class Test
{
  static void Main() {
    Type[] t = {
      typeof(int),
      typeof(System.Int32),
      typeof(string),
      typeof(double[])
    };
    for (int i = 0; i < t.Length; i++) {
      Console.WriteLine(t[i].Name);
    }
  }
}
```

produces the following output:

```
Int32
Int32
String
Double[]
```

Note that `int` and `System.Int32` are the same type.

7.5.12 checked and unchecked operators

The `checked` and `unchecked` operators are used to control the **overflow checking context** for integral-type arithmetic operations and conversions.

checked-expression:
   checked (*expression*)

unchecked-expression:
   unchecked (*expression*)

The `checked` operator evaluates the contained expression in a checked context, and the `unchecked` operator evaluates the contained expression in an unchecked context. A *checked-expression* or *unchecked-expression* corresponds exactly to a *parenthesized-expression* (section 7.5.3), except that the contained expression is evaluated in the given overflow checking context.

The overflow checking context can also be controlled through the `checked` and `unchecked` statements (section 8.11).

The following operations are affected by the overflow checking context established by the checked and unchecked operators and statements:

- The predefined ++ and -- unary operators (section 7.5.9 and section 7.6.7), when the operand is of an integral type.
- The predefined - unary operator (section 7.6.2), when the operand is of an integral type.
- The predefined +, -, *, and / binary operators (section 7.7), when both operands are of integral types.
- Explicit numeric conversions (section 6.2.1) from one integral type to another integral type.

When one of the above operations produce a result that is too large to represent in the destination type, the context in which the operation is performed controls the resulting behavior:

- In a checked context, if the operation is a constant expression (section 7.15), a compile-time error occurs. Otherwise, when the operation is performed at run-time, an OverflowException is thrown.
- In an unchecked context, the result is truncated by discarding any high-order bits that do not fit in the destination type.

When a non-constant expression (an expression that is evaluated at run-time) is not enclosed by any checked or unchecked operators or statements, the effect of an overflow during the run-time evaluation of the expression depends on external factors (such as compiler switches and execution environment configuration). The effect is however guaranteed to be either that of a checked evaluation or that of an unchecked evaluation.

For constant expressions (expressions that can be fully evaluated at compile-time), the default overflow checking context is always checked. Unless a constant expression is explicitly placed in an unchecked context, overflows that occur during the compile-time evaluation of the expression always cause compile-time errors.

In the example

```
class Test
{
    static int x = 1000000;
    static int y = 1000000;
    static int F() {
        return checked(x * y);    // Throws OverflowException
    }
    static int G() {
        return unchecked(x * y);  // Returns -727379968
    }
    static int H() {
        return x * y;             // Depends on default
    }
}
```

no compile-time errors are reported since neither of the expressions can be evaluated at compile-time. At run-time, the F() method throws an OverflowException, and the G() method returns –727379968 (the lower 32 bits of the out-of-range result). The behavior of the H() method depends on the default overflow checking context for the compilation, but it is either the same as F() or the same as G().

In the example

```
class Test
{
   const int x = 1000000;
   const int y = 1000000;
   static int F() {
      return checked(x * y);     // Compile error, overflow
   }
   static int G() {
      return unchecked(x * y);   // Returns -727379968
   }
   static int H() {
      return x * y;              // Compile error, overflow
   }
}
```

the overflows that occur when evaluating the constant expressions in F() and H() cause compile-time errors to be reported because the expressions are evaluated in a checked context. An overflow also occurs when evaluating the constant expression in G(), but since the evaluation takes place in an unchecked context, the overflow is not reported.

The checked and unchecked operators only affect the overflow checking context for those operations that are textually contained within the "(" and ")" tokens. The operators have no effect on function members that are invoked as a result of evaluating the contained expression. In the example

```
class Test
{
   static int Multiply(int x, int y) {
      return x * y;
   }
   static int F() {
      return checked(Multiply(1000000, 1000000));
   }
}
```

the use of checked in F() does not affect the evaluation of x * y in Multiply(), and x * y is therefore evaluated in the default overflow checking context.

The unchecked operator is convenient when writing constants of the signed integral types in hexadecimal notation. For example:

```
class Test
{
    public const int AllBits = unchecked((int)0xFFFFFFFF);
    public const int HighBit = unchecked((int)0x80000000);
}
```

Both of the hexadecimal constants above are of type uint. Because the constants are outside the int range, without the unchecked operator, the casts to int would produce compile-time errors.

7.6 Unary expressions

unary-expression:
   primary-expression
  + *unary-expression*
  - *unary-expression*
  ! *unary-expression*
  ~ *unary-expression*
  * *unary-expression*
  & *unary-expression*
   pre-increment-expression
   pre-decrement-expression
   cast-expression

7.6.1 Unary plus operator

For an operation of the form +x, unary operator overload resolution (section 7.2.3) is applied to select a specific operator implementation. The operand is converted to the parameter type of the selected operator, and the type of the result is the return type of the operator. The predefined unary plus operators are:

```
int operator +(int x);
uint operator +(uint x);
long operator +(long x);
ulong operator +(ulong x);
float operator +(float x);
double operator +(double x);
decimal operator +(decimal x);
```

For each of these operators, the result is simply the value of the operand.

7.6.2 Unary minus operator

For an operation of the form -x, unary operator overload resolution (section 7.2.3) is applied to select a specific operator implementation. The operand is converted to the parameter type of the selected operator, and the type of the result is the return type of the operator. The predefined negation operators are:

- Integer negation:

```
int operator -(int x);
long operator -(long x);
```

The result is computed by subtracting x from zero. In a checked context, if the value of x is the maximum negative int or long, an OverflowException is thrown. In an unchecked context, if the value of x is the maximum negative int or long, the result is that same value and the overflow is not reported.

If the operand of the negation operator is of type uint, it is converted to type long, and the type of the result is long. An exception is the rule that permits the int value -2147483648 (-2^{31}) to be written as a decimal integer literal (section 2.4.4.2).

If the operand of the negation operator is of type ulong, an error occurs. An exception is the rule that permits the long value -9223372036854775808 (-2^{63}) to be written as decimal integer literal (section 2.4.4.2).

- Floating-point negation:

```
float operator -(float x);
double operator -(double x);
```

The result is the value of x with its sign inverted. If x is NaN, the result is also NaN.

- Decimal negation:

```
decimal operator -(decimal x);
```

The result is computed by subtracting x from zero.

7.6.3 Logical negation operator

For an operation of the form !x, unary operator overload resolution (section 7.2.3) is applied to select a specific operator implementation. The operand is converted to the parameter type of the selected operator, and the type of the result is the return type of the operator. Only one predefined logical negation operator exists:

```
bool operator !(bool x);
```

This operator computes the logical negation of the operand: If the operand is true, the result is false. If the operand is false, the result is true.

7.6.4 Bitwise complement operator

For an operation of the form ~x, unary operator overload resolution (section 7.2.3) is applied to select a specific operator implementation. The operand is converted to the parameter type of the selected operator, and the type of the result is the return type of the operator. The predefined bitwise complement operators are:

```
int operator ~(int x);
uint operator ~(uint x);
long operator ~(long x);
ulong operator ~(ulong x);
```

For each of these operators, the result of the operation is the bitwise complement of x.

Every enumeration type E implicitly provides the following bitwise complement operator:

```
E operator ~(E x);
```

The result of evaluating ~x, where x is an expression of an enumeration type E with an underlying type U, is exactly the same as evaluating (E)(~(U)x).

7.6.5 Indirection operator

7.6.6 Address operator

7.6.7 Prefix increment and decrement operators

pre-increment-expression:
   ++ unary-expression

pre-decrement-expression:
   -- unary-expression

The operand of a prefix increment or decrement operation must be an expression classified as a variable, a property access, or an indexer access. The result of the operation is a value of the same type as the operand.

If the operand of a prefix increment or decrement operation is a property or indexer access, the property or indexer must have both a get and a set accessor. If this is not the case, a compile-time error occurs.

Unary operator overload resolution (section 7.2.3) is applied to select a specific operator implementation. Predefined ++ and -- operators exist for the following types: sbyte, byte, short, ushort, int, uint, long, ulong, char, float, double, decimal, and any enum type. The predefined ++ operators return the value produced by adding 1 to the operand, and the predefined -- operators return the value produced by subtracting 1 from the operand.

The run-time processing of a prefix increment or decrement operation of the form ++x or --x consists of the following steps:

- If x is olassified as a variable:
  - x is evaluated to produce the variable.
  - The selected operator is invoked with the value of x as its argument.
  - The value returned by the operator is stored in the location given by the evaluation of x.
  - The value returned by the operator becomes the result of the operation.
- If x is classified as a property or indexer access:
  - The instance expression (if x is not `static`) and the argument list (if x is an indexer access) associated with x are evaluated, and the results are used in the subsequent `get` and `set` accessor invocations.
  - The `get` accessor of x is invoked.
  - The selected operator is invoked with the value returned by the `get` accessor as its argument.
  - The `set` accessor of x is invoked with the value returned by the operator as its `value` argument.
  - The value returned by the operator becomes the result of the operation.

The ++ and -- operators also support postfix notation, as described in section 7.5.9. The result of x++ or x-- is the value of x *before* the operation, whereas the result of ++x or --x is the value of x *after* the operation. In either case, x itself has the same value after the operation.

An `operator ++` or `operator --` implementation can be invoked using either postfix or prefix notation. It is not possible to have separate operator implementations for the two notations.

7.6.8 Cast expressions

A *cast-expression* is used to explicitly convert an expression to a given type.

cast-expression:
    (*type*) *unary-expression*

A *cast-expression* of the form (T)E, where T is a *type* and E is a *unary-expression*, performs an explicit conversion (section 6.2) of the value of E to type T. If no explicit conversion exists from the type of E to T, an error occurs. Otherwise, the result is the value produced by the explicit conversion. The result is always classified as a value, even if E denotes a variable.

The grammar for a *cast-expression* leads to certain syntactic ambiguities. For example, the expression (x)-y could either be interpreted as a *cast-expression* (a cast of -y to type x) or as an *additive-expression* combined with a *parenthesized-expression* (which computes the value x - y).

To resolve *cast-expression* ambiguities, the following rule exists: A sequence of one or more *token*s (section 2.4) enclosed in parentheses is considered the start of a *cast-expression* only if at least one of the following are true:

- The sequence of tokens is correct grammar for a *type*, but not for an *expression*.
- The sequence of tokens is correct grammar for a *type*, and the token immediately following the closing parentheses is the token "~", the token "!", the token "(", an *identifier* (section 2.4.1), a *literal* (section 2.4.4), or any *keyword* (section 2.4.3) except is.

The above rules mean that only if the construct is unambiguously a *cast-expression* is it considered a *cast-expression*.

The term "correct grammar" above means only that the sequence of tokens must conform to the particular grammatical production. It specifically does not consider the actual meaning of any constituent identifiers. For example, if x and y are identifiers, then x.y is correct grammar for a type, even if x.y doesn't actually denote a type.

From the disambiguation rules it follows that, if x and y are identifiers, (x)y, (x)(y), and (x)(-y) are *cast-expression*s, but (x)-y is not, even if x identifies a type. However, if x is a keyword that identifies a predefined type (such as int), then all four forms are *cast-expression*s (because such a keyword could not possibly be an expression by itself).

7.7 Arithmetic operators

The *, /, %, +, and - operators are called the arithmetic operators.

multiplicative-expression:
    unary-expression
    multiplicative-expression * unary-expression*
    multiplicative-expression / *unary-expression*
    multiplicative-expression % *unary-expression*

additive-expression:
    multiplicative-expression
    additive-expression + *multiplicative-expression*
    additive-expression - *multiplicative-expression*

7.7.1 Multiplication operator

For an operation of the form x * y, binary operator overload resolution (section 7.2.4) is applied to select a specific operator implementation. The operands are converted to the parameter types of the selected operator, and the type of the result is the return type of the operator.

The predefined multiplication operators are listed below. The operators all compute the product of x and y.

- Integer multiplication:

```
int operator *(int x, int y);
uint operator *(uint x, uint y);
long operator *(long x, long y);
ulong operator *(ulong x, ulong y);
```

In a checked context, if the product is outside the range of the result type, an OverflowException is thrown. In an unchecked context, overflows are not reported and any significant high-order bits of the result are discarded.

- Floating-point multiplication:

```
float operator *(float x, float y);
double operator *(double x, double y);
```

The product is computed according to the rules of IEEE 754 arithmetic. The following table lists the results of all possible combinations of nonzero finite values, zeros, infinities, and NaN's. In the table, x and y are positive finite values. z is the result of x * y. If the result is too large for the destination type, z is infinity. If the result is too small for the destination type, z is zero.

	+y	−y	+0	−0	+∞	−∞	NaN
+x	z	−z	+0	−0	+∞	−∞	NaN
−x	−z	z	−0	+0	−∞	+∞	NaN
+0	+0	−0	+0	−0	NaN	NaN	NaN
−0	−0	+0	−0	+0	NaN	NaN	NaN
+∞	+∞	+∞	NaN	NaN	+∞	+∞	NaN
−∞	−∞	+∞	NaN	NaN	−∞	+∞	NaN
NaN	NaN	NaN	NaN	NaN	NaN	NaN	NaN

- Decimal multiplication:

```
decimal operator *(decimal x, decimal y);
```

If the resulting value is too large to represent in the decimal format, an OverflowException is thrown. If the result value is too small to represent in the decimal format, the result is zero.

7.7.2 Division operator

For an operation of the form x / y, binary operator overload resolution (section 7.2.4) is applied to select a specific operator implementation. The operands are converted to the parameter types of the selected operator, and the type of the result is the return type of the operator.

The predefined division operators are listed below. The operators all compute the quotient of x and y.

- Integer division:

```
int operator /(int x, int y);
uint operator /(uint x, uint y);
long operator /(long x, long y);
ulong operator /(ulong x, ulong y);
```

If the value of the right operand is zero, a DivideByZeroException is thrown.

The division rounds the result towards zero, and the absolute value of the result is the largest possible integer that is less than the absolute value of the quotient of the two operands. The result is zero or positive when the two operands have the same sign and zero or negative when the two operands have opposite signs.

If the left operand is the maximum negative int or long and the right operand is -1, an overflow occurs. In a checked context, this causes an OverflowException to be thrown. In an unchecked context, the overflow is not reported and the result is instead the value of the left operand.

- Floating-point division:

```
float operator /(float x, float y);
double operator /(double x, double y);
```

The quotient is computed according to the rules of IEEE 754 arithmetic. The following table lists the results of all possible combinations of nonzero finite values, zeros, infinities, and NaN's. In the table, x and y are positive finite values. z is the result of x / y. If the result is too large for the destination type, z is infinity. If the result is too small for the destination type, z is zero.

	+y	−y	+0	−0	+∞	−∞	**NaN**
+x	z	−z	+∞	−∞	+0	−0	NaN
−x	−z	z	−∞	+∞	−0	+0	NaN
+0	+0	−0	NaN	NaN	+0	−0	NaN
−0	−0	+0	NaN	NaN	−0	+0	NaN
+∞	+∞	−∞	+∞	−∞	NaN	NaN	NaN
−∞	−∞	+∞	−∞	+∞	NaN	NaN	NaN
NaN	NaN	NaN	NaN	NaN	NaN	NaN	NaN

- Decimal division:

```
decimal operator /(decimal x, decimal y);
```

If the value of the right operand is zero, a `DivideByZeroException` is thrown. If the resulting value is too large to represent in the `decimal` format, an `OverflowException` is thrown. If the result value is too small to represent in the `decimal` format, the result is zero.

7.7.3 Remainder operator

For an operation of the form $x \% y$, binary operator overload resolution (section 7.2.4) is applied to select a specific operator implementation. The operands are converted to the parameter types of the selected operator, and the type of the result is the return type of the operator.

The predefined remainder operators are listed below. The operators all compute the remainder of the division between x and y.

- Integer remainder:

```
int operator %(int x, int y);
uint operator %(uint x, uint y);
long operator %(long x, long y);
ulong operator %(ulong x, ulong y);
```

The result of $x \% y$ is the value produced by $x - (x / y) * y$. If y is zero, a `DivideByZeroException` is thrown. The remainder operator never causes an overflow.

- Floating-point remainder:

```
float operator %(float x, float y);
double operator %(double x, double y);
```

The following table lists the results of all possible combinations of nonzero finite values, zeros, infinities, and NaN's. In the table, x and y are positive finite values. z is the result of $x \% y$ and is computed as $x - n * y$, where n is the largest possible integer that is less than or equal to x / y. This method of computing the remainder is analogous to that used for integer operands, but differs from the IEEE 754 definition (in which n is the integer closest to x / y).

	+y	−y	+0	−0	+∞	−∞	NaN
+x	z	z	NaN	NaN	x	x	NaN
−x	−z	−z	NaN	NaN	−x	−x	NaN
+0	+0	+0	NaN	NaN	+0	+0	NaN
−0	−0	−0	NaN	NaN	−0	−0	NaN
+∞	NaN	NaN	NaN	NaN	NaN	NaN	NaN
−∞	NaN	NaN	NaN	NaN	NaN	NaN	NaN
NaN	NaN	NaN	NaN	NaN	NaN	NaN	NaN

- Decimal remainder:

```
decimal operator %(decimal x, decimal y);
```

If the value of the right operand is zero, a `DivideByZeroException` is thrown. If the resulting value is too large to represent in the `decimal` format, an `OverflowException` is thrown. If the result value is too small to represent in the `decimal` format, the result is zero.

7.7.4 Addition operator

For an operation of the form $x + y$, binary operator overload resolution (section 7.2.4) is applied to select a specific operator implementation. The operands are converted to the parameter types of the selected operator, and the type of the result is the return type of the operator.

The predefined addition operators are listed below. For numeric and enumeration types, the predefined addition operators compute the sum of the two operands. When one or both operands are of type string, the predefined addition operators concatenate the string representation of the operands.

- Integer addition:

```
int operator +(int x, int y);
uint operator +(uint x, uint y);
long operator +(long x, long y);
ulong operator +(ulong x, ulong y);
```

In a `checked` context, if the sum is outside the range of the result type, an `OverflowException` is thrown. In an `unchecked` context, overflows are not reported and any significant high-order bits of the result are discarded.

- Floating-point addition:

```
float operator +(float x, float y);
double operator +(double x, double y);
```

The sum is computed according to the rules of IEEE 754 arithmetic. The following table lists the results of all possible combinations of nonzero finite values, zeros, infinities, and NaN's. In the table, x and y are nonzero finite values, and z is the result of $x + y$. If x and y have the same magnitude but opposite signs, z is positive zero. If $x + y$ is too large to represent in the destination type, z is an infinity with the same sign as $x + y$. If $x + y$ is too small to represent in the destination type, z is a zero with the same sign as $x + y$.

	y	+0	−0	+∞	−∞	NaN
x	z	x	x	+∞	−∞	NaN
+0	y	+0	+0	+∞	−∞	NaN
−0	y	+0	−0	+∞	−∞	NaN
+∞	+∞	+∞	+∞	+∞	NaN	NaN
−∞	−∞	−∞	−∞	NaN	−∞	NaN
NaN	NaN	NaN	NaN	NaN	NaN	NaN

- Decimal addition:

```
decimal operator +(decimal x, decimal y);
```

If the resulting value is too large to represent in the decimal format, an OverflowException is thrown. If the result value is too small to represent in the decimal format, the result is zero.

- Enumeration addition. Every enumeration type implicitly provides the following predefined operators, where E is the enum type, and U is the underlying type of E:

```
E operator +(E x, U y);
E operator +(U x, E y);
```

The operators are evaluated exactly as (E)((U)x + (U)y).

- String concatenation:

```
string operator +(string x, string y);
string operator +(string x, object y);
string operator +(object x, string y);
```

The binary + operator performs string concatenation when one or both operands are of type string. If an operand of string concatenation is null, an empty string is substituted. Otherwise, any non-string argument is converted to its string representation by invoking the virtual ToString() method inherited from type object. If ToString() returns null, an empty string is substituted.

The result of the string concatenation operator is a string that consists of the characters of the left operand followed by the characters of the right operand. The string concatenation operator never returns a null value. An OutOfMemoryException may be thrown if there is not enough memory available to allocate the resulting string.

- Delegate combination. Every delegate type implicitly provides the following predefined operator, where D is the delegate type:

```
D operator +(D x, D y);
```

The binary + operator performs delegate combination when one or both operands are of a delegate type D. If the first operand is null, then the result of the operation is the value of the second operand. Otherwise, if the second operand is null, then the result of the operation is the value of the first operand. Otherwise, if D is a combinable delegate type (section 15.1.1) then the result of the operation is a new delegate instance that, when invoked, invokes the first operand and then invokes the second operand. Otherwise, D is not a combinable delegate type, and a MulticastNotSupportedException is thrown.

7.7.5 Subtraction operator

For an operation of the form x - y, binary operator overload resolution (section 7.2.4) is applied to select a specific operator implementation. The operands are converted to the parameter types of the selected operator, and the type of the result is the return type of the operator.

The predefined subtraction operators are listed below. The operators all subtract y from x.

- Integer subtraction:

```
int operator -(int x, int y);
uint operator -(uint x, uint y);
long operator -(long x, long y);
ulong operator -(ulong x, ulong y);
```

In a checked context, if the difference is outside the range of the result type, an OverflowException is thrown. In an unchecked context, overflows are not reported and any significant high-order bits of the result are discarded.

- Floating-point subtraction:

```
float operator -(float x, float y);
double operator -(double x, double y);
```

The difference is computed according to the rules of IEEE 754 arithmetic. The following table lists the results of all possible combinations of nonzero finite values, zeros, infinities, and NaN's. In the table, x and y are nonzero finite values, and z is the result of x - y. If x and y are equal, z is positive zero. If x - y is too large to represent in the destination type, z is an infinity with the same sign as x - y. If x - y is too small to represent in the destination type, z is a zero with the same sign as x - y.

	y	+0	−0	+∞	−∞	**NaN**
x	z	x	x	−∞	+∞	NaN
+0	−y	+0	+0	−∞	+∞	NaN
−0	−y	−0	+0	−∞	+∞	NaN
+∞	+∞	+∞	+∞	NaN	+∞	NaN
−∞	−∞	−∞	−∞	−∞	NaN	NaN
NaN	NaN	NaN	NaN	NaN	NaN	NaN

- Decimal subtraction:

```
decimal operator -(decimal x, decimal y);
```

If the resulting value is too large to represent in the decimal format, an OverflowException is thrown. If the result value is too small to represent in the decimal format, the result is zero.

- Enumeration subtraction. Every enumeration type implicitly provides the following predefined operator, where E is the enum type, and U is the underlying type of E:

```
U operator -(E x, E y);
```

This operator is evaluated exactly as (U)((U)x - (U)y). In other words, the operator computes the difference between the ordinal values of x and y, and the type of the result is the underlying type of the enumeration.

```
E operator -(E x, U y);
```

This operator is evaluated exactly as (E)((U)x - y). In other words, the operator subtracts a value from the underlying type of the enumeration, yielding a value of the enumeration.

- Delegate removal. Every delegate type implicitly provides the following predefined operator, where D is the delegate type:

```
D operator -(D x, D y);
```

The binary - operator performs delegate removal when one or both operands are of a delegate type D.

7.8 Shift operators

The << and >> operators are used to perform bit shifting operations.

shift-expression:
   additive-expression
   shift-expression << *additive-expression*
   shift-expression >> *additive-expression*

For an operation of the form x << count or x >> count, binary operator overload resolution (section 7.2.4) is applied to select a specific operator implementation. The operands are converted to the parameter types of the selected operator, and the type of the result is the return type of the operator.

When declaring an overloaded shift operator, the type of the first operand must always be the class or struct containing the operator declaration, and the type of the second operand must always be `int`.

The predefined shift operators are listed below.

- Shift left:

```
int operator <<(int x, int count);
uint operator <<(uint x, int count);
long operator <<(long x, int count);
ulong operator <<(ulong x, int count);
```

The `<<` operator shifts `x` left by a number of bits computed as described below.

The high-order bits of `x` are discarded, the remaining bits are shifted left, and the low-order empty bit positions are set to zero.

- Shift right:

```
int operator >>(int x, int count);
uint operator >>(uint x, int count);
long operator >>(long x, int count);
ulong operator >>(ulong x, int count);
```

The `>>` operator shifts `x` right by a number of bits computed as described below.

When `x` is of type `int` or `long`, the low-order bits of `x` are discarded, the remaining bits are shifted right, and the high-order empty bit positions are set to zero if `x` is non-negative and set to one if `x` is negative.

When `x` is of type `uint` or `ulong`, the low-order bits of `x` are discarded, the remaining bits are shifted right, and the high-order empty bit positions are set to zero.

For the predefined operators, the number of bits to shift is computed as follows:

- When the type of `x` is `int` or `uint`, the shift count is given by the low-order five bits of `count`. In other words, the shift count is computed from `count & 0x1F`.
- When the type of `x` is `long` or `ulong`, the shift count is given by the low-order six bits of `count`. In other words, the shift count is computed from `count & 0x3F`.

If the resulting shift count is zero, the shift operators simply return the value of `x`.

Shift operations never cause overflows and produce the same results in `checked` and `unchecked` contexts.

When the left operand of the `>>` operator is of a signed integral type, the operator performs an *arithmetic* shift right wherein the value of the most significant bit (the sign bit) of the operand is propagated to the high-order empty bit positions. When the left operand of the `>>` operator is of an unsigned integral type, the operator performs a *logical* shift right wherein high-order empty bit positions are always set to zero. To perform the opposite operation of that inferred from the operand type, explicit casts can be used. For example, if `x` is a variable of type `int`, the operation `(int)((uint)x >> y)` performs a logical shift right of `x`.

7.9 Relational operators

The ==, !=, <, >, <=, >=, is and as operators are called the relational operators.

relational-expression:
 shift-expression
 relational-expression < *shift-expression*
 relational-expression > *shift-expression*
 relational-expression <= *shift-expression*
 relational-expression >= *shift-expression*
 relational-expression is *type*
 relational-expression as *type*

equality-expression:
 relational-expression
 equality-expression == *relational-expression*
 equality-expression != *relational-expression*

The is operator is described in section 7.9.9 and the as operator is described in section 7.9.10.

The ==, !=, <, >, <= and >= operators are ***comparison operators***. For an operation of the form x *op* y, where *op* is a comparison operator, overload resolution (section 7.2.4) is applied to select a specific operator implementation. The operands are converted to the parameter types of the selected operator, and the type of the result is the return type of the operator.

The predefined comparison operators are described in the following sections.
All predefined comparison operators return a result of type bool, as described in the following table.

Operation	Result
x == y	true if x is equal to y, false otherwise
x != y	true if x is not equal to y, false otherwise
x < y	true if x is less than y, false otherwise
x > y	true if x is greater than y, false otherwise
x <= y	true if x is less than or equal to y, false otherwise
x >= y	true if x is greater than or equal to y, false otherwise

7.9.1 Integer comparison operators

The predefined integer comparison operators are:

```
bool operator ==(int x, int y);
bool operator ==(uint x, uint y);
bool operator ==(long x, long y);
bool operator ==(ulong x, ulong y);
bool operator !=(int x, int y);
bool operator !=(uint x, uint y);
bool operator !=(long x, long y);
bool operator !=(ulong x, ulong y);
bool operator <(int x, int y);
bool operator <(uint x, uint y);
bool operator <(long x, long y);
bool operator <(ulong x, ulong y);
bool operator >(int x, int y);
bool operator >(uint x, uint y);
bool operator >(long x, long y);
bool operator >(ulong x, ulong y);
bool operator <=(int x, int y);
bool operator <=(uint x, uint y);
bool operator <=(long x, long y);
bool operator <=(ulong x, ulong y);
bool operator >=(int x, int y);
bool operator >=(uint x, uint y);
bool operator >=(long x, long y);
bool operator >=(ulong x, ulong y);
```

Each of these operators compare the numeric values of the two integer operands and return a `bool` value that indicates whether the particular relation is `true` or `false`.

7.9.2 Floating-point comparison operators

The predefined floating-point comparison operators are:

```
bool operator ==(float x, float y);
bool operator ==(double x, double y);
bool operator !=(float x, float y);
bool operator !=(double x, double y);
bool operator <(float x, float y);
bool operator <(double x, double y);
```

```
bool operator >(float x, float y);
bool operator >(double x, double y);
bool operator <=(float x, float y);
bool operator <=(double x, double y);
bool operator >=(float x, float y);
bool operator >=(double x, double y);
```

The operators compare the operands according to the rules of the IEEE 754 standard:

- If either operand is NaN, the result is `false` for all operators except `!=`, and `true` for the `!=` operator. For any two operands, `x != y` always produces the same result as `!(x == y)`. However, when one or both operands are NaN, the `<`, `>`, `<=`, and `>=` operators *do not* produce the same results as the logical negation of the opposite operator. For example, if either of `x` and `y` is NaN, then `x < y` is `false`, but `!(x >= y)` is `true`.

- When neither operand is NaN, the operators compare the values of the two floating-point operands with respect to the ordering

```
-∞ < -max < ... < -min < -0.0 == +0.0 < +min < ... < +max < +∞
```

where `min` and `max` are the smallest and largest positive finite values that can be represented in the given floating-point format. Notable effects of this ordering are:

- Negative and positive zero are considered equal.
- A negative infinity is considered less than all other values, but equal to another negative infinity.
- A positive infinity is considered greater than all other values, but equal to another positive infinity.

7.9.3 Decimal comparison operators

The predefined decimal comparison operators are:

```
bool operator ==(decimal x, decimal y);
bool operator !=(decimal x, decimal y);
bool operator <(decimal x, decimal y);
bool operator >(decimal x, decimal y);
bool operator <=(decimal x, decimal y);
bool operator >=(decimal x, decimal y);
```

Each of these operators compare the numeric values of the two decimal operands and return a `bool` value that indicates whether the particular relation is `true` or `false`.

7.9.4 Boolean equality operators

The predefined boolean equality operators are:

```
bool operator ==(bool x, bool y);
bool operator !=(bool x, bool y);
```

The result of == is `true` if both x and y are `true` or if both x and y are `false`. Otherwise, the result is `false`.

The result of != is `false` if both x and y are `true` or if both x and y are `false`. Otherwise, the result is `true`. When the operands are of type `bool`, the != operator produces the same result as the ^ operator.

7.9.5 Enumeration comparison operators

Every enumeration type implicitly provides the following predefined comparison operators:

```
bool operator ==(E x, E y);
bool operator !=(E x, E y);
bool operator <(E x, E y);
bool operator >(E x, E y);
bool operator <=(E x, E y);
bool operator >=(E x, E y);
```

The result of evaluating x *op* y, where x and y are expressions of an enumeration type E with an underlying type U, and *op* is one of the comparison operators, is exactly the same as evaluating ((U)x) *op* ((U)y). In other words, the enumeration type comparison operators simply compare the underlying integral values of the two operands.

7.9.6 Reference type equality operators

The predefined reference type equality operators are:

```
bool operator ==(object x, object y);
bool operator !=(object x, object y);
```

The operators return the result of comparing the two references for equality or non-equality.

Since the predefined reference type equality operators accept operands of type `object`, they apply to all types that do not declare applicable `operator ==` and `operator !=` members. Conversely, any applicable user-defined equality operators effectively hide the predefined reference type equality operators.

The predefined reference type equality operators require the operands to be *reference-type* values or the value `null`, and furthermore require that an implicit conversion exists from the type of either operand to the type of the other operand. Unless both of these conditions are true, a compile-time error occurs. Notable implications of these rules are:

- It is an error to use the predefined reference type equality operators to compare two references that are known to be different at compile-time. For example, if the compile time types of the operands are two class types A and B, and if neither A nor B derives from the other, then it would be impossible for the two operands to reference the same object. Thus, the operation is considered a compile-time error.

- The predefined reference type equality operators do not permit value type operands to be compared. Therefore, unless a struct type declares its own equality operators, it is not possible to compare values of that struct type.

- The predefined reference type equality operators never cause boxing operations to occur for their operands. It would be meaningless to perform such boxing operations, since references to the newly allocated boxed instances would necessarily differ from all other references.

For an operation of the form x == y or x != y, if any applicable `operator ==` or `operator !=` exists, the operator overload resolution (section 7.2.4) rules will select that operator instead of the predefined reference type equality operator. However, it is always possible to select the reference type equality operator by explicitly casting one or both of the operands to type `object`. The example

```
class Test
{
   static void Main() {
      string s = "Test";
      string t = string.Copy(s);
      Console.WriteLine(s == t);
      Console.WriteLine((object)s == t);
      Console.WriteLine(s == (object)t);
      Console.WriteLine((object)s == (object)t);
   }
}
```

produces the output

```
True
False
False
False
```

The s and t variables refer to two distinct string instances containing the same characters. The first comparison outputs True because the predefined string equality operator (section 7.9.7) is selected when both operands are of type string. The remaining comparisons all output False because the predefined reference type equality operator is selected when one or both of the operands are of type object.

Note that the above technique is not meaningful for value types. The example

```
class Test
{
    static void Main() {
        int i = 123;
        int j = 123;
        Console.WriteLine((object)i == (object)j);
    }
}
```

outputs False because the casts create references to two separate instances of boxed int values.

7.9.7 String equality operators

The predefined string equality operators are:

```
bool operator ==(string x, string y);
bool operator !=(string x, string y);
```

Two string values are considered equal when one of the following is true:

- Both values are null.
- Both values are non-null references to string instances that have identical lengths and identical characters in each character position.

The string equality operators compare string *values* rather than string *references*. When two separate string instances contain the exact same sequence of characters, the values of the strings are equal, but the references are different. As described in section 7.9.6, the reference type equality operators can be used to compare string references instead of string values.

7.9.8 Delegate equality operators

Every delegate type D implicitly provides the following predefined comparison operators:

```
bool operator ==(System.Delegate x, D y);
bool operator ==(D x, System.Delegate y);
bool operator !=(System.Delegate x, D y);
bool operator !=(D x, System.Delegate y);
```

Two delegate instances are considered equal as follows:

- If either of the delegate instances is `null`, they are equal if and only if both are `null`.
- If either of the delegate instances was instantiated with another delegate, they are equal if and only if both were instantiated on the same delegate instance. Otherwise,
- If either of the delegate instances is a non-multicast delegate, the are equal if and only if both are non-multicast delegates, and either:
  - both refer to the same static method, or
  - both refer to the same non-static method on the same target object.
- If either of the delegate instances is a multi-cast delegate, they are equal if and only if their invocation lists are the same length, and each delegate in one's invocation list is equal to the corresponding delegate, in order, in the other's invocation list.

Note that delegates of different types can be considered equal by the above definition, as long as they have the same return type and parameter types.

7.9.9 The is operator

The `is` operator is used to dynamically check if the run-time type of an object is compatible with a given type. The result of the operation `e is T`, where `e` is an expression and `T` is a type, is a boolean value indicating whether `e` can successfully be converted to type `T` by a reference conversion, a boxing conversion, or an unboxing conversion. The operation is evaluated as follows:

- If the compile-time type of `e` is the same as `T`, or if an implicit reference conversion (section 6.1.4) or boxing conversion (section 6.1.5) exists from the compile-time type of `e` to `T`:
  - Since `e` is known to always be of the given type, the compiler may issue a warning to this effect.
  - If `e` is of a reference type, the result of the operation is equivalent to evaluating `e != null`.
  - If `e` is of a value type, the result of the operation is `true`.
- Otherwise, if an explicit reference conversion (section 6.2.3) or unboxing conversion (section 6.2.4) exists from the compile-time type of `e` to `T`, a dynamic type check is performed:
  - If the value of `e` is `null`, the result is `false`.
  - Otherwise, let `R` be the run-time type of the instance referenced by `e`. If `R` and `T` are the same type, if `R` is a reference type and an implicit reference conversion from `R` to `T` exists, or if `R` is a value type and `T` is an interface type that is implemented by `R`, the result is `true`.
  - Otherwise, the result is `false`.

- Otherwise, no reference or boxing conversion of e to type T is possible:
  - Since e is known to never be of the given type, the compiler may issue a warning to this effect.
  - The result of the operation is `false`.

Note that the `is` operator only considers reference conversions, boxing conversions, and unboxing conversions. Other conversions, such as user defined conversions, are not considered by the `is` operator.

7.9.10 The as operator

The `as` operator is used to explicitly convert a value to a given reference type using a reference conversion or a boxing conversion. Unlike a cast expression (section 7.6.8), the `as` operator never throws an exception. Instead, if the indicated conversion is not possible, the resulting value is `null`.

In an operation of the form e as T, e must be an expression and T must be a reference type. The type of the result is T, and the result is always classified as a value. The operation is evaluated as follows:

- If the compile-time type of e is the same as T, the result is simply the value of e.
- Otherwise, if an implicit reference conversion (section 6.1.4) or boxing conversion (section 6.1.5) exists from the compile-time type of e to T, this conversion is performed and becomes the result of the operation.
- Otherwise, if an explicit reference conversion (section 6.2.3) exists from the compile-time type of e to T, a dynamic type check is performed:
  - If the value of e is `null`, the result is the value `null` with the compile-time type T.
  - Otherwise, let R be the run-time type of the instance referenced by e. If R and T are the same type, if R is a reference type and an implicit reference conversion from R to T exists, or if R is a value type and T is an interface type that is implemented by R, the result is the reference given by e with the compile-time type T.
  - Otherwise, the result is the value `null` with the compile-time type T.
- Otherwise, the indicated conversion is never possible, and a compile-time error occurs.

Note that the `as` operator only performs reference conversions and boxing conversions. Other conversions, such as user defined conversions, are not possible with the `as` operator and should instead be performed using cast expressions.

7.10 Logical operators

The &, ^, and | operators are called the logical operators.

and-expression:
   equality-expression
   and-expression & *equality-expression*

exclusive-or-expression:
   and-expression
   exclusive-or-expression ^ *and-expression*

inclusive-or-expression:
   exclusive-or-expression
   inclusive-or-expression | *exclusive-or-expression*

For an operation of the form x *op* y, where *op* is one of the logical operators, overload resolution (section 7.2.4) is applied to select a specific operator implementation. The operands are converted to the parameter types of the selected operator, and the type of the result is the return type of the operator.

The predefined logical operators are described in the following sections.

7.10.1 Integer logical operators

The predefined integer logical operators are:

```
int operator &(int x, int y);
uint operator &(uint x, uint y);
long operator &(long x, long y);
ulong operator &(ulong x, ulong y);
int operator |(int x, int y);
uint operator |(uint x, uint y);
long operator |(long x, long y);
ulong operator |(ulong x, ulong y);
int operator ^(int x, int y);
uint operator ^(uint x, uint y);
long operator ^(long x, long y);
ulong operator ^(ulong x, ulong y);
```

The & operator computes the bitwise logical AND of the two operands, the | operator computes the bitwise logical OR of the two operands, and the ^ operator computes the bitwise logical exclusive OR of the two operands. No overflows are possible from these operations.

7.10.2 Enumeration logical operators

Every enumeration type E implicitly provides the following predefined logical operators:

```
E operator &(E x, E y);
E operator |(E x, E y);
E operator ^(E x, E y);
```

The result of evaluating x *op* y, where x and y are expressions of an enumeration type E with an underlying type U, and *op* is one of the logical operators, is exactly the same as evaluating (E)((U)x) *op* ((U)y). In other words, the enumeration type logical operators simply perform the logical operation on the underlying type of the two operands.

7.10.3 Boolean logical operators

The predefined boolean logical operators are:

```
bool operator &(bool x, bool y);
bool operator |(bool x, bool y);
bool operator ^(bool x, bool y);
```

The result of x & y is true if both x and y are true. Otherwise, the result is false.

The result of x | y is true if either x or y is true. Otherwise, the result is false.

The result of x ^ y is true if x is true and y is false, or x is false and y is true. Otherwise, the result is false. When the operands are of type bool, the ^ operator computes the same result as the != operator.

7.11 Conditional logical operators

The && and || operators are called the conditional logical operators. They are at times also called the "short-circuiting" logical operators.

conditional-and-expression:
   inclusive-or-expression
   conditional-and-expression && *inclusive-or-expression*

conditional-or-expression:
   conditional-and-expression
   conditional-or-expression || *conditional-and-expression*

The && and || operators are conditional versions of the & and | operators:

- The operation x && y corresponds to the operation x & y, except that y is evaluated only if x is true.

- The operation x || y corresponds to the operation x | y, except that y is evaluated only if x is false.

An operation of the form x && y or x || y is processed by applying overload resolution (section 7.2.4) as if the operation was written x & y or x | y. Then,

- If overload resolution fails to find a single best operator, or if overload resolution selects one of the predefined integer logical operators, an error occurs.
- Otherwise, if the selected operator is one of the predefined boolean logical operators (section 7.10.2), the operation is processed as described in section 7.11.1.
- Otherwise, the selected operator is a user-defined operator, and the operation is processed as described in section 7.11.2.

It is not possible to directly overload the conditional logical operators. However, because the conditional logical operators are evaluated in terms of the regular logical operators, overloads of the regular logical operators are, with certain restrictions, also considered overloads of the conditional logical operators. This is described further in section 7.11.2.

7.11.1 Boolean conditional logical operators

When the operands of && or || are of type bool, or when the operands are of types that do not define an applicable operator & or operator |, but do define implicit conversions to bool, the operation is processed as follows:

- The operation x && y is evaluated as x? y: false. In other words, x is first evaluated and converted to type bool. Then, if x is true, y is evaluated and converted to type bool, and this becomes the result of the operation. Otherwise, the result of the operation is false.
- The operation x || y is evaluated as x? true: y. In other words, x is first evaluated and converted to type bool. Then, if x is true, the result of the operation is true. Otherwise, y is evaluated and converted to type bool, and this becomes the result of the operation.

7.11.2 User-defined conditional logical operators

When the operands of && or || are of types that declare an applicable user-defined operator & or operator |, both of the following must be true, where T is the type in which the selected operator is declared:

- The return type and the type of each parameter of the selected operator must be T. In other words, the operator must compute the logical AND or the logical OR of two operands of type T, and must return a result of type T.
- T must contain declarations of operator true and operator false.

A compile-time error occurs if either of these requirements is not satisfied. Otherwise, the `&&` or `||` operation is evaluated by combining the user-defined `operator true` or `operator false` with the selected user-defined operator:

- The operation x `&&` y is evaluated as `T.false(x)? x: T.&(x, y)`, where `T.false(x)` is an invocation of the `operator false` declared in `T`, and `T.&(x, y)` is an invocation of the selected `operator &`. In other words, x is first evaluated and `operator false` is invoked on the result to determine if x is definitely false. Then, if x is definitely false, the result of the operation is the value previously computed for x. Otherwise, y is evaluated, and the selected `operator &` is invoked on the value previously computed for x and the value computed for y to produce the result of the operation.

- The operation x `||` y is evaluated as `T.true(x)? x: T.|(x, y)`, where `T.true(x)` is an invocation of the `operator true` declared in `T`, and `T.|(x, y)` is an invocation of the selected `operator |`. In other words, x is first evaluated and `operator true` is invoked on the result to determine if x is definitely true. Then, if x is definitely true, the result of the operation is the value previously computed for x. Otherwise, y is evaluated, and the selected `operator |` is invoked on the value previously computed for x and the value computed for y to produce the result of the operation.

In either of these operations, the expression given by x is only evaluated once, and the expression given by y is either not evaluated or evaluated exactly once.

For an example of a type that implements `operator true` and `operator false`, see section 11.4.2.

7.12 Conditional operator

The `?:` operator is called the conditional operator. It is at times also called the ternary operator.

conditional-expression:
  conditional-or-expression
  conditional-or-expression `?` *expression* `:` *expression*

A conditional expression of the form `b? x: y` first evaluates the condition `b`. Then, if `b` is `true`, x is evaluated and becomes the result of the operation. Otherwise, y is evaluated and becomes the result of the operation. A conditional expression never evaluates both x and y.

The conditional operator is right-associative, meaning that operations are grouped from right to left. For example, an expression of the form `a? b: c? d: e` is evaluated as `a? b: (c? d: e)`.

The first operand of the `?:` operator must be an expression of a type that can be implicitly converted to `bool`, or an expression of a type that implements `operator true`. If neither of these requirements are satisfied, a compile-time error occurs.

The second and third operands of the ?: operator control the type of the conditional expression. Let X and Y be the types of the second and third operands. Then,

- If X and Y are the same type, then this is the type of the conditional expression.
- Otherwise, if an implicit conversion (section 6.1) exists from X to Y, but not from Y to X, then Y is the type of the conditional expression.
- Otherwise, if an implicit conversion (section 6.1) exists from Y to X, but not from X to Y, then X is the type of the conditional expression.
- Otherwise, no expression type can be determined, and a compile-time error occurs.

The run-time processing of a conditional expression of the form b? x: y consists of the following steps:

- First, b is evaluated, and the bool value of b is determined:
  - If an implicit conversion from the type of b to bool exists, then this implicit conversion is performed to produce a bool value.
  - Otherwise, the operator true defined by the type of b is invoked to produce a bool value.
- If the bool value produced by the step above is true, then x is evaluated and converted to the type of the conditional expression, and this becomes the result of the conditional expression.
- Otherwise, y is evaluated and converted to the type of the conditional expression, and this becomes the result of the conditional expression.

7.13 Assignment operators

The assignment operators assign a new value to a variable, a property, or an indexer element.

assignment:
    unary-expression   assignment-operator   expression

assignment-operator: one of
    =   +=   -=   *=   /=   %=   &= |=   ^=   <<=   >>=

The left operand of an assignment must be an expression classified as a variable, a property access, or an indexer access.

The = operator is called the ***simple assignment operator***. It assigns the value of the right operand to the variable, property, or indexer element given by the left operand. The simple assignment operator is described in section 7.13.1.

The operators formed by prefixing a binary operator with an = character are called the ***compound assignment operators***. These operators perform the indicated operation on the two operands, and then assign the resulting value to the variable, property, or indexer element given by the left operand. The compound assignment operators are described in section 7.13.2.

The assignment operators are right-associative, meaning that operations are grouped from right to left. For example, an expression of the form a = b = c is evaluated as a = (b = c).

7.13.1 Simple assignment

The = operator is called the simple assignment operator. In a simple assignment, the right operand must be an expression of a type that is implicitly convertible to the type of the left operand. The operation assigns the value of the right operand to the variable, property, or indexer element given by the left operand.

The result of a simple assignment expression is the value assigned to the left operand. The result has the same type as the left operand and is always classified as a value.

If the left operand is a property or indexer access, the property or indexer must have a set accessor. If this is not the case, a compile-time error occurs.

The run-time processing of a simple assignment of the form x = y consists of the following steps:

- If x is classified as a variable:
  - x is evaluated to produce the variable.
  - y is evaluated and, if required, converted to the type of x through an implicit conversion (section 6.1).
  - If the variable given by x is an array element of a *reference-type*, a run-time check is performed to ensure that the value computed for y is compatible with the array instance of which x is an element. The check succeeds if y is null, or if an implicit reference conversion (section 6.1.4) exists from the actual type of the instance referenced by y to the actual element type of the array instance containing x. Otherwise, an ArrayTypeMismatchException is thrown.
  - The value resulting from the evaluation and conversion of y is stored into the location given by the evaluation of x.
- If x is classified as a property or indexer access:
  - The instance expression (if x is not static) and the argument list (if x is an indexer access) associated with x are evaluated, and the results are used in the subsequent set accessor invocation.
  - y is evaluated and, if required, converted to the type of x through an implicit conversion (section 6.1).
  - The set accessor of x is invoked with the value computed for y as its value argument.

The array co-variance rules (section 12.5) permit a value of an array type A[] to be a reference to an instance of an array type B[], provided an implicit reference conversion exists from B to A. Because of these rules, assignment to an array element of a *reference-type* requires a run-time check to ensure that the value being assigned is compatible with the array instance. In the example

```
string[] sa = new string[10];
object[] oa = sa;
oa[0] = null;             // Ok
oa[1] = "Hello";          // Ok
oa[2] = new ArrayList();  // ArrayTypeMismatchException
```

the last assignment causes an ArrayTypeMismatchException to be thrown because an instance of ArrayList cannot be stored in an element of a string[].

When a property or indexer declared in a *struct-type* is the target of an assignment, the instance expression associated with the property or indexer access must be classified as a variable. If the instance expression is classified as a value, a compile-time error occurs.

Given the declarations:

```
struct Point
{
   int x, y;
   public Point(int x, int y) {
      this.x = x;
      this.y = y;
   }
   public int X {
      get { return x; }
      set { x = value; }
   }
   public int Y {
      get { return y; }
      set { y = value; }
   }
}
struct Rectangle
{
   Point a, b;
   public Rectangle(Point a, Point b) {
      this.a = a;
      this.b = b;
   }
```

(continued)

(continued)

```
public Point A {
    get { return a; }
    set { a = value; }
}
public Point B {
    get { return b; }
    set { b = value; }
}
}
```

in the example

```
Point p = new Point();
p.X = 100;
p.Y = 100;
Rectangle r = new Rectangle();
r.A = new Point(10, 10);
r.B = p;
```

the assignments to `p.X`, `p.Y`, `r.A`, and `r.B` are permitted because `p` and `r` are variables. However, in the example

```
Rectangle r = new Rectangle();
r.A.X = 10;
r.A.Y = 10;
r.B.X = 100;
r.B.Y = 100;
```

the assignments are all invalid, since `r.A` and `r.B` are not variables.

7.13.2 Compound assignment

An operation of the form x *op=* y is processed by applying binary operator overload resolution (section 7.2.4) as if the operation was written x *op* y. Then,

- If the return type of the selected operator is *implicitly* convertible to the type of x, the operation is evaluated as x = x *op* y, except that x is evaluated only once.

- Otherwise, if the selected operator is a predefined operator, if the return type of the selected operator is *explicitly* convertible to the type of x, and if y is *implicitly* convertible to the type of x, then the operation is evaluated as x = (T)(x *op* y), where T is the type of x, except that x is evaluated only once.

- Otherwise, the compound assignment is invalid, and a compile-time error occurs.

The term "evaluated only once" means that in the evaluation of x *op* y, the results of any constituent expressions of x are temporarily saved and then reused when performing the assignment to x. For example, in the assignment `A()[B()] += C()`, where A is a method returning `int[]`, and B and C are methods returning `int`, the methods are invoked only once, in the order A, B, C.

When the left operand of a compound assignment is a property access or indexer access, the property or indexer must have both a `get` accessor and a `set` accessor. If this is not the case, a compile-time error occurs.

The second rule above permits x *op=* y to be evaluated as x = (T)(x *op* y) in certain contexts. The rule exists such that the predefined operators can be used as compound operators when the left operand is of type `sbyte`, `byte`, `short`, `ushort`, or `char`. Even when both arguments are of one of those types, the predefined operators produce a result of type `int`, as described in section 7.2.6.2. Thus, without a cast it would not be possible to assign the result to the left operand.

The intuitive effect of the rule for predefined operators is simply that x *op=* y is permitted if both of x *op* y and x = y are permitted. In the example

```
byte b = 0;
char ch = '\0';
int i = 0;
b += 1;          // Ok
b += 1000;       // Error, b = 1000 not permitted
b += i;          // Error, b = i not permitted
b += (byte)i;    // Ok
ch += 1;         // Error, ch = 1 not permitted
ch += (char)1;   // Ok
```

the intuitive reason for each error is that a corresponding simple assignment would also have been an error.

7.13.3 Event assignment

7.14 Expression

An *expression* is either a *conditional-expression* or an *assignment*.

expression:
    conditional-expression
    assignment

7.15 Constant expressions

A *constant-expression* is an expression that can be fully evaluated at compile-time.

constant-expression:
  expression

The type of a constant expression can be one of the following: sbyte, byte, short, ushort, int, uint, long, ulong, char, float, double, decimal, bool, string, any enumeration type, or the null type. The following constructs are permitted in constant expressions:

- Literals (including the null literal).
- References to const members of class and struct types.
- References to members of enumeration types.
- Parenthesized sub-expressions.
- Cast expressions, provided the target type is one of the types listed above.
- The predefined +, -, !, and ~ unary operators.
- The predefined +, -, *, /, %, <<, >>, &, |, ^, &&, ||, ==, !=, <, >, <=, and => binary operators, provided each operand is of a type listed above.
- The ?: conditional operator.

Whenever an expression is of one of the types listed above and contains only the constructs listed above, the expression is evaluated at compile-time. This is true even if the expression is a sub-expression of a larger expression that contains non-constant constructs.

The compile-time evaluation of constant expressions uses the same rules as run-time evaluation of non-constant expressions, except that where run-time evaluation would have thrown an exception, compile-time evaluation causes a compile-time error to occur.

Unless a constant expression is explicitly placed in an unchecked context, overflows that occur in integral-type arithmetic operations and conversions during the compile-time evaluation of the expression always cause compile-time errors (section 7.5.12).

Constant expressions occur in the contexts listed below. In these contexts, an error occurs if an expression cannot be fully evaluated at compile-time.

- Constant declarations (section 10.3).
- Enumeration member declarations (section 14.3).
- case labels of a switch statement (section 8.7.2).
- goto case statements (section 8.9.3).
- Dimension lengths in an array creation expression (section 7.5.10.2) that includes an initializer.
- Attributes (section 17).

An implicit constant expression conversion (section 6.1.6) permits a constant expression of type `int` to be converted to `sbyte`, `byte`, `short`, `ushort`, `uint`, or `ulong`, provided the value of the constant expression is within the range of the destination type.

7.16 Boolean expressions

A *boolean-expression* is an expression that yields a result of type `bool`.

boolean-expression:
    expression

The controlling conditional expression of an *if-statement* (section 8.7.1), *while-statement* (section 8.8.1), *do-statement* (section 8.8.2), or *for-statement* (section 8.8.3) is a *boolean-expression*. The controlling conditional expression of the `?:` operator (section 7.12) follows the same rules as a *boolean-expression*, but for reasons of operator precedence is classified as a *conditional-or-expression*.

A *boolean-expression* is required to be of a type that can be implicitly converted to `bool` or of a type that implements `operator true`. If neither of these requirements are satisfied, a compile-time error occurs.

When a boolean expression is of a type that cannot be implicitly converted to `bool` but does implement `operator true`, then following evaluation of the expression, the `operator true` implementation provided by the type is invoked to produce a `bool` value.

The `DBBool` struct type in section 11.4.2 provides an example of a type that implements `operator true`.

8. Statements

C# provides a variety of statements. Most of these statements will be familiar to developers who have programmed in C and C++.

statement:
    labeled-statement
    declaration-statement
    embedded-statement

embedded-statement:
    block
    empty-statement
    expression-statement
    selection-statement
    iteration-statement
    jump-statement
    try-statement
    checked-statement
    unchecked-statement
    lock-statement
    using-statement

The *embedded-statement* nonterminal is used for statements that appear within other statements. The use of *embedded-statement* rather than *statement* excludes the use of declaration statements and labeled statements in these contexts. For example, the code

```
void F(bool b) {
   if (b)
      int i = 44;
}
```

is in error because an if statement requires an *embedded-statement* rather than a *statement* for its if branch. If this code were permitted, then the variable i would be declared, but it could never be used.

8.1 End points and reachability

Every statement has an **end point**. In intuitive terms, the end point of a statement is the location that immediately follows the statement. The execution rules for composite statements (statements that contain embedded statements) specify the action that is taken when control reaches the end point of an embedded statement. For example, when control reaches the end point of a statement in a block, control is transferred to the next statement in the block.

If a statement can possibly be reached by execution, the statement is said to be *reachable*. Conversely, if there is no possibility that a statement will be executed, the statement is said to be *unreachable*.

In the example

```
void F() {
    Console.WriteLine("reachable");
    goto Label;
    Console.WriteLine("unreachable");
    Label:
    Console.WriteLine("reachable");
}
```

the second `Console.WriteLine` invocation is unreachable because there is no possibility that the statement will be executed.

A warning is reported if the compiler determines that a statement is unreachable. It is specifically not an error for a statement to be unreachable.

To determine whether a particular statement or end point is reachable, the compiler performs flow analysis according to the reachability rules defined for each statement. The flow analysis takes into account the values of constant expressions (section 7.15) that control the behavior of statements, but the possible values of non-constant expressions are not considered. In other words, for purposes of control flow analysis, a non-constant expression of a given type is considered to have any possible value of that type.

In the example

```
void F() {
    const int i = 1;
    if (i == 2) Console.WriteLine("unreachable");
}
```

the boolean expression of the `if` statement is a constant expression because both operands of the `==` operator are constants. The constant expression is evaluated at compile-time, producing the value `false`, and the `Console.WriteLine` invocation is therefore considered unreachable. However, if `i` is changed to be a local variable

```
void F() {
    int i = 1;
    if (i == 2) Console.WriteLine("reachable");
}
```

the `Console.WriteLine` invocation is considered reachable, even though it will in reality never be executed.

The *block* of a function member is always considered reachable. By successively evaluating the reachability rules of each statement in a block, the reachability of any given statement can be determined.

In the example

```
void F(int x) {
   Console.WriteLine("start");
   if (x < 0) Console.WriteLine("negative");
}
```

the reachability of the second `Console.WriteLine` is determined as follows:

- First, because the block of the `F` method is reachable, the first `Console.WriteLine` statement is reachable.
- Next, because the first `Console.WriteLine` statement is reachable, its end point is reachable.
- Next, because the end point of the first `Console.WriteLine` statement is reachable, the `if` statement is reachable.
- Finally, because the boolean expression of the `if` statement does not have the constant value `false`, the second `Console.WriteLine` statement is reachable.

There are two situations in which it is an error for the end point of a statement to be reachable:

- Because the `switch` statement does not permit a switch section to "fall through" to the next switch section, it is an error for the end point of the statement list of a switch section to be reachable. If this error occurs, it is typically an indication that a `break` statement is missing.
- It is an error for the end point of the block of a function member that computes a value to be reachable. If this error occurs, it is typically an indication that a `return` statement is missing.

8.2 Blocks

A *block* permits multiple statements to be written in contexts where a single statement is allowed.

block:
    { *statement-list*_{opt} }

A *block* consists of an optional *statement-list* (section 8.2.1), enclosed in braces. If the statement list is omitted, the block is said to be empty.

A block may contain declaration statements (section 8.5). The scope of a local variable or constant declared in a block extends from the declaration to the end of the block.

Within a block, the meaning of a name used in an expression context must always be the same (section 7.5.2.1).

A block is executed as follows:

- If the block is empty, control is transferred to the end point of the block.
- If the block is not empty, control is transferred to the statement list. When and if control reaches the end point of the statement list, control is transferred to the end point of the block.

The statement list of a block is reachable if the block itself is reachable.

The end point of a block is reachable if the block is empty or if the end point of the statement list is reachable.

8.2.1 Statement lists

A *statement list* consists of one or more statements written in sequence. Statement lists occur in *block*s (section 8.2) and in *switch-block*s (section 8.7.2).

statement-list:
  statement
  statement-list   statement

A statement list is executed by transferring control to the first statement. When and if control reaches the end point of a statement, control is transferred to the next statement. When and if control reaches the end point of the last statement, control is transferred to the end point of the statement list.

A statement in a statement list is reachable if at least one of the following is true:

- The statement is the first statement and the statement list itself is reachable.
- The end point of the preceding statement is reachable.
- The statement is a labeled statement and the label is referenced by a reachable `goto` statement.

The end point of a statement list is reachable if the end point of the last statement in the list is reachable.

8.3 The empty statement

An *empty-statement* does nothing.

empty-statement:
  ;

An empty statement is used when there are no operations to perform in a context where a statement is required.

Execution of an empty statement simply transfers control to the end point of the statement. Thus, the end point of an empty statement is reachable if the empty statement is reachable.

An empty statement can be used when writing a `while` statement with a null body:

```
bool ProcessMessage() {…}
void ProcessMessages() {
   while (ProcessMessage())
      ;
}
```

Also, an empty statement can be used to declare a label just before the closing "}"of a block:

```
void F() {
   …
if (done) goto exit;
   …
exit: ;
}
```

8.4 Labeled statements

A *labeled-statement* permits a statement to be prefixed by a label. Labeled statements are permitted blocks, but are not permitted as embedded statements.

labeled-statement:
   identifier : *statement*

A labeled statement declares a label with the name given by the *identifier*. The scope of a label is the block in which the label is declared, including any nested blocks. It is an error for two labels with the same name to have overlapping scopes.

A label can be referenced from `goto` statements (section 8.9.3) within the scope of the label. This means that `goto` statements can transfer control inside blocks and out of blocks, but never into blocks.

Labels have their own declaration space and do not interfere with other identifiers. The example

```
int F(int x) {
   if (x >= 0) goto x;
   x = -x;
   x: return x;
}
```

is valid and uses the name x as both a parameter and a label.

Execution of a labeled statement corresponds exactly to execution of the statement following the label.

In addition to the reachability provided by normal flow of control, a labeled statement is reachable if the label is referenced by a reachable `goto` statement.

8.5 Declaration statements

A *declaration-statement* declares a local variable or constant. Declaration statements are permitted in blocks, but are not permitted as embedded statements.

declaration-statement:
    local-variable-declaration ;
    local-constant-declaration ;

8.5.1 Local variable declarations

A *local-variable-declaration* declares one or more local variables.

local-variable-declaration:
    type   variable-declarators

variable-declarators:
    variable-declarator
    variable-declarators , variable-declarator

variable-declarator:
    identifier
    identifier = variable-initializer

variable-initializer:
    expression
    array-initializer

The *type* of a *local-variable-declaration* specifies the type of the variables introduced by the declaration. The type is followed by a list of *variable-declarator*s, each of which introduces a new variable. A *variable-declarator* consists of an *identifier* that names the variable, optionally followed by an "=" token and a *variable-initializer* that gives the initial value of the variable.

The value of a local variable is obtained in an expression using a *simple-name* (section 7.5.2), and the value of a local variable is modified using an *assignment* (section 7.13). A local variable must be definitely assigned (section 5.3) at each location where its value is obtained.

The scope of a local variable starts immediately after its identifier in the declaration and extends to the end of the block containing the declaration. Within the scope of a local variable, it is an error to declare another local variable or constant with the same name.

A local variable declaration that declares multiple variables is equivalent to multiple declarations of single variables with the same type. Furthermore, a variable initializer in a local variable declaration corresponds exactly to an assignment statement that is inserted immediately after the declaration.

The example

```
void F() {
   int x = 1, y, z = x * 2;
}
```

corresponds exactly to

```
void F() {
   int x; x = 1;
   int y;
   int z; z = x * 2;
}
```

8.5.2 Local constant declarations

A *local-constant-declaration* declares one or more local constants.

local-constant-declaration:
   const *type   constant-declarators*

constant-declarators:
   constant-declarator
   constant-declarators , constant-declarator

constant-declarator:
   identifier = constant-expression

The *type* of a *local-constant-declaration* specifies the type of the constants introduced by the declaration. The type is followed by a list of *constant-declarator*s, each of which introduces a new constant. A *constant-declarator* consists of an *identifier* that names the constant, followed by an "=" token, followed by a *constant-expression* (section 7.15) that gives the value of the constant.

The *type* and *constant-expression* of a local constant declaration must follow the same rules as those of a constant member declaration (section 10.3).

The value of a local constant is obtained in an expression using a *simple-name* (section 7.5.2).

The scope of a local constant extends from its declaration to the end of the block containing the declaration. The scope of a local constant does not include the *constant-expression* that provides its value. Within the scope of a local constant, it is an error to declare another local variable or constant with the same name.

8.6 Expression statements

An *expression-statement* evaluates a given expression. The value computed by the expression, if any, is discarded.

expression-statement:
  statement-expression ;

statement-expression:
  invocation-expression
  object-creation-expression
  assignment
  post-increment-expression
  post-decrement-expression
  pre-increment-expression
  pre-decrement-expression

Not all expressions are permitted as statements. In particular, expressions such as $x + y$ and $x == 1$ that have no side-effects, but merely compute a value (which will be discarded), are not permitted as statements.

Execution of an expression statement evaluates the contained expression and then transfers control to the end point of the expression statement.

8.7 Selection statements

Selection statements select one of a number of possible statements for execution based on the value of a controlling expression.

selection-statement:
  if-statement
  switch-statement

8.7.1 The if statement

The `if` statement selects a statement for execution based on the value of a boolean expression.

if-statement:
  `if` `(` *boolean-expression* `)` *embedded-statement*
  `if` `(` *boolean-expression* `)` *embedded-statement* `else` *embedded-statement*
boolean-expression:
  expression

An else part is associated with the nearest preceding if statement that does not already have an else part. Thus, an if statement of the form

```
if (x) if (y) F(); else G();
```

is equivalent to

```
if (x) {
    if (y) {
        F();
    }
    else {
        G();
    }
}
```

An if statement is executed as follows:

- The *boolean-expression* (section 7.16) is evaluated.
- If the boolean expression yields true, control is transferred to the first embedded statement. When and if control reaches the end point of that statement, control is transferred to the end point of the if statement.
- If the boolean expression yields false and if an else part is present, control is transferred to the second embedded statement. When and if control reaches the end point of that statement, control is transferred to the end point of the if statement.
- If the boolean expression yields false and if an else part is not present, control is transferred to the end point of the if statement.

The first embedded statement of an if statement is reachable if the if statement is reachable and the boolean expression does not have the constant value false.

The second embedded statement of an if statement, if present, is reachable if the if statement is reachable and the boolean expression does not have the constant value true.

The end point of an if statement is reachable if the end point of at least one of its embedded statements is reachable. In addition, the end point of an if statement with no else part is reachable if the if statement is reachable and the boolean expression does not have the constant value true.

8.7.2 The switch statement

The `switch` statement executes the statements that are associated with the value of the controlling expression.

switch-statement:
    `switch` (*expression*) *switch-block*

switch-block:
    { *switch-sections_{opt}* }

switch-sections:
    switch-section
    switch-sections   switch-section

switch-section:
    switch-labels   statement-list

switch-labels:
    switch-label
    switch-labels   switch-label

switch-label:
    `case` *constant-expression* :
    `default` :

A *switch-statement* consists of the keyword `switch`, followed by a parenthesized expression (called the switch expression), followed by a *switch-block*. The *switch-block* consists of zero or more *switch-section*s, enclosed in braces. Each *switch-section* consists of one or more *switch-labels* followed by a *statement-list* (section 8.2.1).

The **governing type** of a `switch` statement is established by the switch expression. If the type of the switch expression is `sbyte`, `byte`, `short`, `ushort`, `int`, `uint`, `long`, `ulong`, `char`, `string`, or an *enum-type*, then that is the governing type of the `switch` statement. Otherwise, exactly one user-defined implicit conversion (section 6.4) must exist from the type of the switch expression to one of the following possible governing types: `sbyte`, `byte`, `short`, `ushort`, `int`, `uint`, `long`, `ulong`, `char`, `string`. If no such implicit conversion exists, or if more that one such implicit conversion exists, a compile-time error occurs.

The constant expression of each `case` label must denote a value of a type that is implicitly convertible (section 6.1) to the governing type of the `switch` statement. A compile-time error occurs if two or more `case` labels in the same `switch` statement specify the same constant value.

There can be at most one `default` label in a switch statement.

A `switch` statement is executed as follows:

- The switch expression is evaluated and converted to the governing type.
- If one of the constants specified in a `case` label Is equal to the value of the switch expression, control is transferred to the statement list following the matched `case` label.
- If no constant matches the value of the switch expression and if a `default` label is present, control is transferred to the statement list following the `default` label.
- If no constant matches the value of the switch expression and if no `default` label is present, control is transferred to the end point of the `switch` statement.

If the end point of the statement list of a switch section is reachable, a compile-time error occurs. This is known as the "no fall through" rule. The example

```
switch (i) {
case 0:
   CaseZero();
   break;
case 1:
   CaseOne();
   break;
default:
   CaseOthers();
   break;
}
```

is valid because no switch section has a reachable end point. Unlike C and C++, execution of a switch section is not permitted to "fall through" to the next switch section, and the example

```
switch (i) {
case 0:
   CaseZero();
case 1:
   CaseZeroOrOne();
default:
   CaseAny();
}
```

is in error. When execution of a switch section is to be followed by execution of another switch section, an explicit `goto case` or `goto default` statement must be used:

```
switch (i) {
case 0:
   CaseZero();
   goto case 1;
```

(continued)

(continued)

```
case 1:
   CaseZeroOrOne();
   goto default;
default:
   CaseAny();
   break;
}
```

Multiple labels are permitted in a *switch-section*. The example

```
switch (i) {
case 0:
   CaseZero();
   break;
case 1:
   CaseOne();
   break;
case 2:
default:
   CaseTwo();
   break;
}
```

is legal. The example does not violate the "no fall through" rule because the labels `case 2:` and `default:` are part of the same *switch-section*.

The "no fall through" rule prevents a common class of bugs that occur in C and C++ when `break` statements are accidentally omitted. Also, because of this rule, the switch sections of a `switch` statement can be arbitrarily rearranged without affecting the behavior of the statement. For example, the sections of the `switch` statement above can be reversed without affecting the behavior of the statement:

```
switch (i) {
default:
   CaseAny();
   break;
case 1:
   CaseZeroOrOne();
   goto default;
case 0:
   CaseZero();
   goto case 1;
}
```

The statement list of a switch section typically ends in a `break`, `goto case`, or `goto default` statement, but any construct that renders the end point of the statement list unreachable is permitted. For example, a `while` statement controlled by the boolean expression `true` is known to never reach its end point. Likewise, a `throw` or `return` statement always transfer control elsewhere and never reaches its end point. Thus, the following example is valid:

```
switch (i) {
case 0:
   while (true) F();
case 1:
   throw new ArgumentException();
case 2:
   return;
}
```

The governing type of a `switch` statement may be the type `string`. For example:

```
void DoCommand(string command) {
   switch (command.ToLower()) {
   case "run":
      DoRun();
      break;
   case "save":
      DoSave();
      break;
   case "quit":
      DoQuit();
      break;
   default:
      InvalidCommand(command);
      break;
   }
}
```

Like the string equality operators (section 7.9.7), the `switch` statement is case sensitive and will execute a given switch section only if the switch expression string exactly matches a `case` label constant. As illustrated by the example above, a `switch` statement can be made case insensitive by converting the switch expression string to lower case and writing all `case` label constants in lower case.

When the governing type of a `switch` statement is `string`, the value `null` is permitted as a case label constant.

A *switch-block* may contain declaration statements (section 8.5). The scope of a local variable or constant declared in a switch block extends from the declaration to the end of the switch block.

Within a switch block, the meaning of a name used in an expression context must always be the same (section 7.5.2.1).

The statement list of a given switch section is reachable if the `switch` statement is reachable and at least one of the following is true:

- The switch expression is a non-constant value.
- The switch expression is a constant value that matches a `case` label in the switch section.
- The switch expression is a constant value that doesn't match any `case` label, and the switch section contains the `default` label.
- A switch label of the switch section is referenced by a reachable `goto case` or `goto default` statement.

The end point of a `switch` statement is reachable if at least one of the following is true:

- The `switch` statement contains a reachable `break` statement that exits the `switch` statement.
- The `switch` statement is reachable, the switch expression is a non-constant value, and no `default` label is present.
- The `switch` statement is reachable, the switch expression is a constant value that doesn't match any `case` label, and no `default` label is present.

8.8 Iteration statements

Iteration statements repeatedly execute an embedded statement.

iteration-statement:
    while-statement
    do-statement
    for-statement
    foreach-statement

8.8.1 The while statement

The `while` statement conditionally executes an embedded statement zero or more times.

while-statement:
    `while` (*boolean-expression*) *embedded-statement*

A `while` statement is executed as follows:

- The *boolean-expression* (section 7.16) is evaluated.

- If the boolean expression yields `true`, control is transferred to the embedded statement. When and if control reaches the end point of the embedded statement (possibly from execution of a `continue` statement), control is transferred to the beginning of the `while` statement.
- If the boolean expression yields `false`, control is transferred to the end point of the `while` statement.

Within the embedded statement of a `while` statement, a `break` statement (section 8.9.1) may be used to transfer control to the end point of the `while` statement (thus ending iteration of the embedded statement), and a `continue` statement (section 8.9.2) may be used to transfer control to the end point of the embedded statement (thus performing another iteration of the `while` statement).

The embedded statement of a `while` statement is reachable if the `while` statement is reachable and the boolean expression does not have the constant value `false`.

The end point of a `while` statement is reachable if at least one of the following is true:

- The `while` statement contains a reachable `break` statement that exits the `while` statement.
- The `while` statement is reachable and the boolean expression does not have the constant value `true`.

8.8.2 The do statement

The `do` statement conditionally executes an embedded statement one or more times.

do-statement:
    `do` *embedded-statement* `while` (*boolean-expression*) ;

A `do` statement is executed as follows:

- Control is transferred to the embedded statement.
- When and if control reaches the end point of the embedded statement (possibly from execution of a `continue` statement), the *boolean-expression* (section 7.16) is evaluated. If the boolean expression yields `true`, control is transferred to the beginning of the `do` statement. Otherwise, control is transferred to the end point of the `do` statement.

Within the embedded statement of a `do` statement, a `break` statement (section 8.9.1) may be used to transfer control to the end point of the `do` statement (thus ending iteration of the embedded statement), and a `continue` statement (section 8.9.2) may be used to transfer control to the end point of the embedded statement (thus performing another iteration of the `do` statement).

The embedded statement of a `do` statement is reachable if the `do` statement is reachable.

The end point of a do statement is reachable if at least one of the following is true:

- The do statement contains a reachable break statement that exits the do statement.
- The end point of the embedded statement is reachable and the boolean expression does not have the constant value true.

8.8.3 The for statement

The for statement evaluates a sequence of initialization expressions and then, while a condition is true, repeatedly executes an embedded statement and evaluates a sequence of iteration expressions.

for-statement:
    for (*for-initializer*$_{opt}$; *for-condition*$_{opt}$; *for-iterator*$_{opt}$) *embedded-statement*
for-initializer:
    local-variable-declaration
    statement-expression-list
for-condition:
    boolean-expression
for-iterator:
    statement-expression-list
statement-expression-list:
    statement-expression
    statement-expression-list , *statement-expression*

The *for-initializer*, if present, consists of either a *local-variable-declaration* (section 8.5.1) or a list of *statement-expression*s (section 8.6) separated by commas. The scope of a local variable declared by a *for-initializer* starts at the *variable-declarator* for the variable and extends to the end of the embedded statement. The scope includes the *for-condition* and the *for-iterator*.

The *for-condition*, if present, must be a *boolean-expression* (section 7.16).

The *for-iterator*, if present, consists of a list of *statement-expression*s (section 8.6) separated by commas.

A for statement is executed as follows:

- If a *for-initializer* is present, the variable initializers or statement expressions are executed in the order they are written. This step is only performed once.
- If a *for-condition* is present, it is evaluated.

- If the *for-condition* is not present or if the evaluation yields `true`, control is transferred to the embedded statement. When and if control reaches the end point of the embedded statement (possibly from execution of a `continue` statement), the expressions of the *for-iterator*, if any, are evaluated in sequence, and then another iteration is performed, starting with evaluation of the *for-condition* in the step above.
- If the *for-condition* is present and the evaluation yields `false`, control is transferred to the end point of the `for` statement.

Within the embedded statement of a `for` statement, a `break` statement (section 8.9.1) may be used to transfer control to the end point of the `for` statement (thus ending iteration of the embedded statement), and a `continue` statement (section 8.9.2) may be used to transfer control to the end point of the embedded statement (thus executing another iteration of the `for` statement).

The embedded statement of a `for` statement is reachable if one of the following is true:

- The `for` statement is reachable and no *for-condition* is present.
- The `for` statement is reachable and a *for-condition* is present and does not have the constant value `false`.

The end point of a `for` statement is reachable if at least one of the following is true:

- The `for` statement contains a reachable `break` statement that exits the `for` statement.
- The `for` statement is reachable and a *for-condition* is present and does not have the constant value `true`.

8.8.4 The foreach statement

The `foreach` statement enumerates the elements of a collection, executing an embedded statement for each element of the collection.

foreach-statement:
    foreach (*type identifier* in *expression*) *embedded-statement*

The *type* and *identifier* of a `foreach` statement declare the **iteration variable** of the statement. The iteration variable corresponds to a read-only local variable with a scope that extends over the embedded statement. During execution of a `foreach` statement, the iteration variable represents the collection element for which an iteration is currently being performed. A compile-time error occurs if the embedded statement attempts to assign to the iteration variable or pass the iteration variable as a `ref` or `out` parameter.

The type of the *expression* of a `foreach` statement must be a collection type (as defined below), and an explicit conversion (section 6.2) must exist from the element type of the collection to the type of the iteration variable.

A type `c` is said to be a ***collection type*** if all of the following are true:

- `C` contains a `public` instance method with the signature `GetEnumerator()` that returns a *struct-type*, *class-type*, or *interface-type*, in the following called `E`.

- `E` contains a `public` instance method with the signature `MoveNext()` and the return type `bool`.

- `E` contains a `public` instance property named `Current` that permits reading. The type of this property is said to be the ***element type*** of the collection type.

The `System.Array` type (section 12.1.1) is a collection type, and since all array types derive from `System.Array`, any array type expression is permitted in a `foreach` statement. For single-dimensional arrays, the `foreach` statement enumerates the array elements in increasing index order, starting with index 0 and ending with index `Length - 1`. For multi-dimensional arrays, the indices of the rightmost dimension are increased first.

A `foreach` statement is executed as follows:

- The collection expression is evaluated to produce an instance of the collection type. This instance is referred to as `c` in the following. If `c` is of a *reference-type* and has the value `null`, a `NullReferenceException` is thrown.

- An enumerator instance is obtained by evaluating the method invocation `c.GetEnumerator()`. The returned enumerator is stored in a temporary local variable, in the following referred to as `e`. It is not possible for the embedded statement to access this temporary variable. If `e` is of a *reference-type* and has the value `null`, a `NullReferenceException` is thrown.

- The enumerator is advanced to the next element by evaluating the method invocation `e.MoveNext()`.

- If the value returned by `e.MoveNext()` is `true`, the following steps are performed:

  - The current enumerator value is obtained by evaluating the property access `e.Current`, and the value is converted to the type of the iteration variable by an explicit conversion (section 6.2). The resulting value is stored in the iteration variable such that it can be accessed in the embedded statement.

  - Control is transferred to the embedded statement. When and if control reaches the end point of the embedded statement (possibly from execution of a `continue` statement), another `foreach` iteration is performed, starting with the step above that advances the enumerator.

- If the value returned by `e.MoveNext()` is `false`, control is transferred to the end point of the `foreach` statement.

Within the embedded statement of a `foreach` statement, a `break` statement (section 8.9.1) may be used to transfer control to the end point of the `foreach` statement (thus ending iteration of the embedded statement), and a `continue` statement (section 8.9.2) may be used to transfer control to the end point of the embedded statement (thus executing another iteration of the `foreach` statement).

The embedded statement of a `foreach` statement is reachable if the `foreach` statement is reachable. Likewise, the end point of a `foreach` statement is reachable if the `foreach` statement is reachable.

8.9 Jump statements

Jump statements unconditionally transfer control.

jump-statement:
    break-statement
    continue-statement
    goto-statement
    return-statement
    throw-statement

The location to which a jump statement transfers control is called the **target** of the jump statement.

When a jump statement occurs within a block, and when the target of the jump statement is outside that block, the jump statement is said to **exit** the block. While a jump statement may transfer control out of a block, it can never transfer control into a block.

Execution of jump statements is complicated by the presence of intervening `try` statements. In the absence of such `try` statements, a jump statement unconditionally transfers control from the jump statement to its target. In the presence of such intervening `try` statements, execution is more complex. If the jump statement exits one or more `try` blocks with associated `finally` blocks, control is initially transferred to the `finally` block of the innermost `try` statement. When and if control reaches the end point of a `finally` block, control is transferred to the `finally` block of the next enclosing `try` statement. This process is repeated until the `finally` blocks of all intervening `try` statements have been executed.

In the example

```
static void F() {
   while (true) {
      try {
         try {
            Console.WriteLine("Before break");
            break;
         }
         finally {
            Console.WriteLine("Innermost finally block");
         }
      }
```

(continued)

(continued)

```
    finally {
        Console.WriteLine("Outermost finally block");
    }
}
Console.WriteLine("After break");
}
```

the finally blocks associated with two try statements are executed before control is transferred to the target of the jump statement.

8.9.1 The break statement

The `break` statement exits the nearest enclosing `switch`, `while`, `do`, `for`, or `foreach` statement.

break-statement:
```
break  ;
```

The target of a `break` statement is the end point of the nearest enclosing `switch`, `while`, `do`, `for`, or `foreach` statement. If a `break` statement is not enclosed by a `switch`, `while`, `do`, `for`, or `foreach` statement, a compile-time error occurs.

When multiple `switch`, `while`, `do`, `for`, or `foreach` statements are nested within each other, a `break` statement applies only to the innermost statement. To transfer control across multiple nesting levels, a `goto` statement (section 8.9.3) must be used.

A `break` statement cannot exit a `finally` block (section 8.10). When a `break` statement occurs within a `finally` block, the target of the `break` statement must be within the same `finally` block, or otherwise a compile-time error occurs.

A `break` statement is executed as follows:

- If the `break` statement exits one or more `try` blocks with associated `finally` blocks, control is initially transferred to the `finally` block of the innermost `try` statement. When and if control reaches the end point of a `finally` block, control is transferred to the `finally` block of the next enclosing `try` statement. This process is repeated until the `finally` blocks of all intervening `try` statements have been executed.

- Control is transferred to the target of the `break` statement.

Because a `break` statement unconditionally transfers control elsewhere, the end point of a `break` statement is never reachable.

8.9.2 The continue statement

The `continue` statement starts a new iteration of the nearest enclosing `while`, `do`, `for`, or `foreach` statement.

continue-statement:
   `continue ;`

The target of a `continue` statement is the end point of the embedded statement of the nearest enclosing `while`, `do`, `for`, or `foreach` statement. If a `continue` statement is not enclosed by a `while`, `do`, `for`, or `foreach` statement, a compile-time error occurs.

When multiple `while`, `do`, `for`, or `foreach` statements are nested within each other, a `continue` statement applies only to the innermost statement. To transfer control across multiple nesting levels, a `goto` statement (section 8.9.3) must be used.

A `continue` statement cannot exit a `finally` block (section 8.10). When a `continue` statement occurs within a `finally` block, the target of the `continue` statement must be within the same `finally` block, or otherwise a compile-time error occurs.

A `continue` statement is executed as follows:

- If the `continue` statement exits one or more `try` blocks with associated `finally` blocks, control is initially transferred to the `finally` block of the innermost `try` statement. When and if control reaches the end point of a `finally` block, control is transferred to the `finally` block of the next enclosing `try` statement. This process is repeated until the `finally` blocks of all intervening `try` statements have been executed.
- Control is transferred to the target of the `continue` statement.

Because a `continue` statement unconditionally transfers control elsewhere, the end point of a `continue` statement is never reachable.

8.9.3 The goto statement

The `goto` statement transfers control to a statement that is marked by a label.

goto-statement:
   `goto` *identifier* `;`
   `goto case` *constant-expression* `;`
   `goto default ;`

The target of a `goto` *identifier* statement is the labeled statement with the given label. If a label with the given name does not exist in the current function member, or if the `goto` statement is not within the scope of the label, a compile-time error occurs. This rule permits the use of a `goto` statement to transfer control *out of* a nested scope, but not *into* a nested scope. In the example

```
class Test
{
    static void Main(string[] args) {
        int i = 0;
        while (true) {
            Console.WriteLine(i++);
            if (i == 10)
                goto done;
        }
    done:
        Console.WriteLine("Done");
    }
}
```

a `goto` statement is used to transfer control out of a nested scope.

The target of a `goto case` statement is the statement list of the switch section in the nearest enclosing `switch` statement that contains a `case` label with the given constant value. If the `goto case` statement is not enclosed by a `switch` statement, if the *constant-expression* is not implicitly convertible (section 6.1) to the governing type of the nearest enclosing `switch` statement, or if the nearest enclosing `switch` statement does not contain a `case` label with the given constant value, a compile-time error occurs.

The target of a `goto default` statement is the statement list of the switch section in the nearest enclosing `switch` statement (section 8.7.2) that contains a `default` label. If the `goto default` statement is not enclosed by a `switch` statement, or if the nearest enclosing `switch` statement does not contain a `default` label, a compile-time error occurs.

A `goto` statement cannot exit a `finally` block (section 8.10). When a `goto` statement occurs within a `finally` block, the target of the `goto` statement must be within the same `finally` block, or otherwise a compile-time error occurs.

A `goto` statement is executed as follows:

- If the `goto` statement exits one or more `try` blocks with associated `finally` blocks, control is initially transferred to the `finally` block of the innermost `try` statement. When and if control reaches the end point of a `finally` block, control is transferred to the `finally` block of the next enclosing `try` statement. This process is repeated until the `finally` blocks of all intervening `try` statements have been executed.
- Control is transferred to the target of the `goto` statement.

Because a `goto` statement unconditionally transfers control elsewhere, the end point of a `goto` statement is never reachable.

8.9.4 The return statement

The `return` statement returns control to the caller of the function member in which the `return` statement appears.

return-statement:
    `return` *expression*$_{opt}$ `;`

A `return` statement with no expression can be used only in a function member that does not compute a value, that is, a method with the return type `void`, the `set` accessor of a property or indexer, a constructor, or a destructor.

A `return` statement with an expression can only be used only in a function member that computes a value, that is, a method with a non-void return type, the `get` accessor of a property or indexer, or a user-defined operator. An implicit conversion (section 6.1) must exist from the type of the expression to the return type of the containing function member.

It is an error for a `return` statement to appear in a `finally` block (section 8.10).

A `return` statement is executed as follows:

- If the `return` statement specifies an expression, the expression is evaluated and the resulting value is converted to the return type of the containing function member by an implicit conversion. The result of the conversion becomes the value returned to the caller.
- If the `return` statement is enclosed by one or more `try` blocks with associated `finally` blocks, control is initially transferred to the `finally` block of the innermost `try` statement. When and if control reaches the end point of a `finally` block, control is transferred to the `finally` block of the next enclosing `try` statement. This process is repeated until the `finally` blocks of all enclosing `try` statements have been executed.
- Control is returned to the caller of the containing function member.

Because a `return` statement unconditionally transfers control elsewhere, the end point of a `return` statement is never reachable.

8.9.5 The throw statement

The `throw` statement throws an exception.

throw-statement:
    `throw` *expression*$_{opt}$ `;`

A `throw` statement with an expression throws the exception produced by evaluating the expression. The expression must denote a value of the class type `System.Exception` or of a class type that derives from `System.Exception`. If evaluation of the expression produces `null`, a `NullReferenceException` is thrown instead.

A `throw` statement with no expression can be used only in a `catch` block. It re-throws the exception that is currently being handled by the `catch` block.

Because a `throw` statement unconditionally transfers control elsewhere, the end point of a `throw` statement is never reachable.

When an exception is thrown, control is transferred to the first `catch` clause in a `try` statement that can handle the exception. The process that takes place from the point of the exception being thrown to the point of transferring control to a suitable exception handler is known as ***exception propagation***. Propagation of an exception consists of repeatedly evaluating the following steps until a `catch` clause that matches the exception is found. In the descriptions, the ***throw point*** is initially the location at which the exception is thrown.

- In the current function member, each `try` statement that encloses the throw point is examined. For each statement `S`, starting with the innermost `try` statement and ending with the outermost `try` statement, the following steps are evaluated:

  - If the `try` block of `S` encloses the throw point and if S has one or more `catch` clauses, the `catch` clauses are examined in order of appearance to locate a suitable handler for the exception. The first `catch` clause that specifies the exception type or a base type of the exception type is considered a match. A general `catch` clause is considered a match for any exception type. If a matching `catch` clause is located, the exception propagation is completed by transferring control to the block of that `catch` clause.

  - Otherwise, if the `try` block or a `catch` block of `S` encloses the throw point and if `S` has a `finally` block, control is transferred to the `finally` block. If the `finally` block throws another exception, processing of the current exception is terminated. Otherwise, when control reaches the end point of the `finally` block, processing of the current exception is continued.

- If an exception handler was not located in the current function member invocation, the function member invocation is terminated. The steps above are then repeated for the caller of the function member with a throw point corresponding to the statement from which the function member was invoked.

- If the exception processing ends up terminating all function member invocations in the current thread or process, indicating that the thread or process has no handler for the exception, then the thread or process is itself terminated in an implementation-defined fashion.

8.10 The try statement

The `try` statement provides a mechanism for catching exceptions that occur during execution of a block. The `try` statement furthermore provides the ability to specify a block of code that is always executed when control leaves the `try` statement.

try-statement:
> `try`   *block*   *catch-clauses*
> `try`   *block*   *finally-clause*
> `try`   *block*   *catch-clauses*   *finally-clause*

catch-clauses:
> *specific-catch-clauses*   *general-catch-clause*$_{opt}$
> *specific-catch-clauses*$_{opt}$ *general-catch-clause*

specific-catch-clauses:
> *specific-catch-clause*
> *specific-catch-clauses*   *specific-catch-clause*

specific-catch-clause:
> `catch`   (*class-type*   *identifier*$_{opt}$)   *block*

general-catch-clause:
> `catch`   *block*

finally-clause:
> `finally`   *block*

There are three possible forms of `try` statements:

- A `try` block followed by one or more `catch` blocks.
- A `try` block followed by a `finally` block.
- A `try` block followed by one or more `catch` blocks followed by a `finally` block.

When a `catch` clause specifies a *class-type*, the type must be `System.Exception` or a type that derives from `System.Exception`.

When a `catch` clause specifies both a *class-type* and an *identifier*, an **exception variable** of the given name and type is declared. The exception variable corresponds to a local variable with a scope that extends over the `catch` block. During execution of the `catch` block, the exception variable represents the exception currently being handled. For purposes of definite assignment checking, the exception variable is considered definitely assigned in its entire scope.

Unless a `catch` clause includes an exception variable name, it is impossible to access the exception object in the `catch` block.

A `catch` clause that specifies neither an exception type nor an exception variable name is called a general `catch` clause. A `try` statement can only have one general `catch` clause, and if one is present it must be the last `catch` clause.

Though the `throw` statement is restricted to throwing exceptions of type `System.Exception` or a type that derives from `System.Exception`, other languages are not bound by this rule, and so may throw exceptions of other types. A general catch clause can be used to catch such exceptions, and a `throw` statement with no expression can be used to re-throw them.

An error occurs if a `catch` clause specifies a type that is the same as or derived from a type that was specified in an earlier `catch` clause. Because `catch` clauses are examined in order of appearance to locate a handler for an exception, without this restriction it would be possible to write unreachable `catch` clauses.

Within a `catch` block, a `throw` statement (section 8.9.5) with no expression can be used to re-throw the exception that was caught by the `catch` block. Assignments to an exception variable do not alter the exception that is re-thrown.

In the example

```
class Test
{
    static void F() {
        try {
            G();
        }
        catch (Exception e) {
            Console.WriteLine("Exception in F: " + e.Message);
            e = new Exception("F");
            throw;              // re-throw
        }
    }
    static void G() {
        throw new Exception("G");
    }
    static void Main() {
        try {
            F();
        }
        catch (Exception e) {
            Console.WriteLine("Exception in Main: " + e.Message);
        }
    }
}
```

the method F catches an exception, writes some diagnostic information to the console, alters the exception variable, and re-throws the exception. The exception that is re-thrown is the original exception, so the output of the program is:

```
Exception in F: G
Exception in Main: G
```

It is an error for a `break`, `continue`, or `goto` statement to transfer control out of a `finally` block. When a `break`, `continue`, or `goto` statement occurs in a `finally` block, the target of the statement must be within the same `finally` block, or otherwise a compile-time error occurs.

It is an error for a `return` statement to occur in a `finally` block.

A `try` statement is executed as follows:

- Control is transferred to the `try` block.
- When and if control reaches the end point of the `try` block:
  - If the `try` statement has a `finally` block, the `finally` block is executed.
  - Control is transferred to the end point of the `try` statement.
- If an exception is propagated to the `try` statement during execution of the `try` block:
  - The `catch` clauses, if any, are examined in order of appearance to locate a suitable handler for the exception. The first `catch` clause that specifies the exception type or a base type of the exception type is considered a match. A general `catch` clause is considered a match for any exception type. If a matching `catch` clause is located:
    - If the matching `catch` clause declares an exception variable, the exception object is assigned to the exception variable.
    - Control is transferred to the matching `catch` block.
    - When and if control reaches the end point of the `catch` block:
      - If the `try` statement has a `finally` block, the `finally` block is executed.
      - Control is transferred to the end point of the `try` statement.
    - If an exception is propagated to the `try` statement during execution of the `catch` block:
      - If the `try` statement has a `finally` block, the `finally` block is executed.
      - The exception is propagated to the next enclosing `try` statement.
  - If the `try` statement has no `catch` clauses or if no `catch` clause matches the exception:
    - If the `try` statement has a `finally` block, the `finally` block is executed.
    - The exception is propagated to the next enclosing `try` statement.

The statements of a `finally` block are always executed when control leaves a `try` statement. This is true whether the control transfer occurs as a result of normal execution, as a result of executing a `break`, `continue`, `goto`, or `return` statement, or as a result of propagating an exception out of the `try` statement.

If an exception is thrown during execution of a `finally` block, the exception is propagated to the next enclosing `try` statement. If another exception was in the process of being propagated, that exception is lost. The process of propagating an exception is further discussed in the description of the `throw` statement (section 8.9.5).

The `try` block of a `try` statement is reachable if the `try` statement is reachable.

A `catch` block of a `try` statement is reachable if the `try` statement is reachable.

The `finally` block of a `try` statement is reachable if the `try` statement is reachable.

The end point of a `try` statement is reachable if both of the following are true:

- The end point of the `try` block is reachable or the end point of at least one `catch` block is reachable.
- If a `finally` block is present, the end point of the `finally` block is reachable.

8.11 The checked and unchecked statements

The `checked` and `unchecked` statements are used to control the ***overflow checking context*** for integral-type arithmetic operations and conversions.

checked-statement:
   `checked` *block*

unchecked-statement:
   `unchecked` *block*

The `checked` statement causes all expressions in the *block* to be evaluated in a checked context, and the `unchecked` statement causes all expressions in the *block* to be evaluated in an unchecked context.

The `checked` and `unchecked` statements are precisely equivalent to the `checked` and `unchecked` operators (section 7.5.12), except that they operate on blocks instead of expressions.

8.12 The lock statement

The `lock` statement obtains the mutual-exclusion lock for a given object, executes a statement, and then releases the lock.

lock-statement:
   `lock` (*expression*) *embedded-statement*

The expression of a `lock` statement must denote a value of a *reference-type*. An implicit boxing conversion (section 6.1.5) is never performed for the expression of a `lock` statement, and thus it is an error for the expression to denote a value of a *value-type*.

A `lock` statement of the form

```
lock (x) …
```

where x is an expression of a *reference-type*, is precisely equivalent to

```
System.Threading.Monitor.Enter(x);
try {
    …
}
finally {
    System.Threading.Monitor.Exit(x);
}
```

except that x is only evaluated once. The exact behavior of the `Enter` and `Exit` methods of the `System.Threading.Monitor` class is implementation-defined.

The `System.Type` object of a class can conveniently be used as the mutual-exclusion lock for static methods of the class. For example:

```
class Cache
{
    public static void Add(object x) {
        lock (typeof(Cache)) {
            …
        }
    }
    public static void Remove(object x) {
        lock (typeof(Cache)) {
            …
        }
    }
}
```

8.13 The using statement

The `using` statement obtains one or more resources, executes a statement, and then disposes of the resource.

using-statement:
    using (*resource-acquisition*)   *embedded-statement*

resource-acquisition:
    local-variable-declaration
    expression

A **resource** is a class or struct that implements `System.IDisposable`, which includes a single parameterless method named `Dispose`. Code that is using a resource can call `Dispose` to indicate that the resource is no longer needed. If `Dispose` is not called, then automatic disposal eventually occurs as a consequence of garbage collection.

If the form of *resource-acquisition* is *local-variable-declaration* then the type of the *local-variable-declaration* must be `System.IDisposable` or a type that can be implicitly converted to `System.IDisposable`. If the form of *resource-acquisition* is *expression* then this expression must be `System.IDisposable` or a type that can be implicitly converted to `System.IDisposable`.

Local variables declared in a *resource-acquisition* are read-only, and must include an initializer.

A `using` statement is translated into three parts: acquisition, usage, and disposal. Usage of the resource is enclosed in a `try` statement that includes a `finally` clause. This `finally` clause disposes of the resource. If a `null` resource is acquired, then no call to `Dispose` is made, and no exception is thrown.

For example, a `using` statement of the form

```
using (R r1 = new R ()) {
    r1.F();
}
```

is precisely equivalent to

```
R r1 = new R();
try {
    r1.F();
}
finally {
    if (r1 != null) ((IDisposable)r1).Dispose();
}
```

A *resource-acquisition* may acquire multiple resources of a given type. This is equivalent to nested `using` statements. For example, a using statement of the form

```
using (R r1 = new R(), r2 = new R()) {
    r1.F();
    r2.F();
}
```

is precisely equivalent to:

```
using (R r1 = new R())
    using (R r2 = new R()) {
        r1.F();
        r2.F();
    }
```

which is, by expansion, precisely equivalent to:

```
R r1 = new R();
try {
   R r2 = new R();
   try {
      r1.F();
      r2.F();
   }
   finally {
      if (r2 != null) ((IDisposable)r2).Dispose();
   }
}
finally {
   if (r1 != null) ((IDisposable)r1).Dispose();
}
```

9. Namespaces

C# programs are organized using namespaces. Namespaces are used both as an "internal" organization system for a program, and as an "external" organization system—a way of presenting program elements that are exposed to other programs.

Using directives are provided to facilitate the use of namespaces.

9.1 Compilation units

A *compilation-unit* defines the overall structure of a source file. A compilation unit consists of zero or more *using-directive*s followed by zero or more *namespace-member-declaration*s.

compilation-unit:
    using-directives~opt~ *attributes*~opt~ *namespace-member-declarations*~opt~

A C# program consists of one or more compilation units, each contained in a separate source file. When a C# program is compiled, all of the compilation units are processed together. Thus, compilation units can depend on each other, possibly in a circular fashion.

The *using-directives* of a compilation unit affect the *attributes* and *namespace-member-declarations* of that compilation unit, but have no effect on other compilation units.

The *attributes* of a compilation unit permit the specification of attributes for the target assembly and module. Assemblies and modules act as physical containers for types. An assembly may consist of several physically separate modules.

The *namespace-member-declarations* of each compilation unit of a program contribute members to a single declaration space called the global namespace. For example:

File A.cs:

```
class A {}
```

File B.cs:

```
class B {}
```

The two compilation units contribute to the single global namespace, in this case declaring two classes with the fully qualified names A and B. Because the two compilation units contribute to the same declaration space, it would have been an error if each contained a declaration of a member with the same name.

9.2 Namespace declarations

A *namespace-declaration* consists of the keyword `namespace`, followed by a namespace name and body, optionally followed by a semicolon.

namespace-declaration:
    `namespace` *qualified-identifier* *namespace-body* ;*opt*

qualified-identifier:
    identifier
    qualified-identifier . *identifier*

namespace-body:
    { *using-directives*_{opt} *namespace-member-declarations*_{opt} }

A *namespace-declaration* may occur as a top-level declaration in a *compilation-unit* or as a member declaration within another *namespace-declaration*. When a *namespace-declaration* occurs as a top-level declaration in a *compilation-unit*, the namespace becomes a member of the global namespace. When a *namespace-declaration* occurs within another *namespace-declaration*, the inner namespace becomes a member of the outer namespace. In either case, the name of a namespace must be unique within the containing namespace.

Namespaces are implicitly `public` and the declaration of a namespace cannot include any access modifiers.

Within a *namespace-body*, the optional *using-directives* import the names of other namespaces and types, allowing them to be referenced directly instead of through qualified names. The optional *namespace-member-declarations* contribute members to the declaration space of the namespace. Note that all *using-directives* must appear before any member declarations.

The *qualified-identifier* of a *namespace-declaration* may be single identifier or a sequence of identifiers separated by "." tokens. The latter form permits a program to define a nested namespace without lexically nesting several namespace declarations.

For example,

```
namespace N1.N2
{
    class A {}
    class B {}
}
```

is semantically equivalent to

```
namespace N1
{
    namespace N2
    {
        class A {}
        class B {}
    }
}
```

Namespaces are open-ended, and two namespace declarations with the same fully qualified name contribute to the same declaration space (section 3.3). In the example

```
namespace N1.N2
{
    class A {}
}
namespace N1.N2
{
    class B {}
}
```

the two namespace declarations above contribute to the same declaration space, in this case declaring two classes with the fully qualified names `N1.N2.A` and `N1.N2.B`. Because the two declarations contribute to the same declaration space, it would have been an error if each contained a declaration of a member with the same name.

9.3 Using directives

Using directives facilitate the use of namespaces and types defined in other namespaces. Using directives impact the name resolution process of *namespace-or-type-name*s (section 3.8) and *simple-name*s (section 7.5.2), but unlike declarations, using directives do not contribute new members to the underlying declaration spaces of the compilation units or namespaces within which they are used.

using-directives:
    using-directive
    using-directives   using-directive

using-directive:
  using-alias-directive
  using-namespace-directive

A *using-alias-directive* (section 9.3.1) introduces an alias for a namespace or type.

A *using-namespace-directive* (section 9.3.2) imports the type members of a namespace.

The scope of a *using-directive* extends over the *namespace-member-declarations* of its immediately containing compilation unit or namespace body. The scope of a *using-directive* specifically does not include its peer *using-directives*. Thus, peer *using-directives* do not affect each other, and the order in which they are written is insignificant.

9.3.1 Using alias directives

A *using-alias-directive* introduces an identifier that serves as an alias for a namespace or type within the immediately enclosing compilation unit or namespace body.

using-alias-directive:
  using *identifier* = *namespace-or-type-name* ;

Within member declarations in a compilation unit or namespace body that contains a *using-alias-directive*, the identifier introduced by the *using-alias-directive* can be used to reference the given namespace or type. For example:

```
namespace N1.N2
{
   class A {}
}
namespace N3
{
   using A = N1.N2.A;
   class B: A {}
}
```

Here, within member declarations in the N3 namespace, A is an alias for N1.N2.A, and thus class N3.B derives from class N1.N2.A. The same effect can be obtained by creating an alias R for N1.N2 and then referencing R.A:

```
namespace N3
{
   using R = N1.N2;
   class B: R.A {}
}
```

The *identifier* of a *using-alias-directive* must be unique within the declaration space of the compilation unit or namespace that immediately contains the *using-alias-directive*. For example:

```
namespace N3
{
   class A {}
}
namespace N3
{
   using A = N1.N2.A;       // Error, A already exists
}
```

Here, N3 already contains a member A, so it is an error for a *using-alias-directive* to use that identifier. It is likewise an error for two or more *using-alias-directive*s in the same compilation unit or namespace body to declare aliases by the same name.

A *using-alias-directive* makes an alias available within a particular compilation unit or namespace body, but it does not contribute any new members to the underlying declaration space. In other words, a *using-alias-directive* is not transitive but rather affects only the compilation unit or namespace body in which it occurs. In the example

```
namespace N3
{
   using R = N1.N2;
}
namespace N3
{
   class B: R.A {}          // Error, R unknown
}
```

the scope of the *using-alias-directive* that introduces R only extends to member declarations in the namespace body in which it is contained, and R is thus unknown in the second namespace declaration. However, placing the *using-alias-directive* in the containing compilation unit causes the alias to become available within both namespace declarations:

```
using R = N1.N2;
namespace N3
{
   class B: R.A {}
}
namespace N3
{
   class C: R.A {}
}
```

Just like regular members, names introduced by *using-alias-directive*s are hidden by similarly named members in nested scopes. In the example

```
using R = N1.N2;
namespace N3
{
    class R {}
    class B: R.A {}        // Error, R has no member A
}
```

the reference to R.A in the declaration of B causes an error because R refers to N3.R, not N1.N2.

The order in which *using-alias-directive*s are written has no significance, and resolution of the *namespace-or-type-name* referenced by a *using-alias-directive* is neither affected by the *using-alias-directive* itself nor by other *using-directive*s in the immediately containing compilation unit or namespace body. In other words, the *namespace-or-type-name* of a *using-alias-directive* is resolved as if the immediately containing compilation unit or namespace body had no *using-directive*s. In the example

```
namespace N1.N2 {}
namespace N3
{
    using R1 = N1;       // OK
    using R2 = N1.N2;    // OK
    using R3 = R1.N2;    // Error, R1 unknown
}
```

the last *using-alias-directive* is in error because it is not affected by the first *using-alias-directive*.

A *using-alias-directive* can create an alias for any namespace or type, including the namespace within which it appears and any namespace or type nested within that namespace.

Accessing a namespace or type through an alias yields exactly the same result as accessing the namespace or type through its declared name. In other words, given

```
namespace N1.N2
{
    class A {}
}
namespace N3
{
    using R1 = N1;
    using R2 = N1.N2;
    class B
```

```
    {
        N1.N2.A a;        // refers to N1.N2.A
        R1.N2.A b;        // refers to N1.N2.A
        R2.A c;           // refers to N1.N2.A
    }
}
```

the names `N1.N2.A`, `R1.N2.A`, and `R2.A` are completely equivalent and all refer to the class whose fully qualified name is `N1.N2.A`.

9.3.2 Using namespace directives

A *using-namespace-directive* imports the types contained in a namespace into the immediately enclosing compilation unit or namespace body, enabling the identifier of each type to be used without qualification.

using-namespace-directive:
   using *namespace-name* ;

Within member declarations in compilation unit or namespace body that contains a *using-namespace-directive*, the types contained in the given namespace can be referenced directly. For example:

```
namespace N1.N2
{
    class A {}
}
namespace N3
{
    using N1.N2;
    class B: A {}
}
```

Here, within member declarations in the `N3` namespace, the type members of `N1.N2` are directly available, and thus class `N3.B` derives from class `N1.N2.A`.

A *using-namespace-directive* imports the types contained in the given namespace, but specifically does not import nested namespaces. In the example

```
namespace N1.N2
{
    class A {}
}
namespace N3
{
    using N1;
    class B: N2.A {}      // Error, N2 unknown
}
```

the *using-namespace-directive* imports the types contained in N1, but not the namespaces nested in N1. Thus, the reference to N2.A in the declaration of B is in error because no members named N2 are in scope.

Unlike a *using-alias-directive*, a *using-namespace-directive* may import types whose identifiers are already defined within the enclosing compilation unit or namespace body. In effect, names imported by a *using-namespace-directive* are hidden by similarly named members in the enclosing compilation unit or namespace body. For example:

```
namespace N1.N2
{
    class A {}
    class B {}
}
namespace N3
{
    using N1.N2;
    class A {}
}
```

Here, within member declarations in the N3 namespace, A refers to N3.A rather than N1.N2.A.

When more than one namespace imported by *using-namespace-directive*s in the same compilation unit or namespace body contain types by the same name, references to that name are considered ambiguous. In the example

```
namespace N1
{
    class A {}
}
namespace N2
{
    class A {}
}
namespace N3
{
    using N1;
    using N2;
    class B: A {}          // Error, A is ambiguous
}
```

both N1 and N2 contain a member A, and because N3 imports both, referencing A in N3 is an error. In this situation, the conflict can be resolved either through qualification of references to A, or by introducing a *using-alias-directive* that picks a particular A.

For example:

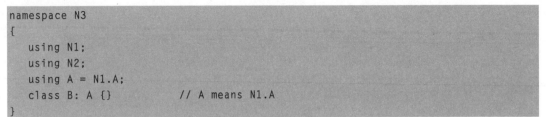

```
namespace N3
{
   using N1;
   using N2;
   using A = N1.A;
   class B: A {}              // A means N1.A
}
```

Like a *using-alias-directive*, a *using-namespace-directive* does not contribute any new members to the underlying declaration space of the compilation unit or namespace, but rather affects only the compilation unit or namespace body in which it appears.

The *namespace-name* referenced by a *using-namespace-directive* is resolved in the same way as the *namespace-or-type-name* referenced by a *using-alias-directive*. Thus, *using-namespace-directive*s in the same compilation unit or namespace body do not affect each other and can be written in any order.

9.4 Namespace members

A *namespace-member-declaration* is either a *namespace-declaration* (section 9.2) or a *type-declaration* (section 9.5).

namespace-member-declarations:
   namespace-member-declaration
   namespace-member-declarations   namespace-member-declaration

namespace-member-declaration:
   namespace-declaration
   type-declaration

A compilation unit or a namespace body can contain *namespace-member-declarations*, and such declarations contribute new members to the underlying declaration space of the containing compilation unit or namespace body.

9.5 Type declarations

A *type-declaration* is either a *class-declaration* (section 10.1), a *struct-declaration* (section 11), an *interface-declaration* (section 13.1), an *enum-declaration* (section 14.1), or a *delegate-declaration* (section 15.1).

type-declaration:
   class-declaration
   struct-declaration
   interface-declaration
   enum-declaration
   delegate-declaration

A *type-declaration* can occur as a top-level declaration in a compilation unit or as a member declaration within a namespace, class, or struct.

When a type declaration for a type T occurs as a top-level declaration in a compilation unit, the fully qualified name of the newly declared type is simply T. When a type declaration for a type T occurs within a namespace, class, or struct, the fully qualified name of the newly declared type is N.T, where N is the fully qualified name of the containing namespace, class, or struct.

A type declared within a class or struct is called a nested type (section 10.2.6).

The permitted access modifiers and the default access for a type declaration depend on the context in which the declaration takes place (section 3.5.1):

- Types declared in compilation units or namespaces can have `public` or `internal` access. The default is `internal` access.
- Types declared in classes can have `public`, `protected internal`, `protected`, `internal`, or `private` access. The default is `private` access.
- Types declared in structs can have `public`, `internal`, or `private` access. The default is `private` access.

10. Classes

A class is a data structure that may contain data members (constants, fields, and events), function members (methods, properties, indexers, operators, constructors, and destructors), and nested types. Class types support inheritance, a mechanism whereby a derived class can extend and specialize a base class.

10.1 Class declarations

A *class-declaration* is a *type-declaration* (section 9.5) that declares a new class.

class-declaration:
  attributes$_{opt}$ *class-modifiers*$_{opt}$ `class` *identifier* *class-base*$_{opt}$ *class-body* `;`$_{opt}$

A *class-declaration* consists of an optional set of *attributes* (section 17), followed by an optional set of *class-modifiers* (section 10.1.1), followed by the keyword `class` and an *identifier* that names the class, followed by an optional *class-base* specification (section 10.1.2), followed by a *class-body* (section 10.1.3), optionally followed by a semicolon.

10.1.1 Class modifiers

A *class-declaration* may optionally include a sequence of class modifiers:

class-modifiers:
  class-modifier
  class-modifiers *class-modifier*

class-modifier:
```
new
public
protected
internal
private
abstract
sealed
```

It is an error for the same modifier to appear multiple times in a class declaration.

The `new` modifier is only permitted on nested classes. It specifies that the class hides an inherited member by the same name, as described in section 10.2.2.

The `public`, `protected`, `internal`, and `private` modifiers control the accessibility of the class. Depending on the context in which the class declaration occurs, some of these modifiers may not be permitted (section 3.5.1).

The `abstract` and `sealed` modifiers are discussed in the following sections.

10.1.1.1 Abstract classes

The `abstract` modifier is used to indicate that a class is incomplete and intended only to be a base class of other classes. An abstract class differs from a non-abstract class is the following ways:

- An abstract class cannot be instantiated directly, and it is an error to use the `new` operator on an abstract class. While it is possible to have variables and values whose compile-time types are abstract, such variables and values will necessarily either be `null` or contain references to instances of non-abstract classes derived from the abstract types.
- An abstract class is permitted (but not required) to contain abstract members.
- An abstract class cannot be sealed.

When a non-abstract class is derived from an abstract class, the non-abstract class must include actual implementations of all inherited abstract members. Such implementations are provided by overriding the abstract members. In the example

```
abstract class A
{
    public abstract void F();
}
abstract class B: A
{
    public void G() {}
}
class C: B
{
    public override void F() {
        // actual implementation of F
    }
}
```

the abstract class A introduces an abstract method F. Class B introduces an additional method G, but doesn't provide an implementation of F. B must therefore also be declared abstract. Class C overrides F and provides an actual implementation. Since there are no outstanding abstract members in C, C is permitted (but not required) to be non-abstract.

10.1.1.2 Sealed classes

The `sealed` modifier is used to prevent derivation from a class. An error occurs if a sealed class is specified as the base class of another class.

A sealed class cannot also be an abstract class.

The `sealed` modifier is primarily used to prevent unintended derivation, but it also enables certain run-time optimizations. In particular, because a sealed class is known to never have any derived classes, it is possible to transform virtual function member invocations on sealed class instances into non-virtual invocations.

10.1.2 Class base specification

A class declaration may include a *class-base* specification which defines the direct base class of the class and the interfaces implemented by the class.

class-base:
   :   *class-type*
   :   *interface-type-list*
   :   *class-type*   ,   *interface-type-list*

interface-type-list:
   interface-type
   interface-type-list   ,   *interface-type*

10.1.2.1 Base classes

When a *class-type* is included in the *class-base*, it specifies the direct base class of the class being declared. If a class declaration has no *class-base*, or if the *class-base* lists only interface types, the direct base class is assumed to be `object`. A class inherits members from its direct base class, as described in section 10.2.1.

In the example

```
class A {}
class B: A {}
```

class `A` is said to be the direct base class of `B`, and `B` is said to be derived from `A`. Since `A` does not explicitly specify a direct base class, its direct base class is implicitly `object`.

The direct base class of a class type must be at least as accessible as the class type itself (section 3.5.4). For example, it is an error for a `public` class to derive from a `private` or `internal` class.

The direct base class of a class type must not be any of the following types: `System.Array`, `System.Delegate`, `System.Enum`, or `System.ValueType`.

The base classes of a class are the direct base class and its base classes. In other words, the set of base classes is the transitive closure of the direct base class relationship. Referring to the example above, the base classes of `B` are `A` and `object`.

Except for class `object`, every class has exactly one direct base class. The `object` class has no direct base class and is the ultimate base class of all other classes.

When a class B derives from a class A, it is an error for A to depend on B. A class *directly depends on* its direct base class (if any) and ***directly depends on*** the class within which it is immediately nested (if any). Given this definition, the complete set of classes upon which a class depends is the transitive closure of the *directly depends on* relationship.

The example

```
class A: B {}
class B: C {}
class C: A {}
```

is in error because the classes circularly depend on themselves. Likewise, the example

```
class A: B.C {}
class B: A
{
    public class C {}
}
```

is in error because A depends on B.C (its direct base class), which depends on B (its immediately enclosing class), which circularly depends on A.

Note that a class does not depend on the classes that are nested within it. In the example

```
class A
{
    class B: A {}
}
```

B depends on A (because A is both its direct base class and its immediately enclosing class), but A does not depend on B (since B is neither a base class nor an enclosing class of A). Thus, the example is valid.

It is not possible to derive from a `sealed` class. In the example

```
sealed class A {}
class B: A {}          // Error, cannot derive from a sealed class
```

class B is in error because it attempts to derive from the `sealed` class A.

10.1.2.2 Interface implementations

A *class-base* specification may include a list of interface types, in which case the class is said to implement the given interface types. Interface implementations are discussed further in section 13.4.

10.1.3 Class body

The *class-body* of a class defines the members of the class.

class-body:
    {   *class-member-declarations*$_{opt}$ }

10.2 Class members

The members of a class consist of the members introduced by its *class-member-declarations* and the members inherited from the direct base class.

class-member-declarations:
    class-member-declaration
    class-member-declarations   *class-member-declaration*

class-member-declaration:
    constant-declaration
    field-declaration
    method-declaration
    property-declaration
    event-declaration
    indexer-declaration
    operator-declaration
    constructor-declaration
    destructor-declaration
    static-constructor-declaration
    type-declaration

The members of a class are divided into the following categories:

- Constants, which represent constant values associated with the class (section 10.3).
- Fields, which are the variables of the class (section 10.4).
- Methods, which implement the computations and actions that can be performed by the class (section 10.5).
- Properties, which define named attributes and the actions associated with reading and writing those attributes (section 10.6).
- Events, which define notifications that are generated by the class (section 10.7).
- Indexers, which permit instances of the class to be indexed in the same way as arrays (section 10.8).
- Operators, which define the expression operators that can be applied to instances of the class (section 10.9).
- Instance constructors, which implement the actions required to initialize instances of the class (section 10.10)

- Destructors, which implement the actions to perform before instances of the class are permanently discarded (section 10.12).
- Static constructors, which implement the actions required to initialize the class itself (section 10.11).
- Types, which represent the types that are local to the class (section 9.5).

Members that contain executable code are collectively known as the *function members* of the class. The function members of a class are the methods, properties, indexers, operators, constructors, and destructors of the class.

A *class-declaration* creates a new declaration space (section 3.3), and the *class-member-declarations* immediately contained by the *class-declaration* introduce new members into this declaration space. The following rules apply to *class-member-declaration*s:

- Constructors and destructors must have the same name as the immediately enclosing class. All other members must have names that differ from the name of the immediately enclosing class.
- The name of a constant, field, property, event, or type must differ from the names of all other members declared in the same class.
- The name of a method must differ from the names of all other non-methods declared in the same class. In addition, the signature (section 3.6) of a method must differ from the signatures of all other methods declared in the same class.
- The signature of an constructor must differ from the signatures of all other constructors declared in the same class.
- The signature of an indexer must differ from the signatures of all other indexers declared in the same class.
- The signature of an operator must differ from the signatures of all other operators declared in the same class.

The inherited members of a class (section 10.2.1) are specifically not part of the declaration space of a class. Thus, a derived class is allowed to declare a member with the same name or signature as an inherited member (which in effect hides the inherited member).

10.2.1 Inheritance

A class ***inherits*** the members of its direct base class. Inheritance means that a class implicitly contains all members of its direct base class, except for the constructors and destructors of the base class. Some important aspects of inheritance are:

- Inheritance is transitive. If C is derived from B, and B is derived from A, then C inherits the members declared in B as well as the members declared in A.
- A derived class *extends* its direct base class. A derived class can add new members to those it inherits, but it cannot remove the definition of an inherited member.

- Constructors and destructors are not inherited, but all other members are, regardless of their declared accessibility (section 3.5). However, depending on their declared accessibility, inherited members may not be accessible in a derived class.

- A derived class can **hide** (section 3.7.1.2) inherited members by declaring new members with the same name or signature. Note however that hiding an inherited member does not remove the member—it merely makes the member inaccessible in the derived class.

- An instance of a class contains a copy of all instance fields declared in the class and its base classes, and an implicit conversion (section 6.1.4) exists from a derived class type to any of its base class types. Thus, a reference to a derived class instance can be treated as a reference to a base class instance.

- A class can declare virtual methods, properties, and indexers, and derived classes can override the implementation of these function members. This enables classes to exhibit polymorphic behavior wherein the actions performed by a function member invocation varies depending on the run-time type of the instance through which the function member is invoked.

10.2.2 The new modifier

A *class-member-declaration* is permitted to declare a member with the same name or signature as an inherited member. When this occurs, the derived class member is said to **hide** the base class member. Hiding an inherited member is not considered an error, but it does cause the compiler to issue a warning. To suppress the warning, the declaration of the derived class member can include a `new` modifier to indicate that the derived member is intended to hide the base member. This topic is discussed further in section 3.7.1.2.

If a `new` modifier is included in a declaration that doesn't hide an inherited member, a warning is issued to that effect. This warning is suppressed by removing the `new` modifier.

It is an error to use the `new` and `override` modifiers in the same declaration.

10.2.3 Access modifiers

A *class-member-declaration* can have any one of the five possible types of declared accessibility (section 3.5.1): `public`, `protected internal`, `protected`, `internal`, or `private`. Except for the `protected internal` combination, it is an error to specify more than one access modifier. When a *class-member-declaration* does not include any access modifiers, the declaration defaults to `private` declared accessibility.

10.2.4 Constituent types

Types that are referenced in the declaration of a member are called the constituent types of the member. Possible constituent types are the type of a constant, field, property, event, or indexer, the return type of a method or operator, and the parameter types of a method, indexer, operator, or constructor. The constituent types of a member must be at least as accessible as the member itself (section 3.5.4).

10.2.5 Static and instance members

Members of a class are either **static members** or **instance members**. Generally speaking, it is useful to think of static members as belonging to classes and instance members as belonging to objects (instances of classes).

When a field, method, property, event, operator, or constructor declaration includes a `static` modifier, it declares a static member. In addition, a constant or type declaration implicitly declares a static member. Static members have the following characteristics:

- When a static member is referenced in a *member-access* (section 7.5.4) of the form `E.M`, `E` must denote a type. It is an error for `E` to denote an instance.
- A static field identifies exactly one storage location. No matter how many instances of a class are created, there is only ever one copy of a static field.
- A static function member (method, property, indexer, operator, or constructor) does not operate on a specific instance, and it is an error to refer to `this` in a static function member.

When a field, method, property, event, indexer, constructor, or destructor declaration does not include a `static` modifier, it declares an instance member. An instance member is sometimes called a non-static member. Instance members have the following characteristics:

- When an instance member is referenced in a *member-access* (section 7.5.4) of the form `E.M`, `E` must denote an instance. It is an error for `E` to denote a type.
- Every instance of a class contains a separate copy of all instance fields of the class.
- An instance function member (method, property accessor, indexer accessor, constructor, or destructor) operates on a given instance of the class, and this instance can be accessed as `this` (section 7.5.7).

The following example illustrates the rules for accessing static and instance members:

```
class Test
{
   int x;
   static int y;
   void F() {
      x = 1;          // Ok, same as this.x = 1
      y = 1;          // Ok, same as Test.y = 1
   }
   static void G() {
      x = 1;          // Error, cannot access this.x
      y = 1;          // Ok, same as Test.y = 1
   }
   static void Main() {
      Test t = new Test();
      t.x = 1;        // Ok
      t.y = 1;        // Error, cannot access static member through instance
      Test.x = 1;     // Error, cannot access instance member through type
      Test.y = 1;     // Ok
   }
}
```

The F method shows that in an instance function member, a *simple-name* (section 7.5.2) can be used to access both instance members and static members. The G method shows that in a static function member, it is an error to access an instance member through a *simple-name*. The Main method shows that in a *member-access* (section 7.5.4), instance members must be accessed through instances, and static members must be accessed through types.

10.2.6 Nested types

10.3 Constants

A **constant** is a class member that represents a constant value: a value that can be computed at compile-time. A *constant-declaration* introduces one or more constants of a given type.

constant-declaration:
    attributes$_{opt}$ constant-modifiers$_{opt}$ const *type constant-declarators* ;

constant-modifiers:
    constant-modifier
    constant-modifiers constant-modifier

constant-modifier:
```
new
public
protected
internal
private
```
constant-declarators:
    constant-declarator
    constant-declarators , *constant-declarator*

constant-declarator:
    identifier = *constant-expression*

A *constant-declaration* may include a set of *attributes* (section 17), a `new` modifier (section 10.2.2), and a valid combination of the four access modifiers (section 10.2.3). The attributes and modifiers apply to all of the members declared by the *constant-declaration*. Even though constants are considered static members, a *constant-declaration* neither requires nor allows a `static` modifier.

The *type* of a *constant-declaration* specifies the type of the members introduced by the declaration. The type is followed by a list of *constant-declarator*s, each of which introduces a new member. A *constant-declarator* consists of an *identifier* that names the member, followed by an "=" token, followed by a *constant-expression* (section 7.15) that gives the value of the member.

The *type* specified in a constant declaration must be `sbyte`, `byte`, `short`, `ushort`, `int`, `uint`, `long`, `ulong`, `char`, `float`, `double`, `decimal`, `bool`, `string`, an *enum-type*, or a *reference-type*. Each *constant-expression* must yield a value of the target type or of a type that can be converted to the target type by an implicit conversion (section 6.1).

The *type* of a constant must be at least as accessible as the constant itself (section 3.5.4).

A constant can itself participate in a *constant-expression*. Thus, a constant may be used in any construct that requires a *constant-expression*. Examples of such constructs include `case` labels, `goto case` statements, `enum` member declarations, attributes, and other constant declarations.

As described in section 7.15, a *constant-expression* is an expression that can be fully evaluated at compile-time. Since the only way to create a non-null value of a *reference-type* other than `string` is to apply the `new` operator, and since the `new` operator is not permitted in a *constant-expression*, the only possible value for constants of *reference-types* other than `string` is `null`.

When a symbolic name for a constant value is desired, but when the type of the value is not permitted in a constant declaration or when the value cannot be computed at compile-time by a *constant-expression*, a `readonly` field (section 10.4.2) may be used instead.

A constant declaration that declares multiple constants is equivalent to multiple declarations of single constants with the same attributes, modifiers, and type.

For example

```
class A
{
    public const double X = 1.0, Y = 2.0, Z = 3.0;
}
```

is equivalent to

```
class A
{
    public const double X = 1.0;
    public const double Y = 2.0;
    public const double Z = 3.0;
}
```

Constants are permitted to depend on other constants within the same program as long as the dependencies are not of a circular nature. The compiler automatically arranges to evaluate the constant declarations in the appropriate order. In the example

```
class A
{
    public const int X = B.Z + 1;
    public const int Y = 10;
}
class B
{
    public const int Z = A.Y + 1;
}
```

the compiler first evaluates Y, then evaluates Z, and finally evaluates X, producing the values 10, 11, and 12. Constant declarations may depend on constants from other programs, but such dependencies are only possible in one direction. Referring to the example above, if A and B were declared in separate programs, it would be possible for A.X to depend on B.Z, but B.Z could then not simultaneously depend on A.Y.

10.4 Fields

A *field* is a member that represents a variable associated with an object or class. A *field-declaration* introduces one or more fields of a given type.

field-declaration:
    *attributes*_{opt} is written as:
    attributes$_{opt}$ *field-modifiers*$_{opt}$ *type* *variable-declarators* ;

field-modifiers:
    field-modifier
    field-modifiers *field-modifier*

field-modifier:
```
new
public
protected
internal
private
static
readonly
```

variable-declarators:
  variable-declarator
  variable-declarators , *variable-declarator*

variable-declarator:
  identifier
  identifier = *variable-initializer*

variable-initializer:
  expression
  array-initializer

A *field-declaration* may include a set of *attributes* (section 17), a `new` modifier (section 10.2.2), a valid combination of the four access modifiers (section 10.2.3), a `static` modifier (section 10.4.1), and a `readonly` modifier (section 10.4.2). The attributes and modifiers apply to all of the members declared by the *field-declaration*.

The *type* of a *field-declaration* specifies the type of the members introduced by the declaration. The type is followed by a list of *variable-declarator*s, each of which introduces a new member. A *variable-declarator* consists of an *identifier* that names the member, optionally followed by an "=" token and a *variable-initializer* (section 10.4.4) that gives the initial value of the member.

The *type* of a field must be at least as accessible as the field itself (section 3.5.4).

The value of a field is obtained in an expression using a *simple-name* (section 7.5.2) or a *member-access* (section 7.5.4). The value of a field is modified using an *assignment* (section 7.13). The value of a field can be both obtained and modified using postfix increment and decrement operators (section 7.5.9) and prefix increment and decrement operators (section 7.6.7).

A field declaration that declares multiple fields is equivalent to multiple declarations of single fields with the same attributes, modifiers, and type. For example

```
class A
{
    public static int X = 1, Y, Z = 100;
}
```

is equivalent to

```
class A
{
  public static int X = 1;
  public static int Y;
  public static int Z = 100;
}
```

10.4.1 Static and instance fields

When a *field-declaration* includes a `static` modifier, the fields introduced by the declaration are **static fields**. When no `static` modifier is present, the fields introduced by the declaration are *instance fields*. Static fields and instance fields are two of the several kinds of variables (section 5) supported by C#, and are at times referred to as **static variables** and **instance variables**.

A static field identifies exactly one storage location. No matter how many instances of a class are created, there is only ever one copy of a static field. A static field comes into existence when the type in which it is declared is loaded, and ceases to exist when the type in which it is declared is unloaded.

Every instance of a class contains a separate copy of all instance fields of the class. An instance field comes into existence when a new instance of its class is created, and ceases to exist when there are no references to that instance and the destructor of the instance has executed.

When a field is referenced in a *member-access* (section 7.5.4) of the form `E.M`, if `M` is a static field, `E` must denote a type, and if `M` is an instance field, E must denote an instance.

The differences between static and instance members are further discussed in section 10.2.5.

10.4.2 Readonly fields

When a *field-declaration* includes a `readonly` modifier, assignments to the fields introduced by the declaration can only occur as part of the declaration or in a constructor in the same class. Specifically, assignments to a `readonly` field are permitted only in the following contexts:

- In the *variable-declarator* that introduces the field (by including a *variable-initializer* in the declaration).
- For an instance field, in the instance constructors of the class that contains the field declaration, or for a static field, in the static constructor of the class the that contains the field declaration. These are also the only contexts in which it is valid to pass a `readonly` field as an `out` or `ref` parameter.

Attempting to assign to a `readonly` field or pass it as an `out` or `ref` parameter in any other context is an error.

10.4.2.1 Using static readonly fields for constants

A `static readonly` field is useful when a symbolic name for a constant value is desired, but when the type of the value is not permitted in a `const` declaration or when the value cannot be computed at compile-time. In the example

```
public class Color
{
    public static readonly Color Black = new Color(0, 0, 0);
    public static readonly Color White = new Color(255, 255, 255);
    public static readonly Color Red = new Color(255, 0, 0);
    public static readonly Color Green = new Color(0, 255, 0);
    public static readonly Color Blue = new Color(0, 0, 255);
    private byte red, green, blue;
    public Color(byte r, byte g, byte b) {
        red = r;
        green = g;
        blue = b;
    }
}
```

the `Black`, `White`, `Red`, `Green`, and `Blue` members cannot be declared as `const` members because their values cannot be computed at compile-time. However, declaring the members as `static readonly` fields has much the same effect.

10.4.2.2 Versioning of constants and static readonly fields

Constants and readonly fields have different binary versioning semantics. When an expression references a constant, the value of the constant is obtained at compile-time, but when an expression references a readonly field, the value of the field is not obtained until run-time. Consider an application that consists of two separate programs:

```
namespace Program1
{
    public class Utils
    {
        public static readonly int X = 1;
    }
}
namespace Program2
{
    class Test
    {
        static void Main() {
            Console.WriteLine(Program1.Utils.X);
        }
    }
}
```

The `Program1` and `Program2` namespaces denote two programs that are compiled separately. Because `Program1.Utils.X` is declared as a static readonly field, the value output by the `Console.WriteLine` statement is not known at compile-time, but rather is obtained at run-time. Thus, if the value of `X` is changed and `Program1` is recompiled, the `Console.WriteLine` statement will output the new value even if `Program2` isn't recompiled. However, had `X` been a constant, the value of `X` would have been obtained at the time `Program2` was compiled, and would remain unaffected by changes in `Program1` until `Program2` is recompiled.

10.4.3 Field initialization

The initial value of a field is the default value (section 5.2) of the field's type. When a class is loaded, all static fields are initialized to their default values, and when an instance of a class is created, all instance fields are initialized to their default values. It is not possible to observe the value of a field before this default initialization has occurred, and a field is thus never "uninitialized". The example

```
class Test
{
   static bool b;
   int i;
   static void Main() {
      Test t = new Test();
      Console.WriteLine("b = {0}, i = {1}", b, t.i);
   }
}
```

produces the output

```
b = False, i = 0
```

because `b` is automatically initialized to its default value when the class is loaded and `i` is automatically initialized to its default value when an instance of the class is created.

10.4.4 Variable initializers

Field declarations may include *variable-initializer*s. For static fields, variable initializers correspond to assignment statements that are executed when the class is loaded. For instance fields, variable initializers correspond to assignment statements that are executed when an instance of the class is created.

The example

```
class Test
{
    static double x = Math.Sqrt(2.0);
    int i = 100;
    string s = "Hello";
    static void Main() {
        Test a = new Test();
        Console.WriteLine("x = {0}, i = {1}, s = {2}", x, a.i, a.s);
    }
}
```

produces the output

```
x = 1.414213562373095, i = 100, s = Hello
```

because an assignment to x occurs when the class is loaded and assignments to i and s occur when an new instance of the class is created.

The default value initialization described in section 10.4.3 occurs for all fields, including fields that have variable initializers. Thus, when a class is loaded, all static fields are first initialized to their default values, and then the static field initializers are executed in textual order. Likewise, when an instance of a class is created, all instance fields are first initialized to their default values, and then the instance field initializers are executed in textual order.

It is possible for static fields with variable initializers to be observed in their default value state, though this is strongly discouraged as a matter of style. The example

```
class Test
{
    static int a = b + 1;
    static int b = a + 1;
    static void Main() {
        Console.WriteLine("a = {0}, b = {1}", a, b);
    }
}
```

exhibits this behavior. Despite the circular definitions of a and b, the program is legal. It produces the output

```
a = 1, b = 2
```

because the static fields a and b are initialized to 0 (the default value for int) before their initializers are executed. When the initializer for a runs, the value of b is zero, and so a is initialized to 1. When the initializer for b runs, the value of a is already 1, and so b is initialized to 2.

10.4.4.1 Static field initialization

The static field variable initializers of a class correspond to a sequence of assignments that are executed immediately upon entry to the static constructor of the class. The variable initializers are executed in the textual order they appear in the class declaration. The class loading and initialization process is described further in section 10.11.

10.4.4.2 Instance field initialization

The instance field variable initializers of a class correspond to a sequence of assignments that are executed immediately upon entry to one of the instance constructors of the class. The variable initializers are executed in the textual order they appear in the class declaration. The class instance creation and initialization process is described further in section 10.10.

A variable initializer for an instance field cannot reference the instance being created. Thus, it is an error to reference this in a variable initializer, as is it an error for a variable initializer to reference any instance member through a *simple-name*. In the example

```
class A
{
   int x = 1;
   int y = x + 1;    // Error, reference to instance member of this
}
```

the variable initializer for y is in error because it references a member of the instance being created.

10.5 Methods

A ***method*** is a member that implements a computation or action that can be performed by an object or class. Methods are declared using *method-declarations*:

method-declaration:
   method-header   method-body

method-header:
   attributes$_{opt}$ method-modifiers$_{opt}$ return-type member-name (formal-parameter-list$_{opt}$)

method-modifiers:
   method-modifier
   method-modifiers   method-modifier

method-modifier:
```
new
public
protected
internal
private
static
virtual
sealed
override
abstract
extern
```

return-type:
> *type*
> void

member-name:
> *identifier*
> *interface-type* . *identifier*

method-body:
> *block*
>
> ;

A *method-declaration* may include a set of *attributes* (section 17), a new modifier (section 10.2.2), an extern modifier (section 10.5.7), a valid combination of the four access modifiers (section 10.2.3), and a valid combination of the static (section 10.5.2), virtual (section 10.5.3), override (section 10.5.4), and abstract (section 10.5.6) modifiers. In addition, a method that includes the override modifier may also include the sealed modifier (section 10.5.5).

The static, virtual, override, and abstract modifiers are mutually exclusive except in one case. The abstract and override modifiers may be used together so that an abstract method can override a virtual one.

The *return-type* of a method declaration specifies the type of the value computed and returned by the method. The *return-type* is void if the method does not return a value.

The *member-name* specifies the name of the method. Unless the method is an explicit interface member implementation, the *member-name* is simply an *identifier*. For an explicit interface member implementation (section 13.4.1) , the *member-name* consists of an *interface-type* followed by a "." and an *identifier*.

The optional *formal-parameter-list* specifies the parameters of the method (section 10.5.1).

The *return-type* and each of the types referenced in the *formal-parameter-list* of a method must be at least as accessible as the method itself (section 3.5.4).

For abstract and extern methods, the *method-body* consists simply of a semicolon. For all other methods, the *method-body* consists of a *block* which specifies the statements to execute when the method is invoked.

The name and the formal parameter list of a method defines the signature (section 3.6) of the method. Specifically, the signature of a method consists of its name and the number, modifiers, and types of its formal parameters. The return type is not part of a method's signature, nor are the names of the formal parameters.

The name of a method must differ from the names of all other non-methods declared in the same class. In addition, the signature of a method must differ from the signatures of all other methods declared in the same class.

10.5.1 Method parameters

The parameters of a method, if any, are declared by the method's *formal-parameter-list*.

formal-parameter-list:
    fixed-parameters
    fixed-parameters , *parameter-array*
    parameter-array

fixed-parameters:
    fixed-parameter
    fixed-parameters , *fixed-parameter*

fixed-parameter:
    attributes$_{opt}$ *parameter-modifier$_{opt}$* *type* *identifier*

parameter-modifier:
    ref
    out

parameter-array:
    attributes$_{opt}$ params *array-type* *identifier*

The formal parameter list consists of one or more *fixed-parameter*s optionally followed by a single *parameter-array*, all separated by commas.

A *fixed-parameter* consists of an optional set of *attributes* (section 17), an optional ref or out modifier, a *type*, and an *identifier*. Each *fixed-parameter* declares a parameter of the given type with the given name.

A *parameter-array* consists of an optional set of *attributes* (section 17), a params modifier, an *array-type*, and an *identifier*. A parameter array declares a single parameter of the given array type with the given name. The *array-type* of a parameter array must be a single-dimensional array type (section 12.1). In a method invocation, a parameter array permits either a single argument of the given array type to be specified, or it permits zero or more arguments of the array element type to be specified. Parameter arrays are further described in section 10.5.1.4.

A method declaration creates a separate declaration space for parameters and local variables. Names are introduced into this declaration space by the formal parameter list of the method and by local variable declarations in the *block* of the method. All names in the declaration space of a method must be unique. Thus, it is an error for a parameter or local variable to have the same name as another parameter or local variable.

A method invocation (section 7.5.5.1) creates a copy, specific to that invocation, of the formal parameters and local variables of the method, and the argument list of the invocation assigns values or variable references to the newly created formal parameters. Within the *block* of a method, formal parameters can be referenced by their identifiers in *simple-name* expressions (section 7.5.2).

There are four kinds of formal parameters:

- Value parameters, which are declared without any modifiers.
- Reference parameters, which are declared with the `ref` modifier.
- Output parameters, which are declared with the `out` modifier.
- Parameter arrays, which are declared with the `params` modifier.

As described in section 3.6, the `ref` and `out` modifiers are part of a method's signature, but the `params` modifier is not.

10.5.1.1 Value parameters

A parameter declared with no modifiers is a value parameter. A value parameter corresponds to a local variable that gets its initial value from the corresponding argument supplied in the method invocation.

When a formal parameter is a value parameter, the corresponding argument in a method invocation must be an expression of a type that is implicitly convertible (section 6.1) to the formal parameter type.

A method is permitted to assign new values to a value parameter. Such assignments only affect the local storage location represented by the value parameter—they have no effect on the actual argument given in the method invocation.

10.5.1.2 Reference parameters

A parameter declared with a `ref` modifier is a reference parameter. Unlike a value parameter, a reference parameter does not create a new storage location. Instead, a reference parameter represents the same storage location as the variable given as the argument in the method invocation.

When a formal parameter is a reference parameter, the corresponding argument in a method invocation must consist of the keyword `ref` followed by a *variable-reference* (section 5.4) of the same type as the formal parameter. A variable must be definitely assigned before it can be passed as a reference parameter.

Within a method, a reference parameter is always considered definitely assigned.

The example

```
class Test
{
   static void Swap(ref int x, ref int y) {
      int temp = x;
      x = y;
      y = temp;
   }
   static void Main() {
      int i = 1, j = 2;
      Swap(ref i, ref j);
      Console.WriteLine("i = {0}, j = {1}", i, j);
   }
}
```

produces the output

```
i = 2, j = 1
```

For the invocation of Swap in Main, x represents i and y represents j. Thus, the invocation has the effect of swapping the values of i and j.

In a method that takes reference parameters it is possible for multiple names to represent the same storage location. In the example

```
class A
{
   string s;
   void F(ref string a, ref string b) {
      s = "One";
      a = "Two";
      b = "Three";
   }
   void G() {
      F(ref s, ref s);
   }
}
```

the invocation of F in G passes a reference to s for both a and b. Thus, for that invocation, the names s, a, and b all refer to the same storage location, and the three assignments all modify the instance field s.

10.5.1.3 Output parameters

A parameter declared with an out modifier is an output parameter. Similar to a reference parameter, an output parameter does not create a new storage location. Instead, an output parameter represents the same storage location as the variable given as the argument in the method invocation.

When a formal parameter is an output parameter, the corresponding argument in a method invocation must consist of the keyword out followed by a *variable-reference* (section 5.4) of the same type as the formal parameter. A variable need not be definitely assigned before it can be passed as an output parameter, but following an invocation where a variable was passed as an output parameter, the variable is considered definitely assigned.

Within a method, just like a local variable, an output parameter is initially considered unassigned and must be definitely assigned before its value is used.

Every output parameter of a method must be definitely assigned before the method returns.

Output parameters are typically used in methods that produce multiple return values. For example:

```
class Test
{
    static void SplitPath(string path, out string dir, out string name) {
        int i = path.Length;
        while (i > 0) {
            char ch = path[i - 1];
            if (ch == '\\' || ch == '/' || ch == ':') break;
            i--;
        }
        dir = path.Substring(0, i);
        name = path.Substring(i);
    }
    static void Main() {
        string dir, name;
        SplitPath("c:\\Windows\\System\\hello.txt", out dir, out name);
        Console.WriteLine(dir);
        Console.WriteLine(name);
    }
}
```

The example produces the output:

```
c:\Windows\System\
hello.txt
```

Note that the dir and name variables can be unassigned before they are passed to SplitPath, and that they are considered definitely assigned following the call.

10.5.1.4 Parameter arrays

A parameter declared with a `params` modifier is a parameter array. If a formal parameter list includes a parameter array, it must be the last parameter in the list and it must be of a single-dimensional array type. For example, the types `string[]` and `string[][]` can be used as the type of a parameter array, but the type `string[,]` can not. It is not possible to combine the `params` modifier with the `ref` and `out` modifiers.

A parameter array permits arguments to be specified in one of two ways in a method invocation:

- The argument given for a parameter array can be a single expression of a type that is implicitly convertible (section 6.1) to the parameter array type. In this case, the parameter array acts precisely like a value parameter.

- Alternatively, the invocation can specify zero or more arguments for the parameter array, where each argument is an expression of a type that is implicitly convertible (section 6.1) to the element type of the parameter array. In this case, the invocation creates an instance of the parameter array type with a length corresponding to the number of arguments, initializes the elements of the array instance with the given argument values, and uses the newly created array instance as the actual argument.

Except for allowing a variable number of arguments in an invocation, a parameter array is precisely equivalent to a value parameter (section 10.5.1.1) of the same type.

The example

```
class Test
{
    static void F(params int[] args) {
        Console.WriteLine("Array contains {0} elements:", args.Length);
        foreach (int i in args) Console.Write(" {0}", i);
        Console.WriteLine();
    }
    static void Main() {
        int[] a = {1, 2, 3};
        F(a);
        F(10, 20, 30, 40);
        F();
    }
}
```

produces the output

```
Array contains 3 elements: 1 2 3
Array contains 4 elements: 10 20 30 40
Array contains 0 elements:
```

The first invocation of F simply passes the array a as a value parameter. The second invocation of F automatically creates a four-element int[] with the given element values and passes that array instance as a value parameter. Likewise, the third invocation of F creates a zero-element int[] and passes that instance as a value parameter. The second and third invocations are precisely equivalent to writing:

```
F(new int[] {10, 20, 30, 40});
F(new int[] {});
```

When performing overload resolution, a method with a parameter array may be applicable either in its normal form or in its expanded form (section 7.4.2.1). The expanded form of a method is available only if the normal form of the method is not applicable and only if a method with the same signature as the expanded form is not already declared in the same type.

The example

```
class Test
{
    static void F(params object[] a) {
        Console.WriteLine("F(object[])");
    }
    static void F() {
        Console.WriteLine("F()");
    }
    static void F(object a0, object a1) {
        Console.WriteLine("F(object,object)");
    }
    static void Main() {
        F();
        F(1);
        F(1, 2);
        F(1, 2, 3);
        F(1, 2, 3, 4);
    }
}
```

produces the output

```
F();
F(object[]);
F(object,object);
F(object[]);
F(object[]);
```

In the example, two of the possible expanded forms of the method with a parameter array are already included in the class as regular methods. These expanded forms are therefore not considered when performing overload resolution, and the first and third method invocations thus select the regular methods. When a class declares a method with a parameter array, it is not uncommon to also include some of the expanded forms as regular methods. By doing so it is possible to avoid the allocation of an array instance that occurs when an expanded form of a method with a parameter array is invoked.

When the type of a parameter array is `object[]`, a potential ambiguity arises between the normal form of the method and the expended form for a single `object` parameter. The reason for the ambiguity is that an `object[]` is itself implicitly convertible to type `object`. The ambiguity presents no problem, however, since it can be resolved by inserting a cast if needed.

The example

```
class Test
{
    static void F(params object[] args) {
        foreach (object o in a) {
            Console.Write(o.GetType().FullName);
            Console.Write(" ");
        }
        Console.WriteLine();
    }
    static void Main() {
        object[] a = {1, "Hello", 123.456};
        object o = a;
        F(a);
        F((object)a);
        F(o);
        F((object[])o);
    }
}
```

produces the output

```
System.Int32 System.String System.Double
System.Object[]
System.Object[]
System.Int32 System.String System.Double
```

In the first and last invocations of F, the normal form of F is applicable because an implicit conversion exists from the argument type to the parameter type (both are of type object[]). Thus, overload resolution selects the normal form of F, and the argument is passed as a regular value parameter. In the second and third invocations, the normal form of F is not applicable because no implicit conversion exists from the argument type to the parameter type (type object cannot be implicitly converted to type object[]). However, the expanded form of F is applicable, and it is therefore selected by overload resolution. As a result, a one-element object[] is created by the invocation, and the single element of the array is initialized with the given argument value (which itself is a reference to an object[]).

10.5.2 Static and instance methods

When a method declaration includes a static modifier, the method is said to be a static method. When no static modifier is present, the method is said to be an instance method.

A static method does not operate on a specific instance, and it is an error to refer to this in a static method. It is furthermore an error to include a virtual, abstract, or override modifier on a static method.

An instance method operates on a given instance of a class, and this instance can be accessed as this (section 7.5.7).

The differences between static and instance members are further discussed in section 10.2.5.

10.5.3 Virtual methods

When an instance method declaration includes a virtual modifier, the method is said to be a virtual method. When no virtual modifier is present, the method is said to be a non-virtual method.

It is an error for a method declaration that includes the virtual modifier to also include any one of the static, abstract, or override modifiers.

The implementation of a non-virtual method is invariant: The implementation is the same whether the method is invoked on an instance of the class in which it is declared or an instance of a derived class. In contrast, the implementation of a virtual method can be changed by derived classes. The process of changing the implementation of an inherited virtual method is known as *overriding* the method (section 10.5.4).

In a virtual method invocation, the *run-time type* of the instance for which the invocation takes place determines the actual method implementation to invoke. In a non-virtual method invocation, the *compile-time type* of the instance is the determining factor. In precise terms, when a method named N is invoked with an argument list A on an instance with a compile-time type C and a run-time type R (where R is either C or a class derived from C), the invocation is processed as follows:

- First, overload resolution is applied to C, N, and A, to select a specific method M from the set of methods declared in and inherited by C. This is described in section 7.5.5.1.
- Then, if M is a non-virtual method, M is invoked.
- Otherwise, M is a virtual method, and the most derived implementation of M with respect to R is invoked.

For every virtual method declared in or inherited by a class, there exists a ***most derived implementation*** of the method with respect to that class. The most derived implementation of a virtual method M with respect to a class R is determined as follows:

- If R contains the introducing virtual declaration of M, then this is the most derived implementation of M.
- Otherwise, if R contains an override of M, then this is the most derived implementation of M.
- Otherwise, the most derived implementation of M is the same as that of the direct base class of R.

The following example illustrates the differences between virtual and non-virtual methods:

```
class A
{
   public void F() { Console.WriteLine("A.F"); }
   public virtual void G() { Console.WriteLine("A.G"); }
}
class B: A
{
   new public void F() { Console.WriteLine("B.F"); }
   public override void G() { Console.WriteLine("B.G"); }
}
class Test
{
   static void Main() {
      B b = new B();
      A a = b;
      a.F();
      b.F();
      a.G();
      b.G();
   }
}
```

In the example, A introduces a non-virtual method F and a virtual method G. The class B introduces a *new* non-virtual method F, thus *hiding* the inherited F, and also *overrides* the inherited method G. The example produces the output:

```
A.F
B.F
B.G
B.G
```

Notice that the statement a.G() invokes B.G, not A.G. This is because the run-time type of the instance (which is B), not the compile-time type of the instance (which is A), determines the actual method implementation to invoke.

Because methods are allowed to hide inherited methods, it is possible for a class to contain several virtual methods with the same signature. This does not present an ambiguity problem, since all but the most derived method are hidden. In the example

```csharp
class A
{
   public virtual void F() { Console.WriteLine("A.F"); }
}
class B: A
{
   public override void F() { Console.WriteLine("B.F"); }
}
class C: B
{
   new public virtual void F() { Console.WriteLine("C.F"); }
}
class D: C
{
   public override void F() { Console.WriteLine("D.F"); }
}
class Test
{
   static void Main() {
      D d = new D();
      A a = d;
      B b = d;
      C c = d;
      a.F();
      b.F();
      c.F();
      d.F();
   }
}
```

the C and D classes contain two virtual methods with the same signature: The one introduced by A and the one introduced by C. The method introduced by C hides the method inherited from A. Thus, the override declaration in D overrides the method introduced by C, and it is not possible for D to override the method introduced by A. The example produces the output:

```
B.F
B.F
D.F
D.F
```

Note that it is possible to invoke the hidden virtual method by accessing an instance of D through a less derived type in which the method is not hidden.

10.5.4 Override methods

When an instance method declaration includes an override modifier, the method is said to be an ***override method***. An override method overrides an inherited virtual method with the same signature. Whereas a virtual method declaration *introduces* a new method, an override method declaration *specializes* an existing inherited virtual method by providing a new implementation of the method.

It is an error for an override method declaration to include any one of the new, static, or virtual modifiers. An override method declaration may include the abstract modifier. This enables a virtual method to be overridden by an abstract method.

The method overridden by an override declaration is known as the ***overridden base method***. For an override method M declared in a class C, the overridden base method is determined by examining each base class of C, starting with the direct base class of C and continuing with each successive direct base class, until an accessible method with the same signature as M is located. For purposes of locating the overridden base method, a method is considered accessible if it is public, if it is protected, if it is protected internal, or if it is internal and declared in the same program as C.

A compile-time error occurs unless all of the following are true for an override declaration:

- An overridden base method can be located as described above.
- The overridden base method is a virtual, abstract, or override method. In other words, the overridden base method cannot be static or non-virtual.
- The overridden base method is not a sealed method.
- The override declaration and the overridden base method have the same declared accessibility. In other words, an override declaration cannot change the accessibility of the virtual method.

An override declaration can access the overridden base method using a *base-access* (section 7.5.8). In the example

```
class A
{
   int x;
   public virtual void PrintFields() {
      Console.WriteLine("x = {0}", x);
   }
}
class B: A
{
   int y;
   public override void PrintFields() {
      base.PrintFields();
      Console.WriteLine("y = {0}", y);
   }
}
```

the `base.PrintFields()` invocation in B invokes the `PrintFields` method declared in A. A *base-access* disables the virtual invocation mechanism and simply treats the base method as a non-virtual method. Had the invocation in B been written `((A)this).PrintFields()`, it would recursively invoke the `PrintFields` method declared in B, not the one declared in A.

Only by including an `override` modifier can a method override another method. In all other cases, a method with the same signature as an inherited method simply hides the inherited method. In the example

```
class A
{
   public virtual void F() {}
}
class B: A
{
   public virtual void F() {}   // Warning, hiding inherited F()
}
```

the F method in B does not include an `override` modifier and therefore does not override the F method in A. Rather, the F method in B hides the method in A, and a warning is reported because the declaration does not include a `new` modifier.

In the example

```
class A
{
   public virtual void F() {}
}
class B: A
{
   new private void F() {}        // Hides A.F within B
}
class C: B
{
   public override void F() {}  // Ok, overrides A.F
}
```

the F method in B hides the virtual F method inherited from A. Since the new F in B has private access, its scope only includes the class body of B and does not extend to C. The declaration of F in C is therefore permitted to override the F inherited from A.

10.5.5 Sealed methods

When an instance method declaration includes a sealed modifier, the method is said to be a **sealed method**. A sealed method overrides an inherited virtual method with the same signature. Whereas a virtual method declaration introduces a new method, an override method declaration specializes an existing inherited virtual method by providing a new implementation of the method.

An override method can also be marked with the sealed modifier. Use of this modifier prevents a derived class from further overriding the method. The sealed modifier can only be used in combination with the override modifier.

The example

```
class A
{
   public virtual void F() {
      Console.WriteLine("A.F");
   }
   public virtual void G() {
      Console.WriteLine("A.G");
   }
}
class B: A
{
   sealed override public void F() {
      Console.WriteLine("B.F");
   }
```

(continued)

(continued)

```
    override public void G() {
        Console.WriteLine("B.G");
    }
}
class C: B
{
    override public void G() {
        Console.WriteLine("C.G");
    }
}
```

the class B provides two override methods: an F method that has the `sealed` modifier and a G method that does not. B's use of the sealed `modifier` prevents C from further overriding F.

10.5.6 Abstract methods

When an instance method declaration includes an `abstract` modifier, the method is said to be an ***abstract method***. An abstract method is implicitly also a virtual method.

An abstract method declaration introduces a new virtual method but does not provide an implementation of the method. Instead, non-abstract derived classes are required to provide their own implementation by overriding the method. Because an abstract method provides no actual implementation, the *method-body* of an abstract method simply consists of a semicolon.

Abstract method declarations are only permitted in abstract classes (section 10.1.1.1).

It is an error for an abstract method declaration to include either the `static` or `virtual` modifiers.

In the example

```
public abstract class Shape
{
    public abstract void Paint(Graphics g, Rectangle r);
}
public class Ellipse: Shape
{
    public override void Paint(Graphics g, Rectangle r) {
        g.drawEllipse(r);
    }
}
```

```
public class Box: Shape
{
   public override void Paint(Graphics g, Rectangle r) {
      g.drawRect(r);
   }
}
```

the Shape class defines the abstract notion of a geometrical shape object that can paint itself. The Paint method is abstract because there is no meaningful default implementation. The Ellipse and Box classes are concrete Shape implementations. Because theses classes are non-abstract, they are required to override the Paint method and provide an actual implementation.

It is an error for a *base-access* (section 7.5.8) to reference an abstract method. In the example

```
class A
{
   public abstract void F();
}
class B: A
{
   public override void F() {
      base.F();                 // Error, base.F is abstract
   }
}
```

an error is reported for the base.F() invocation because it references an abstract method.

An abstract method declaration is permitted to override a virtual method. This allows an abstract class to force re-implementation of the method in derived classes, and makes the original implementation of the method unavailable. In the example

```
class A
{
   public virtual void F() {
      Console.WriteLine("A.F");
   }
}
abstract class B: A
{
   public abstract override void F();
}
```

(continued)

(continued)

```
class C: B
{
   public override void F() {
      Console.WriteLine("C.F");
   }
}
```

the class A declares a virtual method, the class B override this method with an abstract method, and the class C overrides to provide its own implementation.

10.5.7 External methods

When a method declaration includes an `extern` modifier, the method is said to be an ***external method***. External methods are implemented externally, using a language other than C#. Because an external method declaration provides no actual implementation, the *method-body* of an external method simply consists of a semicolon.

The `extern` modifier is typically used in conjunction with a `DllImport` attribute (section B.8), allowing external methods to be implemented by DLLs (Dynamic Link Libraries). The execution environment may support other mechanisms whereby implementations of external methods can be provided.

It is an error for an external method declaration to also include the `abstract` modifier. When an external method includes a `DllImport` attribute, the method declaration must also include a `static` modifier.

This example demonstrates use of the `extern` modifier and the `DllImport` attribute:

```
class Path
{
   [DllImport("kernel32", setLastError=true)]
   static extern bool CreateDirectory(string name, SecurityAttributes sa);
   [DllImport("kernel32", setLastError=true)]
   static extern bool RemoveDirectory(string name);
   [DllImport("kernel32", setLastError=true)]
   static extern int GetCurrentDirectory(int bufSize, StringBuilder buf);
   [DllImport("kernel32", setLastError=true)]
   static extern bool SetCurrentDirectory(string name);
}
```

10.5.8 Method body

The *method-body* of a method declaration consists either of a *block* or a semicolon.

Abstract and external method declarations do not provide a method implementation, and the method body of an abstract or external method simply consists of a semicolon. For all other methods, the method body is a block (section 8.2) that contains the statements to execute when the method is invoked.

When the return type of a method is `void`, `return` statements (section 8.9.4) in the method body are not permitted to specify an expression. If execution of the method body of a void method completes normally (that is, if control flows off the end of the method body), the method simply returns to the caller.

When the return type of a method is not `void`, each `return` statement in the method body must specify an expression of a type that is implicitly convertible to the return type. Execution of the method body of a value-returning method is required to terminate in a `return` statement that specifies an expression, or in a `throw` statement that throws an exception. It is an error if execution of the method body can complete normally. In other words, in a value-returning method, control is not permitted to flow off the end of the method body.

In the example

```
class A
{
   public int F() {}        // Error, return value required
   public int G() {
      return 1;
   }
   public int H(bool b) {
      if (b) {
         return 1;
      }
      else {
         return 0;
      }
   }
}
```

the value-returning F method is in error because control can flow off the end of the method body. The G and H methods are correct because all possible execution paths end in a return statement that specifies a return value.

10.5.9 Method overloading

The method overload resolution rules are described in section 7.4.2.

10.6 Properties

A ***property*** is a member that provides access to an attribute of an object or a class. Examples of properties include the length of a string, the size of a font, the caption of a window, the name of a customer, and so on. Properties are a natural extension of fields—both are named members with associated types, and the syntax for accessing fields and properties is the same. However, unlike fields, properties do not denote storage locations. Instead, properties have ***accessors*** that specify the statements to execute in order to read or write their values. Properties thus provide a mechanism for associating actions with the reading and writing of an object's attributes, and they furthermore permit such attributes to be computed.

Properties are declared using *property-declaration*s:

property-declaration:
    attributes$_{opt}$ property-modifiers$_{opt}$ type member-name { accessor-declarations }
property-modifiers:
    property-modifier
    property-modifiers property-modifier
property-modifier:
    `new`
    `public`
    `protected`
    `internal`
    `private`
    `static`
    `virtual`
    `sealed`
    `override`
    `abstract`
member-name:
    identifier
    interface-type . identifier

A *property-declaration* may include a set of *attributes* (section 17), a `new` modifier (section 10.2.2), a valid combination of the four access modifiers (section 10.2.3), and a valid combination of the `static` (section 10.5.2), `virtual` (section 10.5.3), `override` (section 10.5.4), and `abstract` (section 10.5.6) modifiers. In addition, a property that includes the `override` modifier may also include the `sealed` modifier (section 10.5.5).

The `static`, `virtual`, `override`, and `abstract` modifiers are mutually exclusive except in one case. The `abstract` and `override` modifiers may be used together so that an abstract property can override a virtual one.

The *type* of a property declaration specifies the type of the property introduced by the declaration, and the *member-name* specifies the name of the property. Unless the property is an explicit interface member implementation, the *member-name* is simply an *Identifier*. For an explicit interface member implementation (section 13.4.1) , the *member-name* consists of an *interface-type* followed by a "." and an *identifier*.

The *type* of a property must be at least as accessible as the property itself (section 3.5.4).

The *accessor-declarations*, which must be enclosed in "{" and "}" tokens, declare the accessors (section 10.6.2) of the property. The accessors specify the executable statements associated with reading and writing the property.

Even though the syntax for accessing a property is the same as that for a field, a property is not classified as a variable. Thus, it is not possible to pass a property as a `ref` or `out` parameter.

10.6.1 Static properties

When a property declaration includes a `static` modifier, the property is said to be a **static property**. When no `static` modifier is present, the property is said to be an **instance property**.

A static property is not associated with a specific instance, and it is an error to refer to `this` in the accessors of a static property. It is furthermore an error to include a `virtual`, `abstract`, or `override` modifier on a static property.

An instance property is associated with a given instance of a class, and this instance can be accessed as `this` (section 7.5.7) in the accessors of the property.

When a property is referenced in a *member-access* (section 7.5.4) of the form `E.M`, if `M` is a static property, `E` must denote a type, and if `M` is an instance property, E must denote an instance.

The differences between static and instance members are further discussed in section 10.2.5.

10.6.2 Accessors

The *accessor-declarations* of a property specify the executable statements associated with reading and writing the property.

accessor-declarations:
    get-accessor-declaration   set-accessor-declaration$_{opt}$
    set-accessor-declaration   get-accessor-declaration$_{opt}$

get-accessor-declaration:
    attributes$_{opt}$ get *accessor-body*

set-accessor-declaration:
  *attributes*_{opt} set *accessor-body*

accessor-body:
  block

  ;

The accessor declarations consist of a *get-accessor-declaration*, a *set-accessor-declaration*, or both. Each accessor declaration consists of the token get or set followed by an *accessor-body*. For abstract properties, the *accessor-body* for each accessor specified is simply a semicolon. For all other accessors, the *accessor-body* is a *block* which specifies the statements to execute when the accessor is invoked.

A get accessor corresponds to a parameterless method with a return value of the property type. Except as the target of an assignment, when a property is referenced in an expression, the get accessor of the property is invoked to compute the value of the property (section 7.1.1). The body of a get accessor must conform to the rules for value-returning methods described in section 10.5.8. In particular, all return statements in the body of a get accessor must specify an expression that is implicitly convertible to the property type. Furthermore, a get accessor is required to terminate in a return statement or a throw statement, and control is not permitted to flow off the end of the get accessor's body.

A set accessor corresponds to a method with a single value parameter of the property type and a void return type. The implicit parameter of a set accessor is always named value. When a property is referenced as the target of an assignment, the set accessor is invoked with an argument that provides the new value (section 7.13.1). The body of a set accessor must conform to the rules for void methods described in section 10.5.8. In particular, return statements in the set accessor body are not permitted to specify an expression. Since a set accessor implicitly has a parameter named value, it is an error for a local variable declaration in a set accessor to use that name.

Based on the presence or absence of the get and set accessors, a property is classified as follows:

- A property that includes both a get accessor and a set accessor is said to be a **read-write** property.

- A property that has only a get accessor is said to be a **read-only** property. It is an error for a read-only property to be the target of an assignment.

- A property that has only a set accessor is said to be a **write-only** property. Except as the target of an assignment, it is an error to reference a write-only property in an expression.

In the example

```
public class Button: Control
{
    private string caption;
    public string Caption {
        get {
            return caption;
        }
        set {
            if (caption != value) {
                caption = value;
                Repaint();
            }
        }
    }
    public override void Paint(Graphics g, Rectangle r) {
        // Painting code goes here
    }
}
```

the Button control declares a public Caption property. The get accessor of the Caption property returns the string stored in the private caption field. The set accessor checks if the new value is different from the current value, and if so, it stores the new value and repaints the control. Properties often follow the pattern shown above: The get accessor simply returns a value stored in a private field, and the set accessor modifies the private field and then performs any additional actions required to fully update the state of the object.

Given the Button class above, the following is an example of use of the Caption property:

```
Button okButton = new Button();
okButton.Caption = "OK";      // Invokes set accessor
string s = okButton.Caption;  // Invokes get accessor
```

Here, the set accessor is invoked by assigning a value to the property, and the get accessor is invoked by referencing the property in an expression.

The get and set accessors of a property are not distinct members, and it is not possible to declare the accessors of a property separately.

The example

```
class A
{
    private string name;
    public string Name {          // Error, duplicate member name
        get { return name; }
    }
    public string Name {          // Error, duplicate member name
        set { name = value; }
    }
}
```

does not declare a single read-write property. Rather, it declares two properties with the same name, one read-only and one write-only. Since two members declared in the same class cannot have the same name, the example causes a compile-time error to occur.

When a derived class declares a property by the same name as an inherited property, the derived property hides the inherited property with respect to both reading and writing. In the example

```
class A
{
    public int P {
        set {…}
    }
}
class B: A
{
    new public int P {
        get {…}
    }
}
```

the P property in B hides the P property in A with respect to both reading and writing. Thus, in the statements

```
B b = new B();
b.P = 1;        // Error, B.P is read-only
((A)b).P = 1;   // Ok, reference to A.P
```

the assignment to b.P causes an error to be reported, since the read-only P property in B hides the write-only P property in A. Note, however, that a cast can be used to access the hidden P property.

Unlike public fields, properties provide a separation between an object's internal state and its public interface. Consider the example:

```
class Label
{
   private int x, y;
   private string caption;
   public Label(int x, int y, string caption) {
      this.x = x;
      this.y = y;
      this.caption = caption;
   }
   public int X {
      get { return x; }
   }
   public int Y {
      get { return y; }
   }
   public Point Location {
      get { return new Point(x, y); }
   }
   public string Caption {
      get { return caption; }
   }
}
```

Here, the `Label` class uses two `int` fields, `x` and `y`, to store its location. The location is publicly exposed both as an `X` and a `Y` property and as a `Location` property of type `Point`. If, in a future version of `Label`, it becomes more convenient to store the location as a `Point` internally, the change can be made without affecting the public interface of the class:

```
class Label
{
   private Point location;
   private string caption;
   public Label(int x, int y, string caption) {
      this.location = new Point(x, y);
      this.caption = caption;
   }
   public int X {
      get { return location.x; }
   }
```

(continued)

(continued)

```
public int Y {
    get { return location.y; }
}
public Point Location {
    get { return location; }
}
public string Caption {
    get { return caption; }
}
}
```

Had x and y instead been `public readonly` fields, it would have been impossible to make such a change to the `Label` class.

Exposing state through properties is not necessarily any less efficient than exposing fields directly. In particular, when a property is non-virtual and contains only a small amount of code, the execution environment may replace calls to accessors with the actual code of the accessors. This process is known as **inlining**, and it makes property access as efficient as field access, yet preserves the increased flexibility of properties.

Since invoking a `get` accessor is conceptually equivalent to reading the value of a field, it is considered bad programming style for `get` accessors to have observable side-effects. In the example

```
class Counter
{
    private int next;
    public int Next {
        get { return next++; }
    }
}
```

the value of the `Next` property depends on the number of times the property has previously been accessed. Thus, accessing the property produces an observable side-effect, and the property should instead be implemented as a method.

The "no side-effects" convention for `get` accessors doesn't mean that `get` accessors should always be written to simply return values stored in fields. Indeed, `get` accessors often compute the value of a property by accessing multiple fields or invoking methods. However, a properly designed `get` accessor performs no actions that cause observable changes in the state of the object.

Properties can be used to delay initialization of a resource until the moment it is first referenced. For example:

```csharp
using System.IO;
public class Console
{
    private static TextReader reader;
    private static TextWriter writer;
    private static TextWriter error;
    public static TextReader In {
        get {
            if (reader == null) {
                reader = new StreamReader(File.OpenStandardInput());
            }
            return reader;
        }
    }
    public static TextWriter Out {
        get {
            if (writer == null) {
                writer = new StreamWriter(File.OpenStandardOutput());
            }
            return writer;
        }
    }
    public static TextWriter Error {
        get {
            if (error == null) {
                error = new StreamWriter(File.OpenStandardError());
            }
            return error;
        }
    }
}
```

The `Console` class contains three properties, `In`, `Out`, and `Error`, that represent the standard input, output, and error devices, respectively. By exposing these members as properties, the `Console` class can delay their initialization until they are actually used. For example, upon first referencing the `Out` property, as in

```csharp
Console.Out.WriteLine("hello, world");
```

the underlying `TextWriter` for the output device is created. But if the application makes no reference to the `In` and `Error` properties, then no objects are created for those devices.

10.6.3 Virtual, sealed, override, and abstract accessors

A property declaration may include a valid combination of the `static`, `virtual`, `override`, and `abstract` modifiers. A property that includes the `override` modifier may also include the `sealed` modifier (section 10.5.5).

The `static`, `virtual`, `override`, and `abstract` modifiers are mutually exclusive except in one case. The `abstract` and `override` modifiers may be used together so that an abstract property can override a virtual one. A `virtual` property declaration specifies that the accessors of the property are virtual. The `virtual` modifier applies to both accessors of a read-write property—it is not possible for only one accessor of a read-write property to be virtual.

An `abstract` property declaration specifies that the accessors of the property are virtual, but does not provide an actual implementation of the accessors. Instead, non-abstract derived classes are required to provide their own implementation for the accessors by overriding the property. Because an accessor for an abstract property declaration provides no actual implementation, its *accessor-body* simply consists of a semicolon.

A property declaration that includes both the `abstract` and `override` modifiers specifies that the property is abstract and overrides a base property. The accessors of such a property are also abstract.

Abstract property declarations are only permitted in abstract classes (section 10.1.1.1). The accessors of an inherited virtual property can be overridden in a derived class by including a property declaration that specifies an `override` directive. This is known as an **overriding property declaration**. An overriding property declaration does not declare a new property. Instead, it simply specializes the implementations of the accessors of an existing virtual property.

An overriding property declaration must specify the exact same accessibility modifiers, type, and name as the inherited property. If the inherited property has only a single accessor (i.e. if the inherited property is read-only or write-only), the overriding property can and must include only that accessor. If the inherited property includes both accessors (i.e. if the inherited property is read-write), the overriding property can include either a single accessor or both accessors.

An overriding property declaration may include the `sealed` modifier. Use of this modifier prevents a derived class from further overriding the property. The accessors of a sealed property are also sealed. It is an error for an overriding property declaration to include a `new` modifier.

Except for differences in declaration and invocation syntax, virtual, sealed, override, and abstract accessors behave exactly like a virtual, sealed, override and abstract methods. Specifically, the rules described in section 10.5.3, section 10.5.4, section 10.5.5, and section 10.5.6 apply as if accessors were methods of a corresponding form:

A `get` accessor corresponds to a parameterless method with a return value of the property type and the same modifiers as the containing property.

A `set` accessor corresponds to a method with a single value parameter of the property type, a `void` return type, and the same modifiers as the containing property.

In the example

```
abstract class A
{
   int y;
   public virtual int X {
      get { return 0; }
   }
   public virtual int Y {
      get { return y; }
      set { y = value; }
   }
   public abstract int Z { get; set; }
}
```

X is a virtual read-only property, Y is a virtual read-write property, and Z is an abstract read-write property. Because Z is abstract, the containing class A must also be declared abstract.

A class that derives from A is show below:

```
class B: A
{
   int z;
   public override int X {
      get { return base.X + 1; }
   }
   public override int Y {
      set { base.Y = value < 0? 0: value; }
   }
   public override int Z {
      get { return z; }
      set { z = value; }
   }
}
```

Here, the declarations of X, Y, and Z are overriding property declarations. Each property declaration exactly matches the accessibility modifiers, type, and name of the corresponding inherited property. The get accessor of X and the set accessor of Y use the base keyword to access the inherited accessors. The declaration of Z overrides both abstract accessors—thus, there are no outstanding abstract function members in B, and B is permitted to be a non-abstract class.

10.7 Events

An **event** is a member that enables an object or class to provide notifications. Clients can attach executable code for events by supplying **event handlers**.

Events are declared using *event-declaration*s:

event-declaration:
    attributes~opt~ *event-modifiers~opt~* `event` *type* *variable-declarators* ;
    attributes~opt~ *event-modifiers~opt~* `event` *type* *member-name* { *event-accessor-declarations* }

event-modifiers:
    event-modifier
    event-modifiers *event-modifier*

event-modifier:
    `new`
    `public`
    `protected`
    `internal`
    `private`
    `static`
    `virtual`
    `sealed`
    `override`
    `abstract`

event-accessor-declarations:
    add-accessor-declaration *remove-accessor-declaration*
    remove-accessor-declaration *add-accessor-declaration*

add-accessor-declaration:
    attributes~opt~ `add` *block*

remove-accessor-declaration:
    attributes~opt~ `remove` *block*

An *event-declaration* may include a set of *attributes* (section 17), a `new` modifier (section 10.2.2), a valid combination of the four access modifiers (section 10.2.3), and a valid combination of the `static` (section 10.5.2), `virtual` (section 10.5.3), `override` (section 10.5.4), and `abstract` (section 10.5.6) modifiers. In addition, an event that includes the `override` modifier may also include the `sealed` modifier (section 10.5.5).

The `static`, `virtual`, `override`, and `abstract` modifiers are mutually exclusive except in one case. The `abstract` and `override` modifiers may be used together so that an abstract event can override a virtual one.

An event declaration may include *event-accessor-declaration*s, or may rely on the compiler to supply such accessors automatically.

An event declaration that omits *event-accessor-declaration*s defines one or more events—one for each of the *variable-declarator*s. The attributes and modifiers apply to all of the members declared by such an *event-declaration*.

An abstract event is declared with an *event-declaration* that omits *event-accessor-declaration*s. It is an error for an *event-declaration* to include both the `abstract` modifier and *event-accessor-declaration*s.

The *type* of an event declaration must be a *delegate-type* (section 4.2), and that *delegate-type* must be at least as accessible as the event itself (section 3.5.4).

An event can be used as the left hand operand of the += and -= operators (section 7.13.3). These operators are used to attach or remove event handlers to or from an event, and the access modifiers of the event control the contexts in which the operations are permitted.

Since += and -= are the only operations that are permitted on an event outside the type that declares the event, external code can add and remove handlers for an event, but cannot in any other way obtain or modify the underlying list of event handlers.

Within the program text of the class or struct that contains the declaration of an event, certain events can be used like fields. To be used in this way, an event must not be abstract, and must not explicitly include *event-accessor-declaration*s. Such an event can be used in any context that permits a field.

In the example

```
public delegate void EventHandler(object sender, EventArgs e);
public class Button: Control
{
    public event EventHandler Click;
    protected void OnClick(EventArgs e) {
        if (Click != null) Click(this, e);
    }
    public void Reset() {
        Click = null;
    }
}
```

`Click` is used as a field within the `Button` class. As the example demonstrates, the field can be examined, modified, and used in delegate invocation expressions. The `OnClick` method in the `Button` class "raises" the `Click` event. The notion of raising an event is precisely equivalent to invoking the delegate represented by the event—thus, there are no special language constructs for raising events. Note that the delegate invocation is preceded by a check that ensures the delegate is non-null.

Outside the declaration of the Button class, the Click member can only be used on the left hand side of the += and -= operators, as in

```
b.Click += new EventHandler(...);
```

which appends a delegate to the invocation list of the Click event, and

```
b.Click -= new EventHandler(...);
```

which removes a delegate from the invocation list of the Click event.

In an operation of the form x += y or x -= y, when x is an event and the reference takes place outside the type that contains the declaration of x, the result of the operation is void (as opposed to the value of x after the assignment). This rule prohibits external code from indirectly examining the underlying delegate of an event.

The following example shows how event handlers are attached to instances of the Button class above:

```
public class LoginDialog: Form
{
   Button OkButton;
   Button CancelButton;
   public LoginDialog() {
      OkButton = new Button(...);
      OkButton.Click += new EventHandler(OkButtonClick);
      CancelButton = new Button(...);
      CancelButton.Click += new EventHandler(CancelButtonClick);
   }
   void OkButtonClick(object sender, EventArgs e) {
      // Handle OkButton.Click event
   }
   void CancelButtonClick(object sender, EventArgs e) {
      // Handle CancelButton.Click event
   }
}
```

Here, the LoginDialog constructor creates two Button instances and attaches event handlers to the Click events.

10.7.1 Event accessors

Event declarations typically omit *event-accessor-declaration*s, as in the Button example above. In cases where the storage cost of one field per event is not acceptable, a class can include *event-accessor-declaration*s and use a private mechanism for storing the list of event handlers.

The *event-accessor-declarations* of an event specify the executable statements associated with adding and removing event handlers.

The accessor declarations consist of an *add-accessor-declaration* and a *remove-accessor-declaration*. Each accessor declaration consists of the token add or remove followed by a *block*. The *block* associated with an *add-accessor-declaration* specifies the statements to execute when an event handler is added, and the *block* associated with a *remove-accessor-declaration* specifies the statements to execute when an event handler is added.

An event accessor, whether an *add-accessor-declaration* or a *remove-accessor-declaration*, corresponds to a method with a single value parameter of the event type and a void return type. The implicit parameter of an event accessor is always named value. When an event is used in an event assignment, the appropriate event accessor is used. If the assignment operator is += then the add accessor is used, and if the assignment operator is -= then the remove accessor is used. In either case, the right hand side of the assignment operator is used as the argument to the event accessor. The block of an *add-accessor-declaration* or a *remove-accessor-declaration* must conform to the rules for void methods described in section 10.5.8. In particular, return statements in such a block are not permitted to specify an expression.

Since an event accessor implicitly has a parameter named value, it is an error for a local variable declaration in an event accessor to use that name.

In the example

```
class Control: Component
{
   // Unique keys for events
   static readonly object mouseDownEventKey = new object();
   static readonly object mouseUpEventKey = new object();
   // Return event handler associated with key
   protected Delegate GetEventHandler(object key) {...}
   // Add event handler associated with key
   protected void AddEventHandler(object key, Delegate handler) {...}
   // Remove event handler associated with key
   protected void RemoveEventHandler(object key, Delegate handler) {...}
   // MouseDown event
   public event MouseEventHandler MouseDown {
      add { AddEventHandler(mouseDownEventKey, value); }
      remove { AddEventHandler(mouseDownEventKey, value); }
   }
   // MouseUp event
   public event MouseEventHandler MouseUp {
      add { AddEventHandler(mouseUpEventKey, value); }
      remove { AddEventHandler(mouseUpEventKey, value); }
   }
}
```

the `Control` class implements an internal storage mechanism for events. The `AddEventHandler` method associates a delegate value with a key, the `GetEventHandler` method returns the delegate currently associated with a key, and the `RemoveEventHandler` method removes a delegate as an event handler for the specified event. Presumably the underlying storage mechanism is designed such that there is no cost for associating a `null` delegate value with a key, and thus unhandled events consume no storage.

10.7.2 Static events

When an event declaration includes a `static` modifier, the event is said to be a **static event**. When no `static` modifier is present, the event is said to be an **instance event**.

A static event is not associated with a specific instance, and it is an error to refer to `this` in the accessors of a static event. It is furthermore an error to include a `virtual`, `abstract`, or `override` modifier on a static event.

An instance event is associated with a given instance of a class, and this instance can be accessed as `this` (section 7.5.7) in the accessors of the event.

When an event is referenced in a *member-access* (section 7.5.4) of the form E.M, if M is a static event, E must denote a type, and if M is an instance event, E must denote an instance.

The differences between static and instance members are further discussed in section 10.2.5.

10.7.3 Virtual, sealed, override, and abstract accessors

An event declaration may include a valid combination of the `static`, `sealed`, `virtual`, `override`, and `abstract` modifiers. An event that includes the `override` modifier may also include the `sealed` modifier (section 10.5.5).

The `static`, `virtual`, `override`, and `abstract` modifiers are mutually exclusive except in one case. The `abstract` and `override` modifiers may be used together so that an abstract event can override a virtual one.

A `virtual` event declaration specifies that the accessors of the event are virtual. The `virtual` modifier applies to both accessors of an event.

An `abstract` event declaration specifies that the accessors of the event are virtual, but does not provide an actual implementation of the accessors. Instead, non-abstract derived classes are required to provide their own implementation for the accessors by overriding the event. Because an accessor for an abstract event declaration provides no actual implementation, its *accessor-body* simply consists of a semicolon.

An event declaration that includes both the `abstract` and `override` modifiers specifies that the event is abstract and overrides a base property. The accessors of such an event are also abstract.

Abstract event declarations are only permitted in abstract classes (section 10.1.1.1).

The accessors of an inherited virtual event can be overridden in a derived class by including an event declaration that specifies an `override` directive. This is known as an ***overriding event declaration***. An overriding event declaration does not declare a new event. Instead, it simply specializes the implementations of the accessors of an existing virtual event.

An overriding event declaration must specify the exact same accessibility modifiers, type, and name as the inherited event.

An overriding event declaration may include the `sealed` modifier. Use of this modifier prevents a derived class from further overriding the event. The accessors of a sealed event are also sealed.

It is an error for an overriding event declaration to include a `new` modifier.

Except for differences in declaration and invocation syntax, virtual, override, and abstract accessors behave exactly like a virtual, sealed, override and abstract methods. Specifically, the rules described in section 10.5.3, section 10.5.4, section 10.5.5, and section 10.5.6 apply as if accessors were methods of a corresponding form. Each accessor corresponds to a method with a single value parameter of the event type, a `void` return type, and the same modifiers as the containing event.

10.8 Indexers

An ***indexer*** is a member that enables an object to be indexed in the same way as an array. Indexers are declared using *indexer-declaration*s:

indexer-declaration:
    attributes$_{opt}$ *indexer-modifiers*$_{opt}$ *indexer-declarator* { *accessor-declarations* }

indexer-modifiers:
    indexer-modifier
    indexer-modifiers indexer-modifier

indexer-modifier:
    `new`
    `public`
    `protected`
    `internal`
    `private`
    `virtual`
    `sealed`
    `override`
    `abstract`

indexer-declarator:
    type `this` [*formal-parameter-list*]
    type *interface-type* . `this` [*formal-parameter-list*]

An *indexer-declaration* may include a set of *attributes* (section 17), a `new` modifier (section 10.2.2), a valid combination of the four access modifiers (section 10.2.3), and a valid combination of the `virtual` (section 10.5.3), `override` (section 10.5.4), and `abstract` (section 10.5.6) modifiers. In addition, an indexer that includes the `override` modifier may also include the `sealed` modifier (section 10.5.5).

The `static`, `virtual`, `override`, and `abstract` modifiers are mutually exclusive except in one case. The `abstract` and `override` modifiers may be used together so that an abstract indexer can override a virtual one.

The *type* of an indexer declaration specifies the element type of the indexer introduced by the declaration. Unless the indexer is an explicit interface member implementation, the *type* is followed by the keyword `this`. For an explicit interface member implementation, the *type* is followed by an *interface-type*, a ".", and the keyword `this`. Unlike other members, indexers do not have user-defined names.

The *formal-parameter-list* specifies the parameters of the indexer. The formal parameter list of an indexer corresponds to that of a method (section 10.5.1), except that at least one parameter must be specified, and that the `ref` and `out` parameter modifiers are not permitted.

The *type* of an indexer and each of the types referenced in the *formal-parameter-list* must be at least as accessible as the indexer itself (section 3.5.4).

The *accessor-declarations*, which must be enclosed in "{" and "}" tokens, declare the accessors of the indexer. The accessors specify the executable statements associated with reading and writing indexer elements.

Even though the syntax for accessing an indexer element is the same as that for an array element, an indexer element is not classified as a variable. Thus, it is not possible to pass an indexer element as a `ref` or `out` parameter.

The formal parameter list of an indexer defines the signature (section 3.6) of the indexer. Specifically, the signature of an indexer consists of the number and types of its formal parameters. The element type is not part of an indexer's signature, nor are the names of the formal parameters.

The signature of an indexer must differ from the signatures of all other indexers declared in the same class.

Indexers and properties are very similar in concept, but differ in the following ways:

- A property is identified by its name, whereas an indexer is identified by its signature.
- A property is accessed through a *simple-name* (section 7.5.2) or a *member-access* (section 7.5.4), whereas an indexer element is accessed through an *element-access* (section 7.5.6.2).
- A property can be a `static` member, whereas an indexer is always an instance member.

- A `get` accessor of a property corresponds to a method with no parameters, whereas a `get` accessor of an indexer corresponds to a method with the same formal parameter list as the indexer.

- A `set` accessor of a property corresponds to a method with a single parameter named `value`, whereas a `set` accessor of an indexer corresponds to a method with the same formal parameter list as the indexer, plus an additional parameter named `value`.

- It is an error for an indexer accessor to declare a local variable with the same name as an indexer parameter.

- In an overriding property declaration, the inherited property is accessed using the syntax `base.P`, where `P` is the property name. In an overriding indexer declaration, the inherited indexer is accessed using the syntax `base[E]`, where `E` is a comma separated list of expressions.

With these differences in mind, all rules defined in section 10.6.2 and section 10.6.3 apply to indexer accessors as well as property accessors.

The example below declares a `BitArray` class that implements an indexer for accessing the individual bits in the bit array.

```
class BitArray
{
    int[] bits;
    int length;
    public BitArray(int length) {
        if (length < 0) throw new ArgumentException();
        bits = new int[((length - 1) >> 5) + 1];
        this.length = length;
    }
    public int Length {
        get { return length; }
    }
    public bool this[int index] {
        get {
            if (index < 0 || index >= length) {
                throw new IndexOutOfRangeException();
            }
            return (bits[index >> 5] & 1 << index) != 0;
        }
        set {
            if (index < 0 || index >= length) {
                throw new IndexOutOfRangeException();
            }
```

(continued)

(continued)

```
        if (value) {
            bits[index >> 5] |= 1 << index;
        }
        else {
            bits[index >> 5] &= ~(1 << index);
        }
    }
    }
}
```

An instance of the BitArray class consumes substantially less memory than a corresponding bool[] (each value occupies only one bit instead of one byte), but it permits the same operations as a bool[].

The following CountPrimes class uses a BitArray and the classical "sieve" algorithm to compute the number of primes between 1 and a given maximum:

```
class CountPrimes
{
    static int Count(int max) {
        BitArray flags = new BitArray(max + 1);
        int count = 1;
        for (int i = 2; i <= max; i++) {
            if (!flags[i]) {
                for (int j = i * 2; j <= max; j += i) flags[j] = true;
                count++;
            }
        }
        return count;
    }
    static void Main(string[] args) {
        int max = int.Parse(args[0]);
        int count = Count(max);
        Console.WriteLine("Found {0} primes between 1 and {1}", count, max);
    }
}
```

Note that the syntax for accessing elements of the BitArray is precisely the same as for a bool[].

10.8.1 Indexer overloading

The indexer overload resolution rules are described in section 7.4.2.

10.9 Operators

An ***operator*** is a member that defines the meaning of an expression operator that can be applied to instances of the class. Operators are declared using *operator-declarations*:

operator-declaration:
    attributes$_{opt}$ operator-modifiers operator-declarator block

operator-modifiers:
    `public static`
    `static public`

operator-declarator:
    unary-operator-declarator
    binary-operator-declarator
    conversion-operator-declarator

unary-operator-declarator:
    type `operator` *overloadable-unary-operator* `(` *type identifier* `)`

overloadable-unary-operator: one of
    `+ - ! ~ ++ -- true false`

binary-operator-declarator:
    type `operator` *overloadable-binary-operator* `(` *type identifier* `,` *type identifier* `)`

overloadable-binary-operator: one of
    `+ - * / % & | ^ << >> == != > < >= <=`

conversion-operator-declarator:
    `implicit operator` *type* `(` *type identifier* `)`
    `explicit operator` *type* `(` *type identifier* `)`

There are three categories of operators: Unary operators (section 10.9.1), binary operators (section 10.9.2), and conversion operators (section 10.9.3).

The following rules apply to all operator declarations:

- An operator declaration must include both a `public` and a `static` modifier, and is not permitted to include any other modifiers.
- The parameter(s) of an operator must be value parameters. It is an error to for an operator declaration to specify `ref` or `out` parameters.
- The signature of an operator must differ from the signatures of all other operators declared in the same class.
- All types referenced in an operator declaration must be at least as accessible as the operator itself (section 3.5.4).

Each operator category imposes additional restrictions, as described in the following sections.

Like other members, operators declared in a base class are inherited by derived classes. Because operator declarations always require the class or struct in which the operator is declared to participate in the signature of the operator, it is not possible for an operator declared in a derived class to hide an operator declared in a base class. Thus, the `new` modifier is never required, and therefore never permitted, in an operator declaration.

For all operators, the operator declaration includes a *block* which specifies the statements to execute when the operator is invoked. The *block* of an operator must conform to the rules for value-returning methods described in section 10.5.8.

Additional information on unary and binary operators can be found in section 7.2.

Additional information on conversion operators can be found in section 6.4.

10.9.1 Unary operators

The following rules apply to unary operator declarations, where T denotes the class or struct type that contains the operator declaration:

- A unary +, -, !, or ~ operator must take a single parameter of type T and can return any type.
- A unary ++ or -- operator must take a single parameter of type T and must return type T.
- A unary `true` or `false` operator must take a single parameter of type T and must return type `bool`.

The signature of a unary operator consists of the operator token (+, -, !, ~, ++, --, `true`, or `false`) and the type of the single formal parameter. The return type is not part of a unary operator's signature, nor is the name of the formal parameter.

The `true` and `false` unary operators require pair-wise declaration. An error occurs if a class declares one of these operators without also declaring the other. The `true` and `false` operators are further described in section 7.16.

10.9.2 Binary operators

A binary operator must take two parameters, at least one of which must be of the class or struct type in which the operator is declared. A binary operator can return any type.

The signature of a binary operator consists of the operator token (+, -, *, /, %, &, |, ^, <<, >>, ==, !=, >, <, >=, or <=) and the types of the two formal parameters. The return type is not part of a binary operator's signature, nor are the names of the formal parameters.

Certain binary operators require pair-wise declaration. For every declaration of either operator of a pair, there must be a matching declaration of the other operator of the pair. Two operator declarations match when they have the same return type and the same type for each parameter. The following operators require pair-wise declaration:

- `operator ==` and `operator !=`
- `operator >` and `operator <`
- `operator >=` and `operator <=`

10.9.3 Conversion operators

A conversion operator declaration introduces a ***user-defined conversion*** (section 6.4) which augments the pre-defined implicit and explicit conversions.

A conversion operator declaration that includes the `implicit` keyword introduces a user-defined implicit conversion. Implicit conversions can occur in a variety of situations, including function member invocations, cast expressions, and assignments. This is described further in section 6.1.

A conversion operator declaration that includes the `explicit` keyword introduces a user-defined explicit conversion. Explicit conversions can occur in cast expressions, and are described further in section 6.2.

A conversion operator converts from a source type, indicated by the parameter type of the conversion operator, to a target type, indicated by the return type of the conversion operator. A class or struct is permitted to declare a conversion from a source type S to a target type T provided all of the following are true:

- S and T are different types.
- Either S or T is the class or struct type in which the operator declaration takes place.
- Neither S nor T is `object` or an *interface-type*.
- T is not a base class of S, and S is not a base class of T.

From the second rule it follows that a conversion operator must either convert to or from the class or struct type in which the operator is declared. For example, it is possible for a class or struct type C to define a conversion from C to `int` and from `int` to C, but not from `int` to `bool`.

It is not possible to redefine a pre-defined conversion. Thus, conversion operators are not allowed to convert from or to `object` because implicit and explicit conversions already exist between `object` and all other types. Likewise, neither of the source and target types of a conversion can be a base type of the other, since a conversion would then already exist.

User-defined conversions are not allowed to convert from or to *interface-type*s. This restriction in particular ensures that no user-defined transformations occur when converting to an *interface-type*, and that a conversion to an *interface-type* succeeds only if the object being converted actually implements the specified *interface-type*.

The signature of a conversion operator consists of the source type and the target type. (Note that this is the only form of member for which the return type participates in the signature.) The `implicit` or `explicit` classification of a conversion operator is not part of the operator's signature. Thus, a class or struct cannot declare both an `implicit` and an `explicit` conversion operator with the same source and target types.

In general, user-defined implicit conversions should be designed to never throw exceptions and never lose information. If a user-defined conversion can give rise to exceptions (for example because the source argument is out of range) or loss of information (such as discarding high-order bits), then that conversion should be defined as an explicit conversion.

In the example

```
public struct Digit
{
   byte value;
   public Digit(byte value) {
      if (value < 0 || value > 9) throw new ArgumentException();
      this.value = value;
   }
   public static implicit operator byte(Digit d) {
      return d.value;
   }
   public static explicit operator Digit(byte b) {
      return new Digit(b);
   }
}
```

the conversion from `Digit` to `byte` is implicit because it never throws exceptions or loses information, but the conversion from `byte` to `Digit` is explicit since `Digit` can only represent a subset of the possible values of a `byte`.

10.10 Instance constructors

An *instance constructor* is a member that implements the actions required to initialize an instance of a class. Constructors are declared using *constructor-declaration*s:

constructor-declaration:
    attributes$_{opt}$ *constructor-modifiers*$_{opt}$ *constructor-declarator* *block*

constructor-modifiers:
    constructor-modifier
    constructor-modifiers *constructor-modifier*

constructor-modifier:
   `public`
   `protected`
   `internal`
   `private`

constructor-declarator:
   identifier (*formal-parameter-list$_{opt}$*) *constructor-initializer$_{opt}$*

constructor-initializer:
   : `base` (*argument-list$_{opt}$*)
   : `this` (*argument-list$_{opt}$*)

A *constructor-declaration* may include a set of *attributes* (section 17) and a valid combination of the four access modifiers (section 10.2.3).

The *identifier* of a *constructor-declarator* must name the class in which the constructor is declared. If any other name is specified, an error occurs.

The optional *formal-parameter-list* of a constructor is subject to the same rules as the *formal-parameter-list* of a method (section 10.5). The formal parameter list defines the signature (section 3.6) of a constructor and governs the process whereby overload resolution (section 7.4.2) selects a particular constructor in an invocation.

Each of the types referenced in the *formal-parameter-list* of a constructor must be at least as accessible as the constructor itself (section 3.5.4).

The optional *constructor-initializer* specifies another constructor to invoke before executing the statements given in the *block* of this constructor. This is described further in section 10.10.1.

The *block* of a constructor declaration specifies the statements to execute in order to initialize a new instance of the class. This corresponds exactly to the *block* of an instance method with a `void` return type (section 10.5.8).

Constructors are not inherited. Thus, a class has no other constructors than those that are actually declared in the class. If a class contains no constructor declarations, a default constructor is automatically provided (section 10.10.4).

Constructors are invoked by *object-creation-expression*s (section 7.5.10.1) and through *constructor-initializer*s.

10.10.1 Constructor initializers

All constructors (except for the constructors of class `object`) implicitly include an invocation of another constructor immediately before the first statement in the *block* of the constructor. The constructor to implicitly invoke is determined by the *constructor-initializer*.

- A constructor initializer of the form `base(…)` causes a constructor from the direct base class to be invoked. The constructor is selected using the overload resolution rules of section 7.4.2. The set of candidate constructors consists of all accessible constructors declared in the direct base class. If the set of candidate constructors is empty, or if a single best constructor cannot be identified, an error occurs.

- A constructor initializer of the form `this(…)` causes a constructor from the class itself to be invoked. The constructor is selected using the overload resolution rules of section 7.4.2. The set of candidate constructors consists of all accessible constructors declared in the class itself. If the set of candidate constructors is empty, or if a single best constructor cannot be identified, an error occurs. If a constructor declaration includes a constructor initializer that invokes the constructor itself, an error occurs.

If a constructor has no constructor initializer, a constructor initializer of the form `base()` is implicitly provided. Thus, a constructor declaration of the form

```
C(…) {…}
```

is exactly equivalent to

```
C(…): base() {…}
```

The scope of the parameters given by the *formal-parameter-list* of a constructor declaration includes the constructor initializer of that declaration. Thus, a constructor initializer is permitted to access the parameters of the constructor. For example:

```
class A
{
    public A(int x, int y) {}
}
class B: A
{
    public B(int x, int y): base(x + y, x - y) {}
}
```

A constructor initializer cannot access the instance being created. It is therefore an error to reference `this` in an argument expression of the constructor initializer, as it is an error for an argument expression to reference any instance member through a *simple-name*.

10.10.2 Instance variable initializers

When a constructor has no constructor initializer or a constructor initializer of the form `base(…)`, the constructor implicitly performs the initializations specified by the *variable-initializer*s of the instance fields declared in the class. This corresponds to a sequence of assignments that are executed immediately upon entry to the constructor and before the implicit invocation of the direct base class constructor. The variable initializers are executed in the textual order they appear in the class declaration.

10.10.3 Constructor execution

It is useful to think of instance variable initializers and constructor initializers as statements that are automatically inserted before the first statement in the *block* of a constructor. The example

```
using System.Collections;
class A
{
   int x = 1, y = -1, count;
   public A() {
      count = 0;
   }
   public A(int n) {
      count = n;
   }
}
class B: A
{
   double sqrt2 = Math.Sqrt(2.0);
   ArrayList items = new ArrayList(100);
   int max;
   public B(): this(100) {
      items.Add("default");
   }
   public B(int n): base(n - 1) {
      max = n;
   }
}
```

contains several variable initializers and also contains constructor initializers of both forms (`base` and `this`). The example corresponds to the code shown below, where each comment indicates an automatically inserted statement (the syntax used for the automatically inserted constructor invocations isn't valid, but merely serves to illustrate the mechanism).

```csharp
using System.Collections;
class A
{
    int x, y, count;
    public A() {
        x = 1;                          // Variable initializer
        y = -1;                         // Variable initializer
        object();                       // Invoke object() constructor
        count = 0;
    }
    public A(int n) {
        x = 1;                          // Variable initializer
        y = -1;                         // Variable initializer
        object();                       // Invoke object() constructor
        count = n;
    }
}
class B: A
{
    double sqrt2;
    ArrayList items;
    int max;
    public B(): this(100) {
        B(100);                         // Invoke B(int) constructor
        items.Add("default");
    }
    public B(int n): base(n - 1) {
        sqrt2 = Math.Sqrt(2.0);         // Variable initializer
        items = new ArrayList(100);     // Variable initializer
        A(n - 1);                       // Invoke A(int) constructor
        max = n;
    }
}
```

Note that variable initializers are transformed into assignment statements, and that these assignment statements are executed *before* the invocation of the base class constructor. This ordering ensures that all instance fields are initialized by their variable initializers before *any* statements that have access to the instance are executed. For example:

```csharp
class A
{
    public A() {
        PrintFields();
    }
    public virtual void PrintFields() {}
}
```

```
class B: A
{
    int x = 1;
    int y;
    public B() {
        y = -1;
    }
    public override void PrintFields() {
        Console.WriteLine("x = {0}, y = {1}", x, y);
    }
}
```

When `new B()` is used to create an instance of B, the following output is produced:

```
x = 1, y = 0
```

The value of x is 1 because the variable initializer is executed before the base class constructor is invoked. However, the value of y is 0 (the default value of an `int`) because the assignment to y is not executed until after the base class constructor returns.

10.10.4 Default constructors

If a class contains no constructor declarations, a default constructor is automatically provided. The default constructor simply invokes the parameterless constructor of the direct base class. If the direct base class does not have an accessible parameterless constructor, an error occurs. If the class is abstract then the declared accessibility for the default constructor is protected. Otherwise, the declared accessibility for the default constructor is public. Thus, the default constructor is always of the form

```
protected C(): base() {}
```

or

```
public C(): base() {}
```

where C is the name of the class.

In the example

```
class Message
{
    object sender;
    string text;
}
```

a default constructor is provided because the class contains no constructor declarations.

Thus, the example is precisely equivalent to

```
class Message
{
    object sender;
    string text;
    public Message(): base() {}
}
```

10.10.5 Private constructors

When a class declares only private constructors it is not possible for other classes to derive from the class or create instances of the class (an exception being classes nested within the class). Private constructors are commonly used in classes that contain only static members. For example:

```
public class Trig
{
    private Trig() {}    // Prevent instantiation
    public const double PI = 3.14159265358979323846;
    public static double Sin(double x) {…}
    public static double Cos(double x) {…}
    public static double Tan(double x) {…}
}
```

The Trig class provides a grouping of related methods and constants, but is not intended to be instantiated. It therefore declares a single private constructor. At least one private constructor must be declared to suppress the automatic generation of a default constructor.

10.10.6 Optional constructor parameters

The this(…) form of constructor initializer is commonly used in conjunction with overloading to implement optional constructor parameters. In the example

```
class Text
{
    public Text(): this(0, 0, null) {}
    public Text(int x, int y): this(x, y, null) {}
    public Text(int x, int y, string s) {
        // Actual constructor implementation
    }
}
```

the first two constructors merely provide the default values for the missing arguments. Both use a this(…) constructor initializer to invoke the third constructor, which actually does the work of initializing the new instance. The effect is that of optional constructor parameters:

```
Text t1 = new Text();              // Same as Text(0, 0, null)
Text t2 = new Text(5, 10);         // Same as Text(5, 10, null)
Text t3 = new Text(5, 20, "Hello");
```

10.11 Static constructors

A *static constructor* is a member that implements the actions required to initialize a class. Static constructors are declared using *static-constructor-declaration*s:

static-constructor-declaration:
    attributes$_{opt}$ `static` *identifier* `(` `)` *block*

A *static-constructor-declaration* may include a set of *attributes* (section 17).

The *identifier* of a *static-constructor-declaration* must name the class in which the static constructor is declared. If any other name is specified, an error occurs.

The *block* of a static constructor declaration specifies the statements to execute in order to initialize the class. This corresponds exactly to the *block* of a static method with a `void` return type (section 10.5.8).

Static constructors are not inherited.

Class loading is the process by which a class is prepared for use in the runtime environment. The loading process is mostly implementation-dependent, though several guarantees are provided:

- A class is loaded before any instance of the class is created.
- A class is loaded before any of its static members are referenced.
- A class is loaded before any types that derive from it are loaded.
- A class cannot be loaded more than once during a single execution of a program.
- If a class has a static constructor then it is automatically called when the class is loaded. Static constructors cannot be invoked explicitly.

The example

```
class Test
{
   static void Main() {
      A.F();
      B.F();
   }
}
class A
{
   static A() {
```

(continued)

(continued)

```
      Console.WriteLine("Init A");
   }
   public static void F() {
      Console.WriteLine("A.F");
   }
}
class B
{
   static B() {
      Console.WriteLine("Init B");
   }
   public static void F() {
      Console.WriteLine("B.F");
   }
}
```

could produce either the output:

```
Init A
A.F
Init B
B.F
```

or the output:

```
Init B
Init A
A.F
B.F
```

because the exact ordering of loading and therefore of static constructor execution is not defined.

The example

```
class Test
{
   static void Main() {
      Console.WriteLine("1");
      B.G();
      Console.WriteLine("2");
   }
}
class A
{
   static A() {
      Console.WriteLine("Init A");
```

```
    }
}
class B: A
{
    static B() {
        Console.WriteLine("Init B");
    }
    public static void G() {
        Console.WriteLine("B.G");
    }
}
```

is guaranteed to produce the output:

```
Init A
Init B
B.G
```

because the static constructor for the class A must execute before the static constructor of the class B, which derives from it.

It is possible to construct circular dependencies that allow static fields with variable initializers to be observed in their default value state.

The example

```
class A
{
    public static int X = B.Y + 1;
}
class B
{
    public static int Y = A.X + 1;
    static void Main() {
        Console.WriteLine("X = {0}, Y = {1}", A.X, B.Y);
    }
}
```

produces the output

```
X = 1, Y = 2
```

To execute the Main method, the system first loads class B. The static constructor of B proceeds to compute the initial value of Y, which recursively causes A to be loaded because the value of A.X is referenced. The static constructor of A in turn proceeds to compute the initial value of X, and in doing so fetches the *default* value of Y, which is zero. A.X is thus initialized to 1. The process of loading A then completes, returning to the calculation of the initial value of Y, the result of which becomes 2.

Had the `Main` method instead been located in class A, the example would have produced the output

```
X = 2, Y = 1
```

Circular references in static field initializers should be avoided since it is generally not possible to determine the order in which classes containing such references are loaded.

10.12 Destructors

A *destructor* is a member that implements the actions required to destruct an instance of a class. Destructors are declared using *destructor-declaration*s:

destructor-declaration:
    attributes_{opt} ~ *identifier* ( ) *block*

A *destructor-declaration* may include a set of *attributes* (section 17).

The *identifier* of a *destructor-declarator* must name the class in which the destructor is declared. If any other name is specified, an error occurs.

The *block* of a destructor declaration specifies the statements to execute in order to destruct an instance of the class. This corresponds exactly to the *block* of an instance method with a `void` return type (section 10.5.8).

Destructors are not inherited. Thus, a class has no other destructors than those that are actually declared in the class.

Destructors are invoked automatically, and cannot be invoked explicitly. An instance becomes eligible for destruction when it is no longer possible for any code to use the instance. Execution of the destructor for the instance may occur at any time after the instance becomes eligible for destruction. When an instance is destructed, the destructors in an inheritance chain are called in order, from most derived to least derived.

11. Structs

Structs are similar to classes in that they represent data structures that can contain data members and function members. But unlike classes, structs are value types and do not require heap allocation. A variable of a struct type directly contains the data of the struct, whereas a variable of a class type contains a reference to the data, the latter known as an object.

Structs are particularly useful for small data structures that have value semantics. Complex numbers, points in a coordinate system, or key-value pairs in a dictionary are all good examples of structs. Key to these data structures is that they have few data members, that they do not require use of inheritance or referential identity, and that they can be conveniently implemented using value semantics where assignment copies the value instead of the reference.

As described in §4.1.3, the simple types provided by C#, such as `int`, `double`, and `bool`, are in fact all struct types. Just as these predefined types are structs, so it is possible to use structs and operator overloading to implement new "primitive" types in the C# language. Two examples of such types are given in section 11.4 at the end of this chapter.

11.1 Struct declarations

A *struct-declaration* is a *type-declaration* (section 9.5) that declares a new struct:

struct-declaration:
    attributes$_{opt}$ *struct-modifiers*$_{opt}$ `struct` *identifier* *struct-interfaces*$_{opt}$
    struct-body `;`$_{opt}$

A *struct-declaration* consists of an optional set of *attributes* (section 17), followed by an optional set of *struct-modifiers* (section 11.1.1), followed by the keyword `struct` and an *identifier* that names the struct, followed by an optional *struct-interfaces* specification (section 11.1.2), followed by a *struct-body* (section 11.1.3), optionally followed by a semicolon.

11.1.1 Struct modifiers

A *struct-declaration* may optionally include a sequence of struct modifiers:

struct-modifiers:
    struct-modifier
    struct-modifiers   struct-modifier

struct-modifier:
    `new`
    `public`
    `protected`
    `internal`
    `private`

It is an error for the same modifier to appear multiple times in a struct declaration.

The modifiers of a struct declaration have the same meaning as those of a class declaration (section 10.1.1). Note, however, that the `abstract` and `sealed` modifiers are not permitted in a struct declaration. Structs cannot be abstract, and because structs do not permit derivation, they are implicitly sealed.

11.1.2 Struct interfaces

A struct declaration may include a *struct-interfaces* specification, in which case the struct is said to implement the given interface types.

struct-interfaces:
    :   *interface-type-list*

Interface implementations are discussed further in section 13.4.

11.1.3 Struct body

The *struct-body* of a struct defines the members of the struct.

struct-body:
    {   *struct-member-declarations*_{opt}   }

11.2 Struct members

The members of a struct consist of the members introduced by its
*struct-member-declaration*s and the members inherited from the `object` type.

struct-member-declarations:
    struct-member-declaration
    struct-member-declarations   struct-member-declaration

struct-member-declaration:
    constant-declaration
    field-declaration
    method-declaration
    property-declaration
    event-declaration
    indexer-declaration
    operator-declaration
    constructor-declaration
    static-constructor-declaration
    type-declaration

Except for the differences noted in section 11.3, the descriptions of class members
provided in section 10.2 through section 10.11 apply to struct members as well.

11.3 Class and struct differences

11.3.1 Value semantics

Structs are value types (section 4.1) and are said to have value semantics. Classes, on
the other hand, are reference types (section 4.2) and are said to have reference
semantics.

A variable of a struct type directly contains the data of the struct, whereas a variable of a
class type contains a reference to the data, the latter known as an object.

With classes, it is possible for two variables to reference the same object, and thus
possible for operations on one variable to affect the object referenced by the other
variable. With structs, the variables each have their own copy of the data, and it is not
possible for operations on one to affect the other. Furthermore, because structs are not
reference types, it is not possible for values of a struct type to be `null`.

Given the declaration

```
struct Point
{
    public int x, y;
    public Point(int x, int y) {
        this.x = x;
        this.y = y;
    }
}
```

the code fragment

```
Point a = new Point(10, 10);
Point b = a;
a.x = 100;
Console.WriteLine(b.x);
```

outputs the value 10. The assignment of a to b creates a copy of the value, and b is thus unaffected by the assignment to a.x. Had Point instead been declared as a class, the output would be 100 because a and b would reference the same object.

11.3.2 Inheritance

All struct types implicitly inherit from class object. A struct declaration may specify a list of implemented interfaces, but it is not possible for a struct declaration to specify a base class.

Struct types are never abstract and are always implicitly sealed. The abstract and sealed modifiers are therefore not permitted in a struct declaration.

Since inheritance isn't supported for structs, the declared accessibility of a struct member cannot be protected or protected internal.

Function members in a struct cannot be abstract or virtual, and the override modifier is allowed only to override methods inherited from the object type.

11.3.3 Assignment

Assignment to a variable of a struct type creates a *copy* of the value being assigned. This differs from assignment to a variable of a class type, which copies the reference but not the object identified by the reference.

Similar to an assignment, when a struct is passed as a value parameter or returned as the result of a function member, a copy of the struct is created. A struct may be passed by reference to a function member using a ref or out parameter.

When a property or indexer of a struct is the target of an assignment, the instance expression associated with the property or indexer access must be classified as a variable. If the instance expression is classified as a value, a compile-time error occurs. This is described in further detail in section 7.13.1.

11.3.4 Default values

As described in section 5.2, several kinds of variables are automatically initialized to their default value when they are created. For variables of class types and other reference types, this default value is null. However, since structs are value types that cannot be null, the default value of a struct is instead the value produced by "zeroing out" the fields of the struct.

Referring to the `Point` struct declared above, the example

```
Point[] a = new Point[100];
```

initializes each `Point` in the array to the value produced by setting the x and y fields to zero.

The default value of a struct corresponds to the value returned by the default constructor of the struct (section 4.1.1). Unlike a class, a struct is not permitted to declare a parameterless constructor. Instead, every struct implicitly has a parameterless constructor, and this constructor always returns the value that results from "zeroing out" the fields of the struct.

Structs must be designed to consider the default initialization state a valid state. In the example

```
struct KeyValuePair
{
    string key;
    string value;
    public KeyValuePair(string key, string value) {
        if (key == null || value == null) throw new ArgumentException();
        this.key = key;
        this.value = value;
    }
}
```

the user-defined constructor protects against null values only where it is explicitly called. In cases where a `KeyValuePair` variable is subject to default value initialization, the `key` and `value` fields will be null, and the struct must be prepared to handle this state.

11.3.5 Boxing and unboxing

A value of a class type can be converted to type `object` or to an interface type that is implemented by the class simply by treating the reference as another type at compile-time. Likewise, a value of type `object` or a value of an interface type can be converted back to a class type without changing the reference (but of course a run-time type check is required in this case).

Since structs are not reference types, these operations are implemented differently for struct types. When a value of a struct type is converted to type `object` or to an interface type that is implemented by the struct, a boxing operation takes place. Likewise, when a value of type `object` or a value of an interface type is converted back to a struct type, an unboxing operation takes place. A key difference from the same operations on class types is that boxing and unboxing *copies* the struct value either into or out of the boxed instance. Thus, following a boxing or unboxing operation, changes made to the unboxed struct are not reflected in the boxed struct.

For further details on boxing and unboxing, see section 4.3.

11.3.6 Meaning of this

Within a constructor or instance function member of a class, `this` is classified as a value. Thus, while `this` can be used to refer to the instance for which the function member was invoked, it is not possible to assign to `this` in a function member of a class.

Within a constructor of a struct, `this` corresponds to an `out` parameter of the struct type, and within an instance function member of a struct, `this` corresponds to a `ref` parameter of the struct type. In both cases, `this` is classified as a variable, and it is possible to modify the entire struct for which the function member was invoked by assigning to `this` or by passing this as a `ref` or `out` parameter.

11.3.7 Field initializers

As described in section 11.3.4, the default value of a struct consists of the value that results from "zeroing out" the fields of the struct. For this reason, a struct does not permit instance field declarations to include variable initializers, and the following example is invalid:

```
struct Point
{
    public int x = 1;  // Error, initializer not permitted
    public int y = 1;  // Error, initializer not permitted
}
```

This restriction applies only to instance fields. Static fields of a struct are permitted to include variable initializers.

11.3.8 Constructors

Unlike a class, a struct is not permitted to declare a parameterless constructor. Instead, every struct implicitly has a parameterless constructor, and this constructor always returns the value that results from "zeroing out" the fields of the struct (section 4.1.1).

A struct constructor is not permitted to include a constructor initializer of the form base(...).

The `this` variable of a struct constructor corresponds to an `out` parameter of the struct type, and similar to an `out` parameter, `this` must be definitely assigned (section 5.3) at every location where the constructor returns.

11.3.9 Destructors

A struct is not permitted to declare a destructor.

11.4 Struct examples

11.4.1 Database integer type

The `DBInt` struct below implements an integer type that can represent the complete set of values of the `int` type, plus an additional state that indicates an unknown value. A type with these characteristics is commonly used in databases.

```
public struct DBInt
{
    // The Null member represents an unknown DBInt value.
    public static readonly DBInt Null = new DBInt();
    // When the defined field is true, this DBInt represents a known value
    // which is stored in the value field. When the defined field is false,
    // this DBInt represents an unknown value, and the value field is 0.
    int value;
    bool defined;
    // Private constructor. Creates a DBInt with a known value.
    DBInt(int value) {
        this.value = value;
        this.defined = true;
    }
    // The IsNull property is true if this DBInt represents an unknown value.
    public bool IsNull { get { return !defined; } }
    // The Value property is the known value of this DBInt, or 0 if this
    // DBInt represents an unknown value.
    public int Value { get { return value; } }
```

(continued)

(continued)

```
// Implicit conversion from int to DBInt.
public static implicit operator DBInt(int x) {
    return new DBInt(x);
}
// Explicit conversion from DBInt to int. Throws an exception if the
// given DBInt represents an unknown value.
public static explicit operator int(DBInt x) {
    if (!x.defined) throw new InvalidOperationException();
    return x.value;
}
public static DBInt operator +(DBInt x) {
    return x;
}
public static DBInt operator -(DBInt x) {
    return x.defined? -x.value: Null;
}
public static DBInt operator +(DBInt x, DBInt y) {
    return x.defined && y.defined? x.value + y.value: Null;
}
public static DBInt operator -(DBInt x, DBInt y) {
    return x.defined && y.defined? x.value - y.value: Null;
}
public static DBInt operator *(DBInt x, DBInt y) {
    return x.defined && y.defined? x.value * y.value: Null;
}
public static DBInt operator /(DBInt x, DBInt y) {
    return x.defined && y.defined? x.value / y.value: Null;
}
public static DBInt operator %(DBInt x, DBInt y) {
    return x.defined && y.defined? x.value % y.value: Null;
}
public static DBBool operator ==(DBInt x, DBInt y) {
    return x.defined && y.defined? x.value == y.value: DBBool.Null;
}
public static DBBool operator !=(DBInt x, DBInt y) {
    return x.defined && y.defined? x.value != y.value: DBBool.Null;
}
public static DBBool operator >(DBInt x, DBInt y) {
    return x.defined && y.defined? x.value > y.value: DBBool.Null;
}
public static DBBool operator <(DBInt x, DBInt y) {
    return x.defined && y.defined? x.value < y.value: DBBool.Null;
}
```

```
    public static DBBool operator >=(DBInt x, DBInt y) {
        return x.defined && y.defined? x.value >= y.value: DBBool.Null;
    }
    public static DBBool operator <=(DBInt x, DBInt y) {
        return x.defined && y.defined? x.value <= y.value: DBBool.Null;
    }
}
```

11.4.2 Database boolean type

The DBBool struct below implements a three-valued logical type. The possible values of this type are DBBool.True, DBBool.False, and DBBool.Null, where the Null member indicates an unknown value. Such three-valued logical types are commonly used in databases.

```
public struct DBBool
{
    // The three possible DBBool values.
    public static readonly DBBool Null = new DBBool(0);
    public static readonly DBBool False = new DBBool(-1);
    public static readonly DBBool True = new DBBool(1);
    // Private field that stores -1, 0, 1 for False, Null, True.
    sbyte value;
    // Private constructor. The value parameter must be -1, 0, or 1.
    DBBool(int value) {
        this.value = (sbyte)value;
    }
    // Properties to examine the value of a DBBool. Return true if this
    // DBBool has the given value, false otherwise.
    public bool IsNull { get { return value == 0; } }
    public bool IsFalse { get { return value < 0; } }
    public bool IsTrue { get { return value > 0; } }
    // Implicit conversion from bool to DBBool. Maps true to DBBool.True and
    // false to DBBool.False.
    public static implicit operator DBBool(bool x) {
        return x? True: False;
    }
    // Explicit conversion from DBBool to bool. Throws an exception if the
    // given DBBool is Null, otherwise returns true or false.
    public static explicit operator bool(DBBool x) {
        if (x.value == 0) throw new InvalidOperationException();
        return x.value > 0;
    }
```

(continued)

(continued)

```csharp
// Equality operator. Returns Null if either operand is Null, otherwise
// returns True or False.
public static DBBool operator ==(DBBool x, DBBool y) {
    if (x.value == 0 || y.value == 0) return Null;
    return x.value == y.value? True: False;
}
// Inequality operator. Returns Null if either operand is Null, otherwise
// returns True or False.
public static DBBool operator !=(DBBool x, DBBool y) {
    if (x.value == 0 || y.value == 0) return Null;
    return x.value != y.value? True: False;
}
// Logical negation operator. Returns True if the operand is False, Null
// if the operand is Null, or False if the operand is True.
public static DBBool operator !(DBBool x) {
    return new DBBool(-x.value);
}
// Logical AND operator. Returns False if either operand is False,
// otherwise Null if either operand is Null, otherwise True.
public static DBBool operator &(DBBool x, DBBool y) {
    return new DBBool(x.value < y.value? x.value: y.value);
}
// Logical OR operator. Returns True if either operand is True, otherwise
// Null if either operand is Null, otherwise False.
public static DBBool operator |(DBBool x, DBBool y) {
    return new DBBool(x.value > y.value? x.value: y.value);
}
// Definitely true operator. Returns true if the operand is True, false
// otherwise.
public static bool operator true(DBBool x) {
    return x.value > 0;
}
// Definitely false operator. Returns true if the operand is False, false
// otherwise.
public static bool operator false(DBBool x) {
    return x.value < 0;
}
}
```

12. Arrays

An array is a data structure that contains a number of variables which are accessed through computed indices. The variables contained in an array, also called the elements of the array, are all of the same type, and this type is called the element type of the array.

An array has a rank which determines the number of indices associated with each array element. The rank of an array is also referred to as the dimensions of the array. An array with a rank of one is called a single-dimensional array, and an array with a rank greater than one is called a multi-dimensional array.

Each dimension of an array has an associated length which is an integral number greater than or equal to zero. The dimension lengths are not part of the type of the array, but rather are established when an instance of the array type is created at run-time. The length of a dimension determines the valid range of indices for that dimension: For a dimension of length N, indices can range from 0 to N - 1 inclusive. The total number of elements in an array is the product of the lengths of each dimension in the array. If one or more of the dimensions of an array have a length of zero, the array is said to be empty.

The element type of an array can be any type, including an array type.

12.1 Array types

An array type is written as a *non-array-type* followed by one or more *rank-specifier*s:

array-type:
    non-array-type   rank-specifiers

non-array-type:
    type

rank-specifiers:
    rank-specifier
    rank-specifiers   rank-specifier

rank-specifier:
    [*dim-separators*$_{opt}$]

dim-separators:
    ,
    dim-separators ,

A *non-array-type* is any *type* that is not itself an *array-type*.

The rank of an array type is given by the leftmost *rank-specifier* in the *array-type*: A *rank-specifier* indicates that the array is an array with a rank of one plus the number of "," tokens in the *rank-specifier*.

The element type of an array type is the type that results from deleting the leftmost *rank-specifier*:

- An array type of the form `T[R]` is an array with rank `R` and a non-array element type `T`.
- An array type of the form `T[R][R₁]…[Rₙ]` is an array with rank `R` and an element type `T[R₁]…[Rₙ]`.

In effect, the *rank-specifier*s are read from left to right *before* the final non-array element type. For example, the type `int[][,,][,]` is a single-dimensional array of three-dimensional arrays of two-dimensional arrays of `int`.

Arrays with a rank of one are called **single-dimensional arrays**. Arrays with a rank greater than one are called **multi-dimensional arrays**, and are also referred to as two-dimensional arrays, three-dimensional arrays, and so on.

At run-time, a value of an array type can be `null` or a reference to an instance of that array type.

12.1.1 The System.Array type

The `System.Array` type is the abstract base type of all array types. An implicit reference conversion (section 6.1.4) exists from any array type to `System.Array`, and an explicit reference conversion (section 6.2.3) exists from `System.Array` to any array type. Note that `System.Array` is itself not an *array-type*. Rather, it is a *class-type* from which all *array-type*s are derived.

At run-time, a value of type `System.Array` can be `null` or a reference to an instance of any array type.

12.2 Array creation

Array instances are created by *array-creation-expression*s (section 7.5.10.2) or by field or local variable declarations that include an *array-initializer* (section 12.6).

When an array instance is created, the rank and length of each dimension are established and then remain constant for the entire lifetime of the instance. In other words, it is not possible to change the rank of an existing array instance, nor is it possible to resize its dimensions.

An array instance created by an *array-creation-expression* is always of an array type. The `System.Array` type is an abstract type that cannot be instantiated.

Elements of arrays created by *array-creation-expression*s are always initialized to their default value (section 5.2).

12.3 Array element access

Array elements are accessed using *element-access* expressions (section 7.5.6.1) of the form $A[I_1, I_2, ..., I_N]$, where A is an expression of an array type and each I_x is an expression of type `int`, `uint`, `long`, `ulong`, or of a type that can be implicitly converted to one or more of these types.. The result of an array element access is a variable, namely the array element selected by the indices.

The elements of an array can be enumerated using a `foreach` statement (section 8.8.4).

12.4 Array members

Every array type inherits the members declared by the `System.Array` type.

12.5 Array covariance

For any two *reference-type*s A and B, if an implicit reference conversion (section 6.1.4) or explicit reference conversion (section 6.2.3) exists from A to B, then the same reference conversion also exists from the array type A[R] to the array type B[R], where R is any given *rank-specifier* (but the same for both array types). This relationship is known as **array covariance**. Array covariance in particular means that a value of an array type A[R] may actually be a reference to an instance of an array type B[R], provided an implicit reference conversion exists from B to A.

Because of array covariance, assignments to elements of reference type arrays include a run-time check which ensures that the value being assigned to the array element is actually of a permitted type (section 7.13.1). For example:

```
class Test
{
   static void Fill(object[] array, int index, int count, object value) {
      for (int i = index; i < index + count; i++) array[i] = value;
   }
   static void Main() {
      string[] strings = new string[100];
      Fill(strings, 0, 100, "Undefined");
      Fill(strings, 0, 10, null);
      Fill(strings, 90, 10, 0);
   }
}
```

The assignment to `array[i]` in the `Fill` method implicitly includes a run-time check which ensures that the object referenced by `value` is either `null` or an instance of a type that is compatible with the actual element type of `array`. In `Main`, the first two invocations of `Fill` succeed, but the third invocation causes an `ArrayTypeMismatchException` to be thrown upon executing the first assignment to `array[i]`. The exception occurs because a boxed `int` cannot be stored in a `string` array.

Array covariance specifically does not extend to arrays of *value-type*s. For example, no conversion exists that permits an `int[]` to be treated as an `object[]`.

12.6 Array initializers

Array initializers may be specified in field declarations (section 10.4), local variable declarations (section 8.5.1), and array creation expressions (section 7.5.10.2):

array-initializer:
    {   *variable-initializer-list*$_{opt}$ }
    {   *variable-initializer-list*   ,   }

variable-initializer-list:
    variable-initializer
    variable-initializer-list   ,   *variable-initializer*

variable-initializer:
    expression
    array-initializer

An array initializer consists of a sequence of variable initializers, enclosed by "{"and "}" tokens and separated by "," tokens. Each variable initializer is an expression or, in the case of a multi-dimensional array, a nested array initializer.

The context in which an array initializer is used determines the type of the array being initialized. In an array creation expression, the array type immediately precedes the initializer. In a field or variable declaration, the array type is the type of the field or variable being declared. When an array initializer is used in a field or variable declaration, such as:

```
int[] a = {0, 2, 4, 6, 8};
```

it is simply shorthand for an equivalent array creation expression:

```
int[] a = new int[] {0, 2, 4, 6, 8}
```

For a single-dimensional array, the array initializer must consist of a sequence of expressions that are assignment compatible with the element type of the array. The expressions initialize array elements in increasing order, starting with the element at index zero. The number of expressions in the array initializer determines the length of the array instance being created. For example, the array initializer above creates an `int[]` instance of length 5 and then initializes the instance with the following values:

```
a[0] = 0; a[1] = 2; a[2] = 4; a[3] = 6; a[4] = 8;
```

For a multi-dimensional array, the array initializer must have as many levels of nesting as there are dimensions in the array. The outermost nesting level corresponds to the leftmost dimension and the innermost nesting level corresponds to the rightmost dimension. The length of each dimension of the array is determined by the number of elements at the corresponding nesting level in the array initializer. For each nested array initializer, the number of elements must be the same as the other array initializers at the same level. The example:

```
int[,] b = {{0, 1}, {2, 3}, {4, 5}, {6, 7}, {8, 9}};
```

creates a two-dimensional array with a length of five for the leftmost dimension and a length of two for the rightmost dimension:

```
int[,] b = new int[5, 2];
```

and then initializes the array instance with the following values:

```
b[0, 0] = 0; b[0, 1] = 1;
b[1, 0] = 2; b[1, 1] = 3;
b[2, 0] = 4; b[2, 1] = 5;
b[3, 0] = 6; b[3, 1] = 7;
b[4, 0] = 8; b[4, 1] = 9;
```

When an array creation expression includes both explicit dimension lengths and an array initializer, the lengths must be constant expressions and the number of elements at each nesting level must match the corresponding dimension length. Some examples:

```
int i = 3;
int[] x = new int[3] {0, 1, 2};     // OK
int[] y = new int[i] {0, 1, 2};     // Error, i not a constant
int[] z = new int[3] {0, 1, 2, 3};  // Error, length/initializer mismatch
```

Here, the initializer for `y` is in error because the dimension length expression is not a constant, and the initializer for `z` is in error because the length and the number of elements in the initializer do not agree.

13. Interfaces

An interface defines a contract. A class or struct that implements an interface must adhere to its contract. An interface may inherit from multiple base interfaces, and a class or struct may implement multiple interfaces.

Interfaces can contain methods, properties, events, and indexers. The interface itself does not provide implementations for the members that it defines. The interface merely specifies the members that must be supplied by classes or interfaces that implement the interface.

13.1 Interface declarations

An *interface-declaration* is a *type-declaration* (section 9.5) that declares a new interface type.

interface-declaration:
    *attributes*_{opt} *interface-modifiers*_{opt} `interface` *identifier interface-base*_{opt}
    interface-body `;`_{opt}

An *interface-declaration* consists of an optional set of *attributes* (section 17), followed by an optional set of *interface-modifiers* (section 13.1.1), followed by the keyword `interface` and an *identifier* that names the interface, optionally followed by an optional *interface-base* specification (section 13.1.2), followed by a *interface-body* (section 13.1.3), optionally followed by a semicolon.

13.1.1 Interface modifiers

An *interface-declaration* may optionally include a sequence of interface modifiers:

interface-modifiers:
    interface-modifier
    interface-modifiers interface-modifier

interface-modifier:
    `new`
    `public`
    `protected`
    `internal`
    `private`

It is an error for the same modifier to appear multiple times in an interface declaration.

The `new` modifier is only permitted on nested interfaces. It specifies that the interface hides an inherited member by the same name, as described in section 10.2.2.

The `public`, `protected`, `internal`, and `private` modifiers control the accessibility of the interface. Depending on the context in which the interface declaration occurs, only some of these modifiers may be permitted (section 3.5.1).

13.1.2 Base interfaces

An interface can inherit from zero or more interfaces, which are called the *explicit base interfaces* of the interface. When an interface has more than zero explicit base interfaces then in the declaration of the interface, the interface identifier is followed by a colon and a comma-separated list of base interface identifiers.

interface-base:
   :   *interface-type-list*

The explicit base interfaces of an interface must be at least as accessible as the interface itself (section 3.5.4). For example, it is an error to specify a `private` or `internal` interface in the *interface-base* of a `public` interface.

It is an error for an interface to directly or indirectly inherit from itself.

The *base interfaces* of an interface are the explicit base interfaces and their base interfaces. In other words, the set of base interfaces is the complete transitive closure of the explicit base interfaces, their explicit base interfaces, and so on. In the example

```
interface IControl
{
   void Paint();
}
interface ITextBox: IControl
{
   void SetText(string text);
}
interface IListBox: IControl
{
   void SetItems(string[] items);
}
interface IComboBox: ITextBox, IListBox {}
```

the base interfaces of `IComboBox` are `IControl`, `ITextBox`, and `IListBox`.

An interface inherits all members of its base interfaces. In other words, the `IComboBox` interface above inherits members `SetText` and `SetItems` as well as `Paint`.

A class or struct that implements an interface also implicitly implements all of the interface's base interfaces.

13.1.3 Interface body

The *interface-body* of an interface defines the members of the interface.

interface-body:
   {   *interface-member-declarations*$_{opt}$ }

13.2 Interface members

The members of an interface are the members inherited from the base interfaces and the members declared by the interface itself.

interface-member-declarations:
   interface-member-declaration
   interface-member-declarations   *interface-member-declaration*

interface-member-declaration:
   interface-method-declaration
   interface-property-declaration
   interface-event-declaration
   interface-indexer-declaration

An interface declaration may declare zero or more members. The members of an interface must be methods, properties, events, or indexers. An interface cannot contain constants, fields, operators, constructors, destructors, static constructors, or types, nor can an interface contain static members of any kind.

All interface members implicitly have public access. It is an error for interface member declarations to include any modifiers. In particular, interface members cannot be declared with the `abstract`, `public`, `protected`, `internal`, `private`, `virtual`, `override`, or `static` modifiers.

The example

```
public delegate void StringListEvent(IStringList sender);
public interface IStringList
{
    void Add(string s);
    int Count { get; }
    event StringListEvent Changed;
    string this[int index] { get; set; }
}
```

declares an interface that contains one each of the possible kinds of members: A method, a property, an event, and an indexer.

An *interface-declaration* creates a new declaration space (section 3.3), and the *interface-member-declarations* immediately contained by the *interface-declaration* introduce new members into this declaration space. The following rules apply to *interface-member-declaration*s:

- The name of a method must differ from the names of all properties and events declared in the same interface. In addition, the signature (section 3.6) of a method must differ from the signatures of all other methods declared in the same interface.
- The name of a property or event must differ from the names of all other members declared in the same interface.
- The signature of an indexer must differ from the signatures of all other indexers declared in the same interface.

The inherited members of an interface are specifically not part of the declaration space of the interface. Thus, an interface is allowed to declare a member with the same name or signature as an inherited member. When this occurs, the derived interface member is said to *hide* the base interface member. Hiding an inherited member is not considered an error, but it does cause the compiler to issue a warning. To suppress the warning, the declaration of the derived interface member must include a `new` modifier to indicate that the derived member is intended to hide the base member. This topic is discussed further in section 3.7.1.2.

If a `new` modifier is included in a declaration that doesn't hide an inherited member, a warning is issued to that effect. This warning is suppressed by removing the `new` modifier.

13.2.1 Interface methods

Interface methods are declared using *interface-method-declaration*s:

interface-method-declaration:
    attributes$_{opt}$ `new`$_{opt}$ *return-type identifier* (*formal-parameter-list*$_{opt}$) ;

The *attributes*, *return-type*, *identifier*, and *formal-parameter-list* of an interface method declaration have the same meaning as those of a method declaration in a class (section 10.5). An interface method declaration is not permitted to specify a method body, and the declaration therefore always ends with a semicolon.

13.2.2 Interface properties

Interface properties are declared using *interface-property-declaration*s:

interface-property-declaration:
    attributes$_{opt}$ new$_{opt}$ *type identifier* { *interface-accessors* }

interface-accessors:
    attributes$_{opt}$ get ;
    attributes$_{opt}$ set ;
    attributes$_{opt}$ get ; *attributes*$_{opt}$ set ;
    attributes$_{opt}$ set ; *attributes*$_{opt}$ get ;

The *attributes*, *type*, and *identifier* of an interface property declaration have the same meaning as those of a property declaration in a class (section 10.6).

The accessors of an interface property declaration correspond to the accessors of a class property declaration (section 10.6.2), except that the accessor body must always be a semicolon. Thus, the accessors simply indicate whether the property is read-write, read-only, or write-only.

13.2.3 Interface events

Interface events are declared using *interface-event-declaration*s:

interface-event-declaration:
    attributes$_{opt}$ new$_{opt}$ event *type identifier* ;

The *attributes*, *type*, and *identifier* of an interface event declaration have the same meaning as those of an event declaration in a class (section 10.7).

13.2.4 Interface indexers

Interface indexers are declared using *interface-indexer-declaration*s:

interface-indexer-declaration:
    attributes$_{opt}$ new$_{opt}$ *type* this [*formal-parameter-list*] { *interface-accessors* }

The *attributes*, *type*, and *formal-parameter-list* of an interface indexer declaration have the same meaning as those of an indexer declaration in a class (section 10.8).

The accessors of an interface indexer declaration correspond to the accessors of a class indexer declaration (section 10.8), except that the accessor body must always be a semicolon. Thus, the accessors simply indicate whether the indexer is read-write, read-only, or write-only.

13.2.5 Interface member access

Interface members are accessed through member access (section 7.5.4) and indexer access (section 7.5.6.2) expressions of the form I.M and I[A], where I is an instance of an interface type, M is a method, property, or event of that interface type, and A is an indexer argument list.

For interfaces that are strictly single-inheritance (each interface in the inheritance chain has exactly zero or one direct base interface), the effects of the member lookup (section 7.3), method invocation (section 7.5.5.1), and indexer access (section 7.5.6.2) rules are exactly the same as for classes and structs: More derived members hide less derived members with the same name or signature. However, for multiple-inheritance interfaces, ambiguities can occur when two or more unrelated base interfaces declare members with the same name or signature. This section shows several examples of such situations. In all cases, explicit casts can be included in the program code to resolve the ambiguities.

In the example

```
interface IList
{
    int Count { get; set; }
}
interface ICounter
{
    void Count(int i);
}
interface IListCounter: IList, ICounter {}
class C
{
    void Test(IListCounter x) {
        x.Count(1);                // Error, Count is ambiguous
        x.Count = 1;               // Error, Count is ambiguous
        ((IList)x).Count = 1;      // Ok, invokes IList.Count.set
        ((ICounter)x).Count(1);    // Ok, invokes ICounter.Count
    }
}
```

the first two statements cause compile-time errors because the member lookup (section 7.3) of Count in IListCounter is ambiguous. As illustrated by the example, the ambiguity is resolved by casting x to the appropriate base interface type. Such casts have no run-time costs—they merely consist of viewing the instance as a less derived type at compile-time.

In the example

```
interface IInteger
{
   void Add(int i);
}
interface IDouble
{
   void Add(double d);
}
interface INumber: IInteger, IDouble {}
class C
{
   void Test(INumber n) {
      n.Add(1);                // Error, both Add methods are applicable
      n.Add(1.0);              // Ok, only IDouble.Add is applicable
      ((IInteger)n).Add(1);    // Ok, only IInteger.Add is a candidate
      ((IDouble)n).Add(1);     // Ok, only IDouble.Add is a candidate
   }
}
```

the invocation n.Add(1) is ambiguous because a method invocation (section 7.5.5.1) requires all overloaded candidate methods to be declared in the same type. However, the invocation n.Add(1.0) is permitted because only IDouble.Add is applicable. When explicit casts are inserted, there is only one candidate method, and thus no ambiguity.

In the example

```
interface IBase
{
   void F(int i);
}
interface ILeft: IBase
{
   new void F(int i);
}
interface IRight: IBase
{
   void G();
}
```

(continued)

(continued)

```
interface IDerived: ILeft, IRight {}
class A
{
   void Test(IDerived d) {
      d.F(1);                 // Invokes ILeft.F
      ((IBase)d).F(1);        // Invokes IBase.F
      ((ILeft)d).F(1);        // Invokes ILeft.F
      ((IRight)d).F(1);       // Invokes IBase.F
   }
}
```

the `IBase.F` member is hidden by the `ILeft.F` member. The invocation `d.F(1)` thus selects `ILeft.F`, even though `IBase.F` appears to not be hidden in the access path that leads through `IRight`.

The intuitive rule for hiding in multiple-inheritance interfaces is simply this: If a member is hidden in any access path, it is hidden in all access paths. Because the access path from `IDerived` to `ILeft` to `IBase` hides `IBase.F`, the member is also hidden in the access path from `IDerived` to `IRight` to `IBase`.

13.3 Fully qualified interface member names

An interface member is sometimes referred to by its *fully qualified name*. The fully qualified name of an interface member consists of the name of the interface in which the member is declared, followed by a dot, followed by the name of the member. For example, given the declarations

```
interface IControl
{
   void Paint();
}
interface ITextBox: IControl
{
   void SetText(string text);
}
```

the fully qualified name of `Paint` is `IControl.Paint` and the fully qualified name of `SetText` is `ITextBox.SetText`.

Note that the fully qualified name of a member references the interface in which the member is declared. Thus, in the example above, it is not possible to refer to `Paint` as `ITextBox.Paint`.

When an interface is part of a namespace, the fully qualified name of an interface member includes the namespace name. For example

```
namespace System
{
   public interface ICloneable
   {
      object Clone();
   }
}
```

Here, the fully qualified name of the Clone method is System.ICloneable.Clone.

13.4 Interface implementations

Interfaces may be implemented by classes and structs. To indicate that a class or struct implements an interface, the interface identifier is included in the base class list of the class or struct.

```
interface ICloneable
{
   object Clone();
}
interface IComparable
{
   int CompareTo(object other);
}
class ListEntry: ICloneable, IComparable
{
   public object Clone() {…}
   public int CompareTo(object other) {…}
}
```

A class or struct that implements an interface also implicitly implements all of the interface's base interfaces. This is true even if the class or struct doesn't explicitly list all base interfaces in the base class list.

```
interface IControl
{
   void Paint();
}
interface ITextBox: IControl
{
   void SetText(string text);
}
class TextBox: ITextBox
{
   public void Paint() {…}
   public void SetText(string text) {…}
}
```

Here, class `TextBox` implements both `IControl` and `ITextBox`.

13.4.1 Explicit interface member implementations

For purposes of implementing interfaces, a class or struct may declare *explicit interface member implementations*. An explicit interface member implementation is a method, property, event, or indexer declaration that references a fully qualified interface member name. For example

```
interface ICloneable
{
   object Clone();
}
interface IComparable
{
   int CompareTo(object other);
}
class ListEntry: ICloneable, IComparable
{
   object ICloneable.Clone() {…}
   int IComparable.CompareTo(object other) {…}
}
```

Here, `ICloneable.Clone` and `IComparable.CompareTo` are explicit interface member implementations.

It is not possible to access an explicit interface member implementation through its fully qualified name in a method invocation, property access, or indexer access. An explicit interface member implementation can only be accessed through an interface instance, and is in that case referenced simply by its member name.

It is an error for an explicit interface member implementation to include access modifiers, as is it an error to include the `abstract`, `virtual`, `override`, or `static` modifiers.

Explicit interface member implementations have different accessibility characteristics than other members. Because explicit interface member implementations are never accessible through their fully qualified name in a method invocation or a property access, they are in a sense private. However, since they can be accessed through an interface instance, they are in a sense also public.

Explicit interface member implementations serve two primary purposes:

- Because explicit interface member implementations are not accessible through class or struct instances, they allow interface implementations to be excluded from the public interface of a class or struct. This is particularly useful when a class or struct implements an internal interface that is of no interest to a consumer of the class or struct.

- Explicit interface member implementations allow disambiguation of interface members with the same signature. Without explicit interface member implementations it would be impossible for a class or struct to have different implementations of interface members with the same signature and return type, as would it be impossible for a class or struct to have any implementation at all of interface members with the same signature but with different return types.

For an explicit interface member implementation to be valid, the class or struct must name an interface in its base class list that contains a member whose fully qualified name, type, and parameter types exactly match those of the explicit interface member implementation. Thus, in the following class

```
class Shape: ICloneable
{
    object ICloneable.Clone() {…}
    int IComparable.CompareTo(object other) {…}
}
```

the declaration of `IComparable.CompareTo` is invalid because `IComparable` is not listed in the base class list of `Shape` and is not a base interface of `ICloneable`. Likewise, in the declarations

```
class Shape: ICloneable
{
    object ICloneable.Clone() {…}
}
class Ellipse: Shape
{
    object ICloneable.Clone() {…}
}
```

the declaration of `ICloneable.Clone` in `Ellipse` is in error because `ICloneable` is not explicitly listed in the base class list of `Ellipse`.

The fully qualified name of an interface member must reference the interface in which the member was declared. Thus, in the declarations

```
interface IControl
{
    void Paint();
}
interface ITextBox: IControl
{
    void SetText(string text);
}
class TextBox: ITextBox
{
    void IControl.Paint() {…}
    void ITextBox.SetText(string text) {…}
}
```

the explicit interface member implementation of `Paint` must be written as `IControl.Paint`.

13.4.2 Interface mapping

A class or struct must provide implementations of all members of the interfaces that are listed in the base class list of the class or struct. The process of locating implementations of interface members in an implementing class or struct is known as *interface mapping*.

Interface mapping for a class or struct `C` locates an implementation for each member of each interface specified in the base class list of `C`. The implementation of a particular interface member `I.M`, where `I` is the interface in which the member `M` is declared, is determined by examining each class or struct `S`, starting with `C` and repeating for each successive base class of `C`, until a match is located:

- If `S` contains a declaration of an explicit interface member implementation that matches `I` and `M`, then this member is the implementation of `I.M`.
- Otherwise, if `S` contains a declaration of a non-static public member that matches `M`, then this member is the implementation of `I.M`.

An error occurs if implementations cannot be located for all members of all interfaces specified in the base class list of `C`. Note that the members of an interface include those members that are inherited from base interfaces.

For purposes of interface mapping, a class member A matches an interface member B when:

- A and B are methods, and the name, type, and formal parameter lists of A and B are identical.
- A and B are properties, the name and type of A and B are identical, and A has the same accessors as B (A is permitted to have additional accessors if it is not an explicit interface member implementation).
- A and B are events, and the name and type of A and B are identical.
- A and B are indexers, the type and formal parameter lists of A and B are identical, and A has the same accessors as B (A is permitted to have additional accessors if it is not an explicit interface member implementation).

Notable implications of the interface mapping algorithm are:

- Explicit interface member implementations take precedence over other members in the same class or struct when determining the class or struct member that implements an interface member.
- Private, protected, and static members do not participate in interface mapping.

In the example

```
interface ICloneable
{
    object Clone();
}
class C: ICloneable
{
    object ICloneable.Clone() {…}
    public object Clone() {…}
}
```

the `ICloneable.Clone` member of C becomes the implementation of `Clone` in `ICloneable` because explicit interface member implementations take precedence over other members.

If a class or struct implements two or more interfaces containing a member with the same name, type, and parameter types, it is possible to map each of those interface members onto a single class or struct member.

For example

```csharp
interface IControl
{
    void Paint();
}
interface IForm
{
    void Paint();
}
class Page: IControl, IForm
{
    public void Paint() {…}
}
```

Here, the `Paint` methods of both `IControl` and `IForm` are mapped onto the `Paint` method in `Page`. It is of course also possible to have separate explicit interface member implementations for the two methods.

If a class or struct implements an interface that contains hidden members, then some members must necessarily be implemented through explicit interface member implementations. For example

```csharp
interface IBase
{
    int P { get; }
}
interface IDerived: IBase
{
    new int P();
}
```

An implementation of this interface would require at least one explicit interface member implementation, and would take one of the following forms

```csharp
class C: IDerived
{
    int IBase.P { get {…} }
    int IDerived.P() {…}
}
class C: IDerived
{
    public int P { get {…} }
    int IDerived.P() {…}
}
```

```
class C: IDerived
{
   int IBase.P { get {…} }
   public int P() {…}
}
```

When a class implements multiple interfaces that have the same base interface, there can be only one implementation of the base interface. In the example

```
interface IControl
{
   void Paint();
}
interface ITextBox: IControl
{
   void SetText(string text);
}
interface IListBox: IControl
{
   void SetItems(string[] items);
}
class ComboBox: IControl, ITextBox, IListBox
{
   void IControl.Paint() {…}
   void ITextBox.SetText(string text) {…}
   void IListBox.SetItems(string[] items) {…}
}
```

it is not possible to have separate implementations for the IControl named in the base class list, the IControl inherited by ITextBox, and the IControl inherited by IListBox. Indeed, there is no notion of a separate identity for these interfaces. Rather, the implementations of ITextBox and IListBox share the same implementation of IControl, and ComboBox is simply considered to implement three interfaces, IControl, ITextBox, and IListBox.

The members of a base class participate in interface mapping. In the example

```
interface Interface1
{
    void F();
}
class Class1
{
    public void F() {}
    public void G() {}
}
class Class2: Class1, Interface1
{
    new public void G() {}
}
```

the method F in Class1 is used in Class2's implementation of Interface1.

13.4.3 Interface implementation inheritance

A class inherits all interface implementations provided by its base classes.

Without explicitly ***re-implementing*** an interface, a derived class cannot in any way alter the interface mappings it inherits from its base classes. For example, in the declarations

```
interface IControl
{
    void Paint();
}
class Control: IControl
{
    public void Paint() {…}
}
class TextBox: Control
{
    new public void Paint() {…}
}
```

the Paint method in TextBox hides the Paint method in Control, but it does not alter the mapping of Control.Paint onto IControl.Paint, and calls to Paint through class instances and interface instances will have the following effects

```
Control c = new Control();
TextBox t = new TextBox();
IControl ic = c;
IControl it = t;
c.Paint();        // invokes Control.Paint();
t.Paint();        // invokes TextBox.Paint();
ic.Paint();       // invokes Control.Paint();
it.Paint();       // invokes Control.Paint();
```

However, when an interface method is mapped onto a virtual method in a class, it is possible for derived classes to override the virtual method and alter the implementation of the interface. For example, rewriting the declarations above to

```
interface IControl
{
    void Paint();
}
class Control: IControl
{
    public virtual void Paint() {…}
}
class TextBox: Control
{
    public override void Paint() {…}
}
```

the following effects will now be observed

```
Control c = new Control();
TextBox t = new TextBox();
IControl ic = c;
IControl it = t;
c.Paint();        // invokes Control.Paint();
t.Paint();        // invokes TextBox.Paint();
ic.Paint();       // invokes Control.Paint();
it.Paint();       // invokes TextBox.Paint();
```

Since explicit interface member implementations cannot be declared virtual, it is not possible to override an explicit interface member implementation. It is however perfectly valid for an explicit interface member implementation to call another method, and that other method can be declared virtual to allow derived classes to override it.

For example

```
interface IControl
{
    void Paint();
}
class Control: IControl
{
    void IControl.Paint() { PaintControl(); }
    protected virtual void PaintControl() {…}
}
class TextBox: Control
{
    protected override void PaintControl() {…}
}
```

Here, classes derived from `Control` can specialize the implementation of `IControl.Paint` by overriding the `PaintControl` method.

13.4.4 Interface re-implementation

A class that inherits an interface implementation is permitted to **re-implement** the interface by including it in the base class list.

A re-implementation of an interface follows exactly the same interface mapping rules as an initial implementation of an interface. Thus, the inherited interface mapping has no effect whatsoever on the interface mapping established for the re-implementation of the interface. For example, in the declarations

```
interface IControl
{
    void Paint();
}
class Control: IControl
{
    void IControl.Paint() {…}
}
class MyControl: Control, IControl
{
    public void Paint() {}
}
```

the fact that `Control` maps `IControl.Paint` onto `Control.IControl.Paint` doesn't affect the re-implementation in `MyControl`, which maps `IControl.Paint` onto `MyControl.Paint`.

Inherited public member declarations and inherited explicit interface member declarations participate in the interface mapping process for re-implemented interfaces.

For example

```
interface IMethods
{
   void F();
   void G();
   void H();
   void I();
}
class Base: IMethods
{
   void IMethods.F() {}
   void IMethods.G() {}
   public void H() {}
   public void I() {}
}
class Derived: Base, IMethods
{
   public void F() {}
   void IMethods.H() {}
}
```

Here, the implementation of IMethods in Derived maps the interface methods onto Derived.F, Base.IMethods.G, Derived.IMethods.H, and Base.I.

When a class implements an interface, it implicitly also implements all of the interface's base interfaces. Likewise, a re-implementation of an interface is also implicitly a re-implementation of all of the interface's base interfaces. For example

```
interface IBase
{
   void F();
}
interface IDerived: IBase
{
   void G();
}
class C: IDerived
{
   void IBase.F() {…}
   void IDerived.G() {…}
}
class D: C, IDerived
{
   public void F() {…}
   public void G() {…}
}
```

Here, the re-implementation of IDerived also re-implements IBase, mapping IBase.F onto D.F.

13.4.5 Abstract classes and interfaces

Like a non-abstract class, an abstract class must provide implementations of all members of the interfaces that are listed in the base class list of the class. However, an abstract class is permitted to map interface methods onto abstract methods. For example

```
interface IMethods
{
   void F();
   void G();
}
abstract class C: IMethods
{
   public abstract void F();
   public abstract void G();
}
```

Here, the implementation of IMethods maps F and G onto abstract methods, which must be overridden in non-abstract classes that derive from C.

Note that explicit interface member implementations cannot be abstract, but explicit interface member implementations are of course permitted to call abstract methods. For example

```
interface IMethods
{
   void F();
   void G();
}
abstract class C: IMethods
{
   void IMethods.F() { FF(); }
   void IMethods.G() { GG(); }
   protected abstract void FF();
   protected abstract void GG();
}
```

Here, non-abstract classes that derive from C would be required to override FF and GG, thus providing the actual implementation of IMethods.

14. Enums

An **_enum type_** is a distinct type with named constants. Enum declarations may appear in the same places that class declarations can occur.

The example

```
enum Color
{
    Red,
    Green,
    Blue
}
```

declares an enum type named `Color` with members `Red`, `Green`, and `Blue`.

14.1 Enum declarations

An enum declaration declares a new enum type. An enum declaration begins with the keyword `enum`, and defines the name, accessibility, underlying type, and members of the enum.

enum-declaration:
    attributes$_{opt}$ _enum-modifiers_$_{opt}$ `enum` _identifier enum-base_$_{opt}$ _enum-body_ `;`$_{opt}$

enum-base:
    `:` _integral-type_

enum-body:
    `{` _enum-member-declarations_$_{opt}$ `}`
    `{` _enum-member-declarations_ `,` `}`

Each enum type has a corresponding integral type called the **_underlying type_** of the enum type. This underlying type must be able to represent all the enumerator values defined in the enumeration. An enum declaration may explicitly declare an underlying type of `byte`, `sbyte`, `short`, `ushort`, `int`, `uint`, `long` or `ulong`. Note that `char` cannot be used as an underlying type. An enum declaration that does not explicitly declare an underlying type has an underlying type of `int`.

The example

```
enum Color: long
{
    Red,
    Green,
    Blue
}
```

declares an enum with an underlying type of `long`. A developer might choose to use an underlying type of `long`, as in the example, to enable the use of values that are in the range of `long` but not in the range of `int`, or to preserve this option for the future.

14.2 Enum modifiers

An *enum-declaration* may optionally include a sequence of enum modifiers:

enum-modifiers:
   enum-modifier
   enum-modifiers *enum-modifier*

enum-modifier:
   new
   public
   protected
   internal
   private

It is an error for the same modifier to appear multiple times in an enum declaration.

The modifiers of an enum declaration have the same meaning as those of a class declaration (section 10.1.1). Note, however, that the `abstract` and `sealed` modifiers are not permitted in an enum declaration. Enums cannot be abstract and do not permit derivation.

14.3 Enum members

The body of an enum type declaration defines zero or more enum members, which are the named constants of the enum type. No two enum members can have the same name.

enum-member-declarations:
   enum-member-declaration
   enum-member-declarations , *enum-member-declaration*

enum-member-declaration:
   *attributes*_{opt} *identifier*
   *attributes*_{opt} *identifier* = *constant-expression*

Each enum member has an associated constant value. The type of this value is the underlying type for the containing enum. The constant value for each enum member must be in the range of the underlying type for the enum. The example

```
enum Color: uint
{
    Red = -1,
    Green = -2,
    Blue = -3
}
```

is in error because the constant values -1, -2, and -3 are not in the range of the underlying integral type uint.

Multiple enum members may share the same associated value. The example

```
enum Color
{
    Red,
    Green,
    Blue,

    Max = Blue
}
```

shows an enum that has two enum members—Blue and Max—that have the same associated value.

The associated value of an enum member is assigned either implicitly or explicitly. If the declaration of the enum member has a *constant-expression* initializer, the value of that constant expression, implicitly converted to the underlying type of the enum, is the associated value of the enum member. If the declaration of the enum member has no initializer, its associated value is set implicitly, as follows:

- If the enum member is the first enum member declared in the enum type, its associated value is zero.
- Otherwise, the associated value of the enum member is obtained by increasing the associated value of the previous enum member by one. This increased value must be within the range of values that can be represented by the underlying type.

The example

```csharp
using System;
enum Color
{
    Red,
    Green = 10,
    Blue
}
class Test
{
    static void Main() {
        Console.WriteLine(StringFromColor(Color.Red));
        Console.WriteLine(StringFromColor(Color.Green));
        Console.WriteLine(StringFromColor(Color.Blue));
    }
    static string StringFromColor(Color c) {
        switch (c) {
            case Color.Red:
                return String.Format("Red = {0}", (int) c);
            case Color.Green:
                return String.Format("Green = {0}", (int) c);
            case Color.Blue:
                return String.Format("Blue = {0}", (int) c);
            default:
                return "Invalid color";
        }
    }
}
```

prints out the enum member names and their associated values. The output is:

```
Red = 0
Blue = 11
Green = 10
```

for the following reasons:

- the enum member Red is automatically assigned the value zero (since it has no initializer and is the first enum member);
- the enum member Green is explicitly given the value 10;
- and the enum member Blue is automatically assigned the value one greater than the member that textually precedes it.

The associated value of an enum member may not, directly or indirectly, use the value of its own associated enum member. Other than this circularity restriction, enum member initializers may freely refer to other enum member initializers, regardless of their textual position. Within an enum member initializer, values of other enum members are always treated as having the type of their underlying type, so that casts are not necessary when referring to other enum members.

The example

```
enum Circular
{
    A = B,
    B
}
```

is invalid because the declarations of A and B are circular. A depends on B explicitly, and B depends on A implicitly.

Enum members are named and scoped in a manner exactly analogous to fields within classes. The scope of an enum member is the body of its containing enum type. Within that scope, enum members can be referred to by their simple name. From all other code, the name of an enum member must be qualified with the name of its enum type. Enum members do not have any declared accessibility—an enum member is accessible if its containing enum type is accessible.

14.4 Enum values and operations

Each enum type defines a distinct type; an explicit enumeration conversion (section 6.2.2) is required to convert between an enum type and an integral type, or between two enum types. The set of values that an enum type can take on is not limited by its enum members. In particular, any value of the underlying type of an enum can be cast to the enum type, and is a distinct valid value of that enum type.

Enum members have the type of their containing enum type (except within other enum member initializers: see section 14.3). The value of an enum member declared in enum type E with associated value v is (E)v.

The following operators can be used on values of enum types: ==, !=, <, >, <=, >= (section 7.9.5), + (section 7.7.4), - (section 7.7.5), ^, &, | (section 7.10.2), ~ (section 7.6.4), ++, -- (section 7.5.9, section 7.6.7), sizeof (section A.5.4).

Every enum type automatically derives from the class System.Enum. Thus, inherited methods and properties of this class can be used on values of an enum type.

15. Delegates

Delegates enable scenarios that other languages—C++, Pascal, Modula, and others—have addressed with function pointers. Unlike C++ function pointers, delegates are fully object oriented; unlike C++ pointers to member functions, delegates encapsulate both an object instance and a method.

A delegate declaration defines a class that extends the class `System.Delegate`. A delegate instance encapsulates a method—a callable entity. For instance methods, a callable entity consists of an instance and a method on the instance. For static methods, a callable entity consists of just a method. If you have a delegate instance and an appropriate set of arguments, you can invoke the delegate with the arguments.

An interesting and useful property of a delegate is that it does not know or care about the class of the object that it references. Any object will do; all that matters is that the method's signature matches the delegate's. This makes delegates perfectly suited for "anonymous" invocation.

15.1 Delegate declarations

A *delegate-declaration* is a *type-declaration* (section 9.5) that declares a new delegate type.

delegate-declaration:
    attributes$_{opt}$ delegate-modifiers$_{opt}$ `delegate` *result-type identifier*
    (*formal-parameter-list$_{opt}$*) ;

delegate-modifiers:
    delegate-modifier
    delegate-modifiers delegate-modifier

delegate-modifier:
    `new`
    `public`
    `protected`
    `internal`
    `private`

It is an error for the same modifier to appear multiple times in a delegate declaration.

The `new` modifier is only permitted on delegates declared within another type. It specifies that the delegate hides an inherited member by the same name, as described in section 10.2.2.

The `public`, `protected`, `internal`, and `private` modifiers control the accessibility of the delegate type. Depending on the context in which the delegate declaration occurs, some of these modifiers may not be permitted (section 3.5.1).

The *formal-parameter-list* identifies the signature of the delegate, and the *result-type* indicates the return type of the delegate. The signature and return type of the delegate must exactly match the signature and return type of any method that the delegate type encapsulates. Delegate types in C# are name equivalent, not structurally equivalent. Two different delegates types that have the same signature and return type are considered **different** delegate types.

A delegate type is a class type that is derived from System.Delegate. Delegate types are implicitly sealed: it is not permissible to derive any type from a delegate type. It is also not permissible to derive a non-delegate class type from System.Delegate. Note that System.Delegate is not itself a delegate type, it is a class type that all delegate types derive from.

C# provides special syntax for delegate instantiation and invocation. Except for instantiation, any operation that can be applied to a class or class instance can also be applied to a delegate class or instance. In particular, it is possible to access members of the System.Delegate type via the usual member access syntax.

15.1.1 Combinable delegate types

Delegate types are classified into two kinds: ***combinable*** and ***non-combinable***. A combinable delegate type must satisfy the following conditions:

- The declared return type of the delegate must be void.
- None of the parameters of the delegate type can be declared as output parameters (section 10.5.1.3).

A run-time exception occurs if an attempt is made to combine (section 7.7.4) two instances of a non-combinable delegate types unless one or the other is null.

15.2 Delegate instantiation

Although delegates behave in most ways like other classes, C# provides special syntax for instantiating a delegate instance. A *delegate-creation-expression* (section 7.5.10.3) is used to create a new instance of a delegate. The newly created delegate instance then refers to either:

- The static method referenced in the *delegate-creation-expression*, or
- The target object (which cannot be null) and instance method referenced in the *delegate-creation-expression*, or
- Another delegate

Once instantiated, delegate instances always refer to the same target object and method.

15.3 Multi-cast delegates

Delegates can be combined using the addition operator (section 7.7.4), and one delegate can be removed from another using the subtraction operator (section 7.7.5). A delegate instance created by combining two or more (non-`null`) delegate instances is called a ***multicast*** delegate instance. For any delegate instance, the ***invocation list*** of the delegate is defined as the ordered list of non-multicast delegates that would be invoked if the delegate instance were invoked. More precisely:

- For a non-multicast delegate instance, the invocation list consists of the delegate instance itself.
- For a multi-cast delegate instance that was created by combining two delegates, the invocation list is the formed by concatenating the invocation lists of the two operands of the addition operation that formed the multi-cast delegate.

15.4 Delegate invocation

C# provides special syntax for invoking a delegate. When a non-multicast delegate is invoked, it invokes the method that the delegate refers to with the same arguments, and returns the same value that the referred to method returns. See section 7.5.5.2 for detailed information on delegate invocation. If an exception occurs during the invocation of a delegate, and the exception is not caught within the method that was invoked, the search for an exception catch clause continues in the method that called the delegate, as if that method had directly called the method that the delegate referred to.

Invocation of a multi-cast delegate proceeds by invocation each of the delegates on the invocation list, in order. Each call is passed the same set of arguments. If the delegate includes reference parameters (section 10.5.1.2), each method invocation will occur with a reference to the same variable; changes to that variable by one method in the invocation list will be "seen" by any later methods in the invocation list.

If an exception occurs during processing of the invocation of a multicast delegate, and the exception is not caught within the method that was invoked, the search for an exception catch clause continues in the method that called the delegate, and any methods later in the invocation list are **not** invoked.

16. Exceptions

Exceptions in C# provide a structured, uniform, and type-safe way of handling both system level and application level error conditions. The exception mechanism is C# is quite similar to that of C++, with a few important differences:

- In C#, all exceptions must be represented by an instance of a class type derived from `System.Exception`. In C++, any value of any type can be used to represent an exception.
- In C#, a finally block (section 8.10) can be used to write termination code that executes in both normal execution and exceptional conditions. Such code is difficult to write in C++ without duplicating code.
- In C#, system-level exceptions such as overflow, divide-by-zero, and null dereferences have well defined exception classes and are on a par with application-level error conditions.

16.1 Causes of exceptions

Exception can be thrown in two different ways.

- A `throw` statement (section 8.9.5) throws an exception immediately and unconditionally. Control never reaches the statement immediately following the `throw`.
- Certain exceptional conditions that arise during the processing of C# statements and expression cause an exception in certain circumstances when the operation cannot be completed normally. For example, an integer division operation (section 7.7.2) throws a `System.DivideByZeroException` if the denominator is zero. See section 16.4 for a list of the various exceptions that can occur in this way.

16.2 The System.Exception class

The `System.Exception` class is the base type of all exceptions. This class has a few notable properties that all exceptions share:

- `Message` is a read-only property that contains a human-readable description of the reason for the exception.
- `InnerException` is a read-only property that contains the "inner exception" for this exception. If this is not `null`, this indicates that the current exception was thrown in response to another exception. The exception that caused the current exception is available in the `InnerException` property.

The value of these properties can be specified in the constructor for `System.Exception`.

16.3 How exceptions are handled

Exception are handled by a `try` statement (section 8.10).

When an exception occurs, the system searches for the nearest `catch` clause than can handle the exception, as determined by the run-time type of the exception. First, the current method is searched for a lexically enclosing `try` statement, and the associated catch clauses of the try statement are considered in order. If that fails, the method that called `try` statement and the current method is searched for a lexically enclosing `try` statement that encloses the point of the call to the current method. This search continues until a `catch` clause is found that can handle the current exception, by naming an exception class that is of the same class, or a base class, of the run-time type of the exception being thrown. A `catch` clause that doesn't name an exception class can handle any exception.

Once a matching catch clause is found, the system transfers control to the first statement of the catch clause. Before execution of the catch clause begins, the system first executes in order any `finally` clauses that were associated with try statements more nested that than the one that caught the exception.

If no matching catch clauses is no found, one of two things occurs:

- If the search for a matching catch clause reaches a static constructor (section 10.11) or static field initializer, then a `System.TypeInitializationException` is thrown at the point that triggered the invocation of the static constructor. The inner exception of the `TypeInitializationException` contains the exception that was originally thrown.

- If the search for matching catch clauses reaches the code that initially started the thread or program, then execution of the thread or program is terminated.

16.4 Common Exception Classes

The following exceptions are thrown by certain C# operations.

`System.OutOfMemoryException`	Thrown when an attempt to allocate memory (via `new`) fails.
`System.StackOverflowException`	Thrown when the execution stack is exhausted by having too many pending method calls; typically indicative of very deep or unbounded recursion.
`System.NullReferenceException`	Thrown when a `null` reference is used in a way that causes the referenced object to be required.
`System.TypeInitializationException`	Thrown when a static constructor throws an exception, and no catch clauses exists to catch in.
`System.InvalidCastException`	Thrown when an explicit conversion from a base type or interface to a derived types fails at run time.
`System.ArrayTypeMismatchException`	Thrown when a store into an array fails because the actual type of the stored element is incompatible with the actual type of the array.
`System.IndexOutOfRangeException`	Thrown when an attempt to index an array via an index that is less than zero or outside the bounds of the array.
`System.MulticastNotSupportedException`	Thrown when an attempt to combine two non-`null` delegates fails, because the delegate type does not have a `void` return type.
`System.ArithmeticException`	A base class for exceptions that occur during arithmetic operations, such as `DivideByZeroException` and `OverflowException`.
`System.DivideByZeroException`	Thrown when an attempt to divide an integral value by zero occurs.
`System.OverflowException`	Thrown when an arithmetic operation in a `checked` context overflows.

17. Attributes

Much of the C# language enables the programmer to specify declarative information about the entities defined in the program. For example, the accessibility of a method in a class is specified by decorating it with the *method-modifiers* public, protected, internal, and private.

C# enables programmers to invent new kinds of declarative information, to specify declarative information for various program entities, and to retrieve attribute information in a run-time environment. For instance, a framework might define a HelpAttribute attribute that can be placed on program elements such as classes and methods to provide a mapping from program elements to documentation for them.

New kinds of declarative information are defined through the declaration of attribute classes (section 17.1), which may have positional and named parameters (section 17.1.2). Declarative information is specified a C# program using *attributes* (section 17.2), and can be retrieved at run-time as attribute instances (section 17.3).

17.1 Attribute classes

The declaration of an ***attribute class*** defines a new kind of ***attribute*** that can be placed on a declaration. A class that derives from the abstract class System.Attribute, whether directly or indirectly, is an attribute class. By convention, attribute classes are named with a suffix of Attribute. Uses of an attribute may either include or omit this suffix.

17.1.1 The AttributeUsage attribute

The AttributeUsage attribute is used to describe how an attribute class can be used.

The AttributeUsage attribute has a positional parameter named that enables an attribute class to specify the kinds of declarations on which it can be used. The example

```
[AttributeUsage(AttributeTargets.Class | AttributeTargets.Interface)]
public class SimpleAttribute: System.Attribute
{}
```

defines an attribute class named SimpleAttribute that can be placed on *class-declaration*s and *interface-declaration*s.

The example

```
[Simple] class Class1 {…}
[Simple] interface Interface1 {…}
```

shows several uses of the `Simple` attribute. The attribute is defined with a class named `SimpleAttribute`, but uses of this attribute may omit the `Attribute` suffix, thus shortening the name to `Simple`. The example above is semantically equivalent to the example

```
[SimpleAttribute] class Class1 {…}
[SimpleAttribute] interface Interface1 {…}
```

The `AttributeUsage` attribute has an `AllowMultiple` named parameter that specifies whether the indicated attribute can be specified more than once for a given entity. If `AllowMultiple` for an attribute is true, then it is a *multi-use attribute class*, and can be specified more than once on an entity. If `AllowMultiple` for an attribute is false or unspecified for an attribute, then it is a *single-use attribute class*, and can be specified at most once on an entity.

The example

```
[AttributeUsage(AttributeTargets.Class, AllowMultiple = true)]
public class AuthorAttribute: System.Attribute {
    public AuthorAttribute(string value);
    public string Value { get {…} }
}
```

defines a multi-use attribute class named `AuthorAttribute`. The example

```
[Author("Brian Kernighan"), Author("Dennis Ritchie")]
class Class1 {…}
```

shows a class declaration with two uses of the `Author` attribute.

The `AttributeUsage` attribute has an `Inherited` named parameter that specifies whether the attribute, when specified on a base class, is also inherited by classes that derive from this base class. If the `Inherited` named parameter is unspecified, then a default value of false is used.

17.1.2 Positional and named parameters

Attribute classes can have *positional parameters* and *named parameters*. Each public constructor for an attribute class defines a valid sequence of positional parameters for the attribute class. Each non-static public read-write field and property for an attribute class defines a named parameter for the attribute class.

The example

```
[AttributeUsage(AttributeTargets.Class)]
public class HelpAttribute: System.Attribute
{
   public HelpAttribute(string url) { // url is a positional parameter
      ...
   }
   public string Topic {   // Topic is a named parameter
      get {...}
      set {...}
   }
   public string Url { get {...} }
}
```

defines an attribute class named HelpAttribute that has one positional parameter (string url) and one named argument (string Topic). The read-only Url property does not define a named parameter. It is non-static and public, but since it is read-only it does not define a named parameter.

The example

```
[HelpAttribute("http://www.mycompany.com/.../Class1.htm")]
class Class1 {
}
[HelpAttribute("http://www.mycompany.com/.../Misc.htm", Topic ="Class2")]
class Class2 {
}
```

shows several uses of the attribute.

17.1.3 Attribute parameter types

By convention, the types of positional and named parameters for an attribute class are limited to the *attribute parameter types*. A type is an attrIbute type if it is one of the following:

- One of the following types: bool, byte, char, double, float, int, long, short, string.
- The type object.
- The type System.Type.
- An enum type provided that it has public accessibility and that the types in which it is nested (if any) also have public accessibility.

17.2 Attribute specification

An **attribute** is a piece of additional declarative information that is specified for a declaration. Attributes can be specified at global scope (to specify attributes on the containing assembly or module) and for *type-declaration*s, *class-member-declaration*s, *interface-member-declaration*s, *enum-member-declaration*s, *property-accessor-declaration*s, *event-accessor-declarations*, and *formal-parameter* declarations.

Attributes are specified in attribute sections. Each attribute section is surrounded in square brackets, with multiple attributes specified in a comma-separated lists. The order in which attributes are specified and the manner in which they are arranged in sections is not significant. For instance, the attribute specifications [A][B], [B][A], [A, B], and [B, A] are equivalent.

attributes:
   attribute-sections

attribute-sections:
   attribute-section
   attribute-sections   attribute-section

attribute-section:
   [*attribute-target-specifier*_{opt}   *attribute-list*   ]
   [*attribute-target-specifier*_{opt}   *attribute-list*   ,]

attribute-target-specifier:
   attribute-target   :

attribute-target:
   assembly
   field
   event
   method
   module
   param
   property
   return
   type

attribute-list:
   attribute
   attribute-list   ,   attribute

attribute:
   *attribute-name   attribute-arguments*_{opt}

attribute-name:
   reserved-attribute-name
   type-name

attribute-arguments:
   (*positional-argument-list*)
   (*positional-argument-list* , *named-argument-list*)
   (*named-argument-list*)

positional-argument-list:
  positional-argument
  positional-argument-list , *positional-argument*

positional-argument:
  attribute-argument-expression

named-argument-list:
  named-argument
  named-argument-list , *named-argument*

named-argument:
  identifier = *attribute-argument-expression*

attribute-argument-expression:
  expression

An attribute consists of an *attribute-name* and an optional list of positional and named arguments. The positional arguments (if any) precede the named arguments.
A positional argument consists of an *attribute-argument-expression*; a named argument consists of a name, followed by an equal sign, followed by an *attribute-argument-expression*.

The *attribute-name* identifies either a reserved attribute or an attribute class. If the form of *attribute-name* is *type-name* then this name must refer to an attribute class. Otherwise, a compile-time error occurs. The example

```
class Class1 {}
[Class1] class Class2 {}   // Error
```

is in error because it attempts to use `Class1`, which is not an attribute class, as an attribute class.

Certain contexts permit the specification of an attribute on more than one target.
A program can explicitly specify the target by including an *attribute-target-specifier*.
In all but one of these contexts, a reasonable default can be employed. Thus, *attribute-target-specifier*s can typically be omitted. The potentially ambiguous contexts are as follows:

- An attribute specified at global scope can apply either to the target assembly or the target module. No default exists for this context, so an *attribute-target-specifier* is always required in this context.

- An attribute specified on a delegate declaration can apply either to the delegate declaration itself or to the return value of this declaration. In the absence of an *attribute-target-specifier*, such an attribute applies to the delegate declaration.

- An attribute specified on a method declaration can apply either to the method declaration itself or to the return value of this declaration. In the absence of an *attribute-target-specifier*, such an attribute applies to the method declaration.

- An attribute specified on an operator declaration can apply either to the operator declaration itself or to the return value of this declaration. In the absence of an *attribute-target-specifier*, such an attribute applies to the operator declaration.

- An attribute specified on non-abstract event declaration that omits event accessors can apply either to the event declaration itself or to the field that is automatically associated with it. In the absence of an *attribute-target-specifier*, such an attribute applies to the event declaration.

- An attribute specified on a get accessor for a property can apply either to the associated method or to the return value of this method. In the absence of an *attribute-target-specifier*, such an attribute applies to the method.

- An attribute specified on a set accessor for a property can apply either to the associated method or to the lone parameter of this method. In the absence of an *attribute-target-specifier*, such an attribute applies to the method.

- An attribute specified on an add or remove accessor for an event can apply either to the associated method or to the lone parameter of this method. In the absence of an *attribute-target-specifier*, such an attribute applies to the method.

By convention, attribute classes are named with a suffix of `Attribute`. An *attribute-name* of the form *type-name* may either include or omit this suffix. An exact match between the *attribute-name* and the name of the attribute class is preferred. The example

```
[AttributeUsage(AttributeTargets.All)]
public class X: System.Attribute
{}
[AttributeUsage(AttributeTargets.All)]
public class XAttribute: System.Attribute
{}
[X]               // refers to X
class Class1 {}
[XAttribute]      // refers to XAttribute
class Class2 {}
```

shows two attribute classes named `X` and `XAttribute`. The attribute `[X]` refers to the class named `X`, and the attribute `[XAttribute]` refers to the attribute class named `[XAttribute]`. If the declaration for class `X` is removed, then both attributes refer to the attribute class named `XAttribute`:

```
[AttributeUsage(AttributeTargets.All)]
public class XAttribute: System.Attribute
{}
[X]              // refers to XAttribute
class Class1 {}
[XAttribute]     // refers to XAttribute
class Class2 {}
```

It is an error to use a single-use attribute class more than once on the same entity. The example

```
[AttributeUsage(AttributeTargets.Class)]
public class HelpStringAttribute: System.Attribute
{
    string value;
    public HelpStringAttribute(string value) {
        this.value = value;
    }
    public string Value { get {…} }
}
[HelpString("Description of Class1")]
[HelpString("Another description of Class1")]
public class Class1 {}
```

is in error because it attempts to use HelpString, which is a single-use attribute class, more than once on the declaration of Class1.

An expression E is an *attribute-argument-expression* if all of the following statements are true:

- The type of E is an attribute parameter type (section 17.1.3).
- At compile-time, the value of E can be resolved to one of the following:
  - A constant value.
  - A System.Type object.
  - A one-dimensional array of *attribute-argument-expression*s.

17.3 Attribute instances

An **attribute instance** is an instance that represents an attribute at run-time. An attribute is defined with an attribute class, positional arguments, and named arguments. An attribute instance is an instance of the attribute class that is initialized with the positional and named arguments.

Retrieval of an attribute instance involves both compile-time and run-time processing, as described in the following sections.

17.3.1 Compilation of an attribute

The compilation of an *attribute* with attribute class T, *positional-argument-list* P and *named-argument-list* N, consists of the following steps:

- Follow the compile-time processing steps for compiling an *object-creation-expression* of the form `new T(P)`. These steps either result in a compile-time error, or determine a constructor on T that can be invoked at run-time. Call this constructor C.
- If the constructor determined in the step above does not have public accessibility, then a compile-time error occurs.
- For each *named-argument* Arg in N:
  - Let Name be the *identifier* of the *named-argument* Arg.
  - Name must identify a non-static read-write public field or property on T. If T has no such field or property, then a compile-time error occurs.
- Keep the following information for run-time instantiation of the attribute instance: the attribute class T, the constructor C on T, the *positional-argument-list* P and the *named-argument-list* N.

17.3.2 Run-time retrieval of an attribute instance

Compilation of an *attribute* yields an attribute class T, constructor C on T, *positional-argument-list* P and *named-argument-list* N. Given this information, an attribute instance can be retrieved at run-time using the following steps:

- Follow the run-time processing steps for executing an *object-creation-expression* of the form T(P), using the constructor C as determined at compile-time. These steps either result in an exception, or produce an instance of T. Call this instance O.
- For each *named-argument* Arg in N, in order:
  - Let Name be the *identifier* of the *named-argument* Arg. If Name does not identify a non-static public read-write field or property on O, then an exception is thrown.
  - Let Value be the result of evaluating the *attribute-argument-expression* of Arg.
  - If Name identifies a field on O, then set this field to the value Value.
  - Otherwise, Name identifies a property on O. Set this property to the value Value.
  - The result is O, an instance of the attribute class T that has been initialized with the *positional-argument-list* P and the *named-argument-list* N.

17.4 Reserved attributes

A small number of attributes affect the language in some way. These attributes include:

- System.AttributeUsageAttribute, which is used to describe the ways in which an attribute class can be used.
- System.ConditionalAttribute, which is used to define conditional methods.
- System.ObsoleteAttribute, which is used to mark a member as obsolete.

17.4.1 The AttributeUsage attribute

The AttributeUsage attribute is used to describe the manner in which the attribute class can be used.

A class that is decorated with the AttributeUsage attribute must derive from System.Attribute, either directly or indirectly. Otherwise, a compile-time error occurs.

```
[AttributeUsage(AttributeTargets.Class)]
public class AttributeUsageAttribute: System.Attribute
{
   public AttributeUsageAttribute(AttributeTargets validOn) {…}
   public virtual bool AllowMultiple { get {…} set {…} }
   public virtual bool Inherited { get {…} set {…} }
   public virtual AttributeTargets ValidOn { get {…} }
}
public enum AttributeTargets
{
   Assembly    = 0x0001,
   Module      = 0x0002,
   Class       = 0x0004,
   Struct      = 0x0008,
   Enum        = 0x0010,
   Constructor = 0x0020,
   Method      = 0x0040,
   Property    = 0x0080,
   Field       = 0x0100,
   Event       = 0x0200,
   Interface   = 0x0400,
   Parameter   = 0x0800,
   Delegate    = 0x1000,
   ReturnValue = 0x2000,
```

(continued)

(continued)

```
  All = Assembly | Module | Class | Struct | Enum | Constructor |
        Method | Property | Field | Event | Interface | Parameter |
        Delegate | ReturnValue,
  ClassMembers  =  Class | Struct | Enum | Constructor | Method |
                   Property | Field | Event | Delegate | Interface,
}
```

17.4.2 The Conditional attribute

The `Conditional` attribute enables the definition of ***conditional methods***. The `Conditional` attribute indicates a condition in the form of a pre-processing identifier. Calls to a conditional method are either included or omitted depending on whether this symbol is defined at the point of the call. If the symbol is defined, then the method call is included if the symbol is undefined, then the call is omitted.

```
[AttributeUsage(AttributeTargets.Method, AllowMultiple = true)]
public class ConditionalAttribute: System.Attribute
{
    public ConditionalAttribute(string conditionalSymbol) {…}
    public string ConditionalSymbol { get {…} }
}
```

A conditional method is subject to the following restrictions:

- The conditional method must be a method in a *class-declaration*. A compile-time error occurs if the `Conditional` attribute is specified on an interface method.

- The conditional method must return have a return type of `void`.

- The conditional method must not be marked with the `override` modifier. A conditional method may be marked with the `virtual` modifier. Overrides of such a method are implicitly conditional, and must not be explicitly marked with a `Conditional` attribute.

- The conditional method must not be an implementation of an interface method. Otherwise, a compile-time error occurs.

Also, a compile-time error occurs if a conditional method is used in a *delegate-creation-expression*. The example

```
#define DEBUG
class Class1
{
    [Conditional("DEBUG")]
    public static void M() {
        Console.WriteLine("Executed Class1.M");
    }
}
```

```
class Class2
{
   public static void Test() {
      Class1.M();
   }
}
```

declares Class1.M as a conditional method. Class2's Test method calls this method. Since the pre-processing symbol DEBUG is defined, if Class2.Test is called, it will call M. If the symbol DEBUG had not been defined, then Class2.Test would not call Class1.M.

It is important to note that the inclusion or exclusion of a call to a conditional method is controlled by the pre-processing identifiers at the point of the call. In the example

```
// Begin class1.cs
   class Class1
   {
      [Conditional("DEBUG")]
      public static void F() {
         Console.WriteLine("Executed Class1.F");
      }
   }
// End class1.cs

// Begin class2.cs
   #define DEBUG
   class Class2
   {
      public static void G {
         Class1.F();            // F is called
      }
   }
// End class2.cs

// Begin class3.cs
   #undef DEBUG
   class Class3
   {
      public static void H {
         Class1.F();            // F is not called
      }
   }
// End class3.cs
```

the classes Class2 and Class3 each contain calls to the conditional method Class1.F, which is conditional based on the presence or absence of DEBUG. Since this symbol is defined in the context of Class2 but not Class3, the call to F in Class2 is actually made, while the call to F in Class3 is omitted.

The use of conditional methods in an inheritance chain can be confusing. Calls made to a conditional method through base, of the form base.M, are subject to the normal conditional method call rules. In the example

```
// Begin class1.cs
   class Class1
   {
      [Conditional("DEBUG")]
      public virtual void M() {
         Console.WriteLine("Class1.M executed");
      }
   }
// End class1.cs

// Begin class2.cs
   class Class2: Class1
   {
      public override void M() {
         Console.WriteLine("Class2.M executed");
         base.M();                  // base.M is not called!
      }
   }
// End class2.cs

// Begin class3.cs
   #define DEBUG
   class Class3
   {
      public static void Test() {
         Class2 c = new Class2();
         c.M();                     // M is called
      }
   }
// End class3.cs
```

Class2 includes a call the M defined in its base class. This call is omitted because the base method is conditional based on the presence of the symbol DEBUG, which is undefined. Thus, the method writes to the console only "Class2.M executed". Judicious use of *pp-declaration*s can eliminate such problems.

17.4.3 The Obsolete attribute

The Obsolete attribute is used to mark program elements that should no longer be used.

```
[AttributeUsage(AttributeTargets.All)]
public class ObsoleteAttribute: System.Attribute
{
    public ObsoleteAttribute(string message) {…}
    public ObsoleteAttribute(string message, bool error) {…}
    public string Message { get {…} }
    public bool IsError{ get {…} }
}
```

A. Unsafe code

The core C# language, as defined in the preceding chapters, differs notably from C and C++ in its omission of pointers as a data type. C# instead provides references and the ability to create objects that are managed by a garbage collector. This design, coupled with other features, makes C# a much safer language than C or C++. In the core C# language it is simply not possible to have an uninitialized variable, a "dangling" pointer, or an expression that indexes an array beyond its bounds. Whole categories of bugs that routinely plague C and C++ programs are thus eliminated.

While practically every pointer type construct in C or C++ has a reference type counterpart in C#, there are nonetheless situations where access to pointer types becomes a necessity. For example, interfacing with the underlying operating system, accessing a memory-mapped device, or implementing a time-critical algorithm may not be possible or practical without access to pointers. To address this need, C# provides the ability to write **unsafe code**.

In unsafe code it is possible to declare and operate on pointers, to perform conversions between pointers and integral types, to take the address of variables, and so forth. In a sense, writing unsafe code is much like writing C code within a C# program.

Unsafe code is in fact a "safe" feature from the perspective of both developers and users. Unsafe code must be clearly marked in the with the modifier `unsafe`, so developers can't possibly use unsafe features accidentally, and the compiler and the execution engine work together to ensure that unsafe code cannot be executed in an untrusted environment.

A.1 Unsafe contexts

The unsafe features of C# are available only in *unsafe contexts*. An unsafe context is introduced by including an `unsafe` modifier in the declaration of a type or a member:

- A declaration of a class, struct, interface, or delegate may include an `unsafe` modifier, in which case the entire textual extent of that type declaration (including the body of the class, struct, or interface) is considered an unsafe context.
- A declaration of a field, method, property, event, indexer, operator, constructor, destructor, or static constructor may include an `unsafe` modifier, in which case the entire textual extent of that member declaration is considered an unsafe context.

In the example

```
public unsafe struct Node
{
    public int Value;
    public Node* Left;
    public Node* Right;
}
```

the `unsafe` modifier specified in the struct declaration causes the entire textual extent of the struct declaration to become an unsafe context. Thus, it is possible to declare the `Left` and `Right` fields to be of a pointer type. The example above could also be written

```
public struct Node
{
    public int Value;
    public unsafe Node* Left;
    public unsafe Node* Right;
}
```

Here, the `unsafe` modifiers in the field declarations cause those declarations to be considered unsafe contexts.

Other than establishing an unsafe context, thus permitting use of pointer types, the `unsafe` modifier has no effect on a type or a member. In the example

```
public class A
{
    public unsafe virtual void F() {
        char* p;
        ...
    }
}
public class B: A
{
    public override void F() {
        base.F();
        ...
    }
}
```

the `unsafe` modifier on the `F` method in `A` simply causes the textual extent of `F` to become an unsafe context in which the unsafe features of the language can be used. In the override of `F` in `B`, there is no need to re-specify the `unsafe` modifier—unless, of course, the `F` method in `B` itself needs access to unsafe features.

The situation is slightly different when a pointer type is part of the method's signature

```
public unsafe class A
{
    public virtual void F(char* p) {…}
}
public class B: A
{
    public unsafe override void F(char* p) {…}
}
```

Here, because F's signature includes a pointer type, it can only be written in an unsafe context. However, the unsafe context can be introduced by either making the entire class unsafe, as is the case in A, or by including an `unsafe` modifier in the method declaration, as is the case in B.

A.2 Pointer types

In an unsafe context, a *type* (section 4) may be a *pointer-type* as well as a *value-type* or a *reference-type*.

type:
   value-type
   reference-type
   pointer-type

A *pointer-type* is written as an *unmanaged-type* or the keyword `void` followed by a `*` token:

pointer-type:
   unmanaged-type `*`
   `void` `*`

unmanaged-type:
   type

The type specified before the `*` in a pointer type is called the **referent type** of the pointer type. It represents the type of the variable to which a value of the pointer type points.

Unlike references (values of reference types), pointers are not tracked by the garbage collector—the garbage collector has no knowledge of pointers and the data to which they point. For this reason a pointer is not permitted to point to a reference or to a structure that contains references, and the referent type of a pointer must be an *unmanaged-type*.

An *unmanaged-type* is any type that isn't a *reference-type* and doesn't contain *reference-type* fields at any level of nesting. In other words, an *unmanaged-type* is one of the following:

- `sbyte`, `byte`, `short`, `ushort`, `int`, `uint`, `long`, `ulong`, `char`, `float`, `double`, `decimal`, or `bool`.
- Any *enum-type*.
- Any *pointer-type*.
- Any user-defined *struct-type* that contains fields of *unmanaged-type*s only.

The intuitive rule for mixing of pointers and references is that referents of references (objects) are permitted to contain pointers, but referents of pointers are not permitted to contain references.

Some examples of pointer types are given in the table below:

Example	Description
`byte*`	Pointer to `byte`
`char*`	Pointer to `char`
`int**`	Pointer to pointer to `int`
`int*[]`	Single-dimensional array of pointers to `int`
`void*`	Pointer to unknown type

A value of a pointer type `T*` represents the *address* of a variable of type `T`. The pointer indirection operator `*` may be used to access this variable. For example, given a variable `P` of type `int*`, the expression `*P` denotes the `int` variable found at the address contained in `P`. Similar to an object reference, a pointer may be `null`. Applying the indirection operator to a `null` pointer causes a `NullReferenceException` to be thrown.

The `void*` type represents a pointer to an unknown type. Because the referent type is unknown, the indirection operator cannot be applied to a pointer of type `void*`. However, a pointer of type `void*` can be cast to any other pointer type (and vice versa).

Pointer types are a separate category of types. Unlike reference types and value types, pointer types to not inherit from `object` and no conversions exist between pointer types and `object`. In particular, boxing and unboxing (section 4.3) is not supported for pointers. However, conversions are permitted between different pointer types and between pointer types and the integral types. This is described in section A.4.

In an unsafe context, several constructs are available for operating on pointers:

- The `*` operator may be used to perform pointer indirection (section A.5.1).
- The `->` operator may be used to access a member of a struct through a pointer (section A.5.2).
- The `[]` operator may be used to index a pointer (section A.5.3).
- The `&` operator may be used to obtain the address of a variable (section A.5.4).

- The ++ and -- operators may be used to increment and decrement pointers (section A.5.5).
- The + and - operators may be used to perform pointer arithmetic (section A.5.6).
- The ==, !=, <, >, <=, and => operators may be used to compare pointers (section A.5.7).
- The stackalloc operator may be used to allocate memory from the call stack (section A.7).
- The fixed statement may be used to temporarily fix a variable so its address can be obtained (section A.6).

A.3 Fixed and moveable variables

The address-of operator (section A.5.4) and the fixed statement (section A.6) divide variables into two categories: **Fixed variables** and **moveable variables**.

Fixed variables reside in storage locations that are unaffected by operation of the garbage collector. Examples of fixed variables include local variables, value parameters, and variables created by dereferencing pointers. Moveable variables on the other hand reside in storage locations that are subject to relocation or disposal by the garbage collector. Examples of moveable variables include fields in objects and elements of arrays.

The & operator (section A.5.4) permits the address of a fixed variable to be obtained with no restrictions. However, because a moveable variable is subject to relocation or disposal by the garbage collector, the address of a moveable variable can only be obtained using a fixed statement (section A.6), and the address remains valid only for the duration of that fixed statement.

In precise terms, a fixed variable is one of the following:

- A variable resulting from a *simple-name* (section 7.5.2) that refers to a local variable or a value parameter.
- A variable resulting from a *member-access* (section 7.5.4) of the form V.I, where V is a fixed variable of a *struct-type*.
- A variable resulting from a *pointer-indirection-expression* (section A.5.1) of the form *P, a *pointer-member-access* (section A.5.2) of the form P->I, or a *pointer-element-access* (section A.5.3) of the form P[E].

All other variables are classified as moveable variables.

Note that a static field is classified as a moveable variable. Also note that a ref or out parameter is classified as a moveable variable, even if the argument given for the parameter is a fixed variable. Finally, note that a variable produced by dereferencing a pointer is always classified as a fixed variable.

A.4 Pointer conversions

In an unsafe context, the set of available implicit and explicit conversions is extended to include pointer types as described in this section.

Implicit pointer conversions can occur in a variety of situations within unsafe contexts, including function member invocations (section 7.4.3), cast expressions (section 7.6.8), and assignments (section 7.13). The implicit pointer conversions are:

- From any *pointer-type* to the type `void*`.
- From the null type to any *pointer-type*.

Explicit pointer conversions can occur only in cast expressions (section 7.6.8) within unsafe contexts. The explicit pointer conversions are:

- From any *pointer-type* to any other *pointer-type*.
- From `int`, `uint`, `long`, or `ulong` to any *pointer-type*.
- From any *pointer-type* to `int`, `uint`, `long`, or `ulong`.

For further details on implicit and explicit conversions, see section 6.1 and section 6.2.

Conversions between two pointer types never change the actual pointer value. In other words, a conversion from one pointer type to another has no effect on the underlying address given by the pointer.

Mappings between pointers and integers are implementation dependent. However, on 32- and 64-bit CPU architectures with a linear address space, conversions of pointers to or from integral types behave exactly as a conversions of `uint` or `ulong` values to or from those integral types.

A.5 Pointers in expressions

In an unsafe context an expression may yield a result of a pointer type, but outside an unsafe context it is an error for an expression to be of a pointer type. In precise terms, outside an unsafe context an error occurs if any *simple-name* (section 7.5.2), *member-access* (section 7.5.4), *invocation-expression* (section 7.5.5), or *element-access* (section 7.5.6) is of a pointer type.

In an unsafe context, the *primary-expression* (section 7.5) and *unary-expression* (section 7.6) productions permit the following additional constructs:

primary-expression:

   ...
   pointer-member-access
   pointer-element-access
   sizeof-expression
   stackalloc-expression

unary-expression:

   ...

   pointer-indirection-expression
   addressof-expression

These constructs are described in the following sections.

A.5.1 Pointer indirection

A *pointer-indirection-expression* consists of an asterisk (∗) followed by a *unary-expression*.

pointer-indirection-expression:
   ∗ *unary-expression*

The unary ∗ operator denotes *pointer indirection* and is used to obtain the variable to which a pointer points. The result of evaluating ∗P, where P is an expression of a pointer type T∗, is a variable of type T. It is an error to apply the unary ∗ operator to an expression of type void∗ or to an expression that isn't of a pointer type.

The effect of applying the unary ∗ operator to a null pointer is implementation defined. In particular, there is no guarantee that this operation throws a NullReferenceException.

For purposes of definite assignment analysis, a variable produced by evaluating an expression of the form ∗P is considered initially assigned (section 5.3.1).

A.5.2 Pointer member access

A *pointer-member-access* consists of a *primary-expression*, followed by a "->" token, followed by an *identifier*.

pointer-member-access:
   primary-expression -> *identifier*

In a pointer member access of the form P->I, P must be an expression of a pointer type other than void∗, and I must denote an accessible member of the type to which P points.

A pointer member access of the form P->I is evaluated exactly as (∗P).I. For a description of the pointer indirection operator (∗), see section A.5.1. For a description of the member access operator (.), see section 7.5.4.

In the example

```
struct Point
{
   public int x;
   public int y;
   public override string ToString() {
      return "(" + x + "," + y + ")";
   }
}
class Test
{
   unsafe static void Main() {
      Point point;
      Point* p = &point;
      p->x = 10;
      p->y = 20;
      Console.WriteLine(p->ToString());
   }
}
```

the `->` operator is used to access fields and invoke a method of a struct through a pointer. Because the operation P->I is precisely equivalent to (*P).I, the Main method could equally well have been written:

```
class Test
{
   unsafe static void Main() {
      Point point;
      Point* p = &point;
      (*p).x = 10;
      (*p).y = 20;
      Console.WriteLine((*p).ToString());
   }
}
```

A.5.3 Pointer element access

A *pointer-element-access* consists of a *primary-expression* followed by an expression enclosed in "[" and "]".

pointer-element-access:
   primary-expression [*expression*]

In a pointer element access of the form P[E], P must be an expression of a pointer type other than void*, and E must be an expression of a type that can be implicitly converted to int, uint, long, or ulong.

A pointer element access of the form P[E] is evaluated exactly as *(P + E). For a description of the pointer indirection operator (*), see section A.5.1. For a description of the pointer addition operator (+), see section A.5.6.

In the example

```
class Test
{
   unsafe static void Main() {
      char* p = stackalloc char[256];
      for (int i = 0; i < 256; i++) p[i] = (char)i;
   }
}
```

a pointer element access is used to initialize the character buffer in a for loop. Because the operation P[E] is precisely equivalent to *(P + E), the example could equally well have been written:

```
class Test
{
   unsafe static void Main() {
      char* p = stackalloc char[256];
      for (int i = 0; i < 256; i++) *(p + i) = (char)i;
   }
}
```

As in C and C++, the pointer element access operator does not check for out-of-bounds errors and the effects of accessing an out-of-bounds element are undefined.

A.5.4 The address-of operator

An *addressof-expression* consists of an ampersand (&) followed by a *unary-expression*.

addressof-expression:
   & *unary-expression*

Given an expression E which is of a type T and is classified as a fixed variable (section A.3), the construct &E computes the address of the variable given by E. The type of the result is T* and is classified as a value. An error occurs if E is not classified as a variable or if E denotes a moveable variable. In the latter case, a fixed statement (section A.6) can be used to temporarily "fix" the variable before obtaining its address.

The & operator does not require its argument to be definitely assigned, but following an & operation, the variable to which the operator is applied is considered definitely assigned in the execution path in which the operation occurs. It is the responsibility of the programmer to ensure that correct initialization of the variable actually does take place in this situation.

In the example

```
unsafe class Test
{
   static void Main() {
       int i;
       int* p = &i;
       *p = 123;
       Console.WriteLine(i);
   }
}
```

i is considered definitely assigned following the &i operation used to initialize p. The assignment to *p in effect initializes i, but the inclusion of this initialization is the responsibility of the programmer, and no compile-time error would occur if the assignment was removed.

The rules of definite assignment for the & operator exist such that redundant initialization of local variables can be avoided. For example, many external APIs take a pointer to a structure which is filled in by the API. Calls to such APIs typically pass the address of a local struct variable, and without the rule, redundant initialization of the struct variable would be required.

A.5.5 Pointer increment and decrement

In an unsafe context, the ++ and -- operators (section 7.5.9 and section 7.6.7) can be applied to pointer variables of all types except void*. Thus, for every pointer type T*, the following operators are implicitly defined:

```
T* operator ++(T* x);
T* operator --(T* x);
```

The operators produce the same results as adding or subtracting the integral value 1 from the pointer argument. In other words, for a pointer variable of type T*, the ++ operator adds sizeof(T) to the address contained in the variable, and the -- operator subtracts sizeof(T) from the address contained in the variable.

If a pointer increment or decrement operation overflows the address range of the underlying CPU architecture, the result is truncated in an implementation dependent fashion, but no exceptions are produced.

A.5.6 Pointer arithmetic

In an unsafe context, the + and - operators (section 7.7.4 and section 7.7.5) can be applied to values of all pointer types except void*. Thus, for every pointer type T*, the following operators are implicitly defined:

```
T* operator +(T* x, int y);
T* operator +(T* x, uint y);
T* operator +(T* x, long y);
T* operator +(T* x, ulong y);
T* operator +(int x, T* y);
T* operator +(uint x, T* y);
T* operator +(long x, T* y);
T* operator +(ulong x, T* y);
T* operator -(T* x, int y);
T* operator -(T* x, uint y);
T* operator -(T* x, long y);
T* operator -(T* x, ulong y);
long operator -(T* x, T* y);
```

Given an expression P of a pointer type T* and an expression N of type int, uint, long, or ulong, the expressions P + N and N + P compute the pointer value of type T* that results from adding N * sizeof(T) to the address given by P. Likewise, the expression P - N computes the pointer value of type T* that results from subtracting N * sizeof(T) from the address given by P.

Given two expressions, P and Q, of a pointer type T*, the expression P - Q computes the difference between the addresses given by P and Q and then divides the difference by sizeof(T). The type of the result is always long. In effect, P - Q is computed as ((long)(P) - (long)(Q)) / sizeof(T).

If a pointer arithmetic operation overflows the address range of the underlying CPU architecture, the result is truncated in an implementation dependent fashion, but no exceptions are produced.

A.5.7 Pointer comparison

In an unsafe context, the ==, !=, <, >, <=, and => operators (section 7.9) can be applied to values of all pointer types. The pointer comparison operators are:

```
bool operator ==(void* x, void* y);
bool operator !=(void* x, void* y);
bool operator <(void* x, void* y);
bool operator >(void* x, void* y);
bool operator <=(void* x, void* y);
bool operator >=(void* x, void* y);
```

Because an implicit conversion exists from any pointer type to the `void*` type, operands of any pointer type can be compared using these operators. The comparison operators compare the addresses given by the two operands as if they were unsigned integers.

A.5.8 The sizeof operator

The `sizeof` operator returns the number of bytes occupied by a variable of a given type. The type specified as an argument to `sizeof` must be an *unmanaged-type* (section A.2).

sizeof-expression:
>   sizeof (*unmanaged-type*)

The result of the `sizeof` operator is a value of type `int`. For certain predefined types, the `sizeof` operator yields a constant value as shown in the table below.

Expression	Result
sizeof(sbyte)	1
sizeof(byte)	1
sizeof(short)	2
sizeof(ushort)	2
sizeof(int)	4
sizeof(uint)	4
sizeof(long)	8
sizeof(ulong)	8
sizeof(char)	2
sizeof(float)	4
sizeof(double)	8
sizeof(bool)	1

For all other types, the result of the `sizeof` operator is implementation dependent and is classified as a value, not a constant.

A.6 The fixed statement

The `fixed` statement is used to "fix" a moveable variable such that its address remains constant for the duration of the statement.

fixed-statement:
>   fixed (*pointer-type fixed-pointer-declarators*) *embedded-statement*

fixed-pointer-declarators:
>   *fixed-pointer-declarator*
>   *fixed-pointer-declarators* , *fixed-pointer-declarator*

fixed-pointer-declarator:
   identifier = & *variable-reference*
   identifier = *expression*

Each *fixed-pointer-declarator* declares a local variable of the given *pointer-type* and initializes the local variable with the address computed by the corresponding *fixed-pointer-initializer*. A local variable declared in a `fixed` statement is accessible in any *fixed-pointer-initializer*s occurring to the left of the declaration, and in the *embedded-statement* of the `fixed` statement. A local variable declared by a `fixed` statement is considered read-only and cannot be assigned to or passed as a `ref` or `out` parameter.

A *fixed-pointer-initializer* can be one of the following:

- The token "&" followed by a *variable-reference* (section 5.4) to a moveable variable (section A.3) of an unmanaged type `T`, provided the type `T*` is implicitly convertible to the pointer type given in the `fixed` statement. In this case, the initializer computes the address of the given variable, and the variable is guaranteed to remain at a fixed address for the duration of the `fixed` statement.

- An expression of an *array-type* with elements of an unmanaged type `T`, provided the type `T*` is implicitly convertible to the pointer type given in the `fixed` statement. In this case, the initializer computes the address of the first element in the array, and the entire array is guaranteed to remain at a fixed address for the duration of the `fixed` statement. A `NullReferenceException` is thrown if the array expression is `null`.

- An expression of type `string`, provided the type `char*` is implicitly convertible to the pointer type given in the `fixed` statement. In this case, the initializer computes the address of the first character in the string, and the entire string is guaranteed to remain at a fixed address for the duration of the `fixed` statement. A `NullReferenceException` is thrown if the string expression is `null`.

For each address computed by a *fixed-pointer-initializer* the `fixed` statement ensures that the variable referenced by the address is not subject to relocation or disposal by the garbage collector for the duration of the `fixed` statement. For example, if the address computed by a *fixed-pointer-initializer* references a field of an object or an element of an array instance, the `fixed` statement guarantees that the containing object instance is not relocated or disposed of during the lifetime of the statement.

It is the programmers responsibility to ensure that pointers created by `fixed` statements do not survive beyond execution of those statements. This for example means that when pointers created by `fixed` statements are passed to external APIs, it is the programmers responsibility to ensure that the APIs retain no memory of these pointers.

The fixed statement is typically implemented by generating tables that describe to the garbage collector which objects are to remain fixed in which regions of executable code. Thus, as long as a garbage collection process doesn't actually occur during execution of a fixed statement, there is very little cost associated with the statement. However, when a garbage collection process does occur, fixed objects may cause fragmentation of the heap (because they can't be moved). For that reason, objects should be fixed only when absolutely necessary and then only for the shortest amount of time possible.

The example

```
unsafe class Test
{
   static int x;
   int y;
   static void F(int* p) {
      *p = 1;
   }
   static void Main() {
      Test t = new Test();
      int[] a = new int[10];
      fixed (int* p = &x) F(p);
      fixed (int* p = &t.y) F(p);
      fixed (int* p = &a[0]) F(p);
      fixed (int* p = a) F(p);
   }
}
```

demonstrates several uses of the fixed statement. The first statement fixes and obtains the address of a static field, the second statement fixes and obtains the address of an instance field, and the third statement fixes and obtains the address of an array element. In each case it would have been an error to use the regular & operator since the variables are all classified as moveable variables.

The third and fourth fixed statements in the example above produce identical results. In general, for an array instance a, specifying &a[0] in a fixed statement is the same as simply specifying a.

Within a fixed statement that obtains pointer p to an array instance a, the pointer values ranging from p to p + a.Length - 1 represent addresses of the elements in the array. Likewise, the variables ranging from p[0] to p[a.Length - 1] represent the actual array elements.

In the example

```
unsafe class Test
{
    static void Fill(int* p, int count, int value) {
        for (; count != 0; count--) *p++ = value;
    }
    static void Main() {
        int[] a = new int[100];
        fixed (int* p = a) Fill(p, 100, -1);
    }
}
```

a `fixed` statement is used to fix an array so its address can be passed to a method that takes a pointer.

A `char*` value produced by fixing a string instance always points to a null-terminated string. Within a fixed statement that obtains a pointer p to a string instance s, the pointer values ranging from p to p + s.Length - 1 represent addresses of the characters in the string, and the pointer value p + s.Length always points to a null character (the character value '\0').

Because strings are immutable, it is the programmers responsibility to ensure that the characters referenced by a pointer to a fixed string are not modified.

The automatic null-termination of strings is particularly convenient when calling external APIs that expect "C-style" strings. Note, however, that a string instance is permitted to contain null characters. If such null characters are present, the string will appear truncated when treated as a null-terminated `char*`.

A.7 Stack allocation

In an unsafe context, a local variable declaration (section 8.5.1) may include a stack allocation initializer which allocates memory from the call stack.

variable-initializer:
  expression
  array-initializer
  stackalloc-initializer

stackalloc-initializer:
  `stackalloc` *unmanaged-type* `[` *expression* `]`

A stack allocation initializer of the form `stackalloc T[E]` requires T to be an unmanaged type (section A.2) and E to be an expression of type `int`. The construct allocates E * sizeof(T) bytes from the call stack and produces a pointer, of type `T*`, to the newly allocated block. If there is not enough memory available to allocate a block of the given size, a `StackOverflowException` is thrown.

There is no way to explicitly free memory allocated using `stackalloc`. Instead, all stack allocated memory blocks created during execution of a function member are automatically discarded when the function member returns. This corresponds to the `alloca` function provided in C and C++.

In the example

```csharp
class Test
{
   unsafe static string IntToString(int value) {
      char* buffer = stackalloc char[16];
      char* p = buffer + 16;
      int n = value >= 0? value: -value;
      do {
         *--p = (char)(n % 10 + '0');
         n /= 10;
      } while (n != 0);
      if (value < 0) *--p = '-';
      return new string(p, (int)(buffer + 16 - p));
   }
   static void Main() {
      Console.WriteLine(IntToString(12345));
      Console.WriteLine(IntToString(-999));
   }
}
```

a `stackalloc` initializer is used in the `IntToString` method to allocate a buffer of 16 characters on the stack. The buffer is automatically discarded when the method returns.

A.8 Dynamic memory allocation

Except for the `stackalloc` operator, C# provides no predefined constructs for managing non-garbage collected memory. Such services are typically provided by supporting class libraries or imported directly from the underlying operating system. For example, the `Memory` class below illustrates how the Heap Functions of the Windows API can be accessed from C#:

```csharp
using System;
using System.Runtime.InteropServices;
public unsafe class Memory
{
   // Handle for the process heap. This handle is used in all calls to the
   // HeapXXX APIs in the methods below.
   static int ph = GetProcessHeap();
```

```
// Private constructor to prevent instantiation.
private Memory() {}
// Allocates a memory block of the given size. The allocated memory is
// automatically initialized to zero.
public static void* Alloc(int size) {
   void* result = HeapAlloc(ph, HEAP_ZERO_MEMORY, size);
   if (result == null) throw new OutOfMemoryException();
   return result;
}
// Copies count bytes from src to dst. The source and destination
// blocks are permitted to overlap.
public static void Copy(void* src, void* dst, int count) {
   byte* ps = (byte*)src;
   byte* pd = (byte*)dst;
   if (ps > pd) {
      for (; count != 0; count--) *pd++ = *ps++;
   }
   else if (ps < pd) {
      for (ps += count, pd += count; count != 0; count--) *--pd = *--ps;
   }
}
// Frees a memory block.
public static void Free(void* block) {
   if (!HeapFree(ph, 0, block)) throw new InvalidOperationException();
}
// Re-allocates a memory block. If the reallocation request is for a
// larger size, the additional region of memory is automatically
// initialized to zero.
public static void* ReAlloc(void* block, int size) {
   void* result = HeapReAlloc(ph, HEAP_ZERO_MEMORY, block, size);
   if (result == null) throw new OutOfMemoryException();
   return result;
}
// Returns the size of a memory block.
public static int SizeOf(void* block) {
   int result = HeapSize(ph, 0, block);
   if (result == -1) throw new InvalidOperationException();
   return result;
}
// Heap API flags
const int HEAP_ZERO_MEMORY = 0x00000008;
// Heap API functions
[DllImport("kernel32")]
static extern int GetProcessHeap();
```

(continued)

(continued)

```
[DllImport("kernel32")]
static extern void* HeapAlloc(int hHeap, int flags, int size);
[DllImport("kernel32")]
static extern bool HeapFree(int hHeap, int flags, void* block);
[DllImport("kernel32")]
static extern void* HeapReAlloc(int hHeap, int flags,
    void* block, int size);
[DllImport("kernel32")]
static extern int HeapSize(int hHeap, int flags, void* block);
}
```

An example that uses the Memory class is given below:

```
class Test
{
    unsafe static void Main() {
        byte* buffer = (byte*)Memory.Alloc(256);
        for (int i = 0; i < 256; i++) buffer[i] = (byte)i;
        byte[] array = new byte[256];
        fixed (byte* p = array) Memory.Copy(buffer, p, 256);
        Memory.Free(buffer);
        for (int i = 0; i < 256; i++) Console.WriteLine(array[i]);
    }
}
```

The example allocates 256 bytes of memory through Memory.Alloc and initializes the memory block with values increasing from 0 to 255. It then allocates a 256 element byte array and uses Memory.Copy to copy the contents of the memory block into the byte array. Finally, the memory block is freed using Memory.Free and the contents of the byte array are output on the console.

B. Interoperability

The attributes described in this chapter are used for creating programs that interoperate with COM programs.

B.1 The ComAliasName attribute

```
namespace System.Runtime.InteropServices
{
    [AttributeUsage(AttributeTargets.Parameter |
                    AttributeTargets.ReturnValue)]
    public class ComAliasName: System.Attribute
    {
        public ComAliasNameAttribute(string value) {…}
        public string Value { get {…} }
    }
}
```

B.2 The ComImport attribute

When placed on a class, the ComImport attribute marks the class as an externally implemented Com class. Such a class declaration enables the use of a C# name to refer to a COM class.

```
namespace System.Runtime.InteropServices
{
    [AttributeUsage(AttributeTargets.Class)]
    public class ComImportAttribute: System.Attribute
    {
        public ComImportAttribute() {…}
    }
}
```

A class that is decorated with the ComImport attribute is subject to the following restrictions:

- It must also be decorated with the Guid attribute, which specifies the CLSID for the COM class being imported. A compile-time error occurs if a class declaration includes the ComImport attribute but fails to include the Guid attribute.
- It must not have any members. (A public constructor with no parameters is automatically provided.)
- It must not derive from a class other than object.

The example

```
using System.Runtime.InteropServices;
[ComImport, Guid("00020810-0000-0000-C000-000000000046")]
class Worksheet {}
class Test
{
    static void Main() {
        Worksheet w = new Worksheet();  // Creates an Excel worksheet
    }
}
```

declares a class Worksheet as a class imported from COM that has a CLSID of "00020810-0000-0000-C000-000000000046". Instantiating a Worksheet instance causes a corresponding COM instantiation.

B.3 The ComRegisterFunction attribute

The presence of the ComRegisterFunction attribute on a method indicates that the method should be called during the COM registration process.

```
namespace System.Runtime.InteropServices
{
    [AttributeUsage(AttributeTargets.Method)]
    public class ComRegisterFunctionAttribute: System.Attribute
    {
        public ComRegisterFunctionAttribute() {…}
    }
}
```

B.4 The ComSourceInterfaces attribute

The ComSourceInterfaces attribute is used to list the source interfaces on the imported coclass.

```
namespace System.Runtime.InteropServices
{
    [AttributeUsage(AttributeTargets.Class)]
    public class ComSourceInterfacesAttribute: System.Attribute
    {
        public ComSourceInterfacesAttribute(string value) {…}
        public string Value { get {…} }
    }
}
```

B.5 The ComUnregisterFunction attribute

The presence of the `ComUnregisterFunction` attribute on a method indicates that the method should be called when the assembly is unregistered for use in COM.

```
namespace System.Runtime.InteropServices
{
    [AttributeUsage(AttributeTargets.Method)]
    public class ComUnregisterFunctionAttribute: System.Attribute
    {
        public ComUnregisterFunctionAttribute() {…}
    }
}
```

B.6 The ComVisible attribute

The `ComVisible` attribute is used to specify whether or not a class or interface is visible in COM.

```
namespace System.Runtime.InteropServices
{
    [AttributeUsage(AttributeTargets.Class |
                    AttributeTargets.Interface |
                    AttributeTargets.Method)]
    public class ComVisibleAttribute: System.Attribute
    {
        public ComVisibleAttribute(bool value) {…}
        public bool Value { get {…} }
    }
}
```

B.7 The DispId attribute

The DispId attribute is used to specify an OLE Automation DISPID. A DISPID is an integral value that identifies a member in a dispinterface.

```
namespace System.Runtime.InteropServices
{
   [AttributeUsage(AttributeTargets.Method | AttributeTargets.Field |
   AttributeTargets.Property)]
   public class DispIdAttribute: System.Attribute
   {
      public DispIdAttribute(int value) {…}
      public int Value { get {…} }
   }
}
```

B.8 The DllImport attribute

The DllImport attribute is used to specify the dll location that contains the implementation of an extern method.

```
namespace System.Runtime.InteropServices
{
   [AttributeUsage(AttributeTargets.Method)]
   public class DllImportAttribute: System.Attribute
   {
      public DllImportAttribute(string dllName) {…}
      public CallingConvention CallingConvention;
      public CharSet CharSet;
      public string EntryPoint;
      public bool ExactSpelling;
      public bool PreserveSig;
      public bool SetLastError;
      public string Value { get {…} }
   }
}
```

Specifically, the DllImport attribute has the following behaviors:

- It can only be placed on method declarations.
- It has a single positional parameter: a dllName parameter that specifies name of the dll in which the imported method can be found.

- It has five named parameters:
  - The `CallingConvention` parameter indicates the calling convention for the entry point. If no `CallingConvention` is specified, a default of `CallingConvention.Winapi` is used.
  - The `CharSet` parameter indicates the character set used in the entry point. If no `CharSet` is specified, a default of `CharSet.Auto` is used.
  - The `EntryPoint` parameter gives the name of the entry point in the dll. If no `EntryPoint` is specified, then the name of the method itself is used.
  - The `ExactSpelling` parameter indicates whether `EntryPoint` must exactly match the spelling of the indicated entry point. If no `ExactSpelling` is specified, a default of `false` is used.
  - The `PreserveSig` parameter indicates whether the signature of the method should be preserved or transformed. When a signature is transformed, it is transformed to one having an HRESULT return value and an additional out parameter named `retval` for the return value. If no `PreserveSig` value is specified, a default of `true` is used.
  - The `SetLastError` parameter indicates whether the method preserves the Win32 "last error". If no `SetLastError` is specified, a default of `false` is used.
- It is a single-use attribute class.

In addition, a method that is decorated with the `DllImport` attribute must have the `extern` modifier.

B.9 The FieldOffset attribute

The `FieldOffset` attribute is used to specify the layout of fields for the struct.

```
namespace System.Runtime.InteropServices
{
    [AttributeUsage(AttributeTargets.Field)]
    public class FieldOffsetAttribute: System.Attribute
    {
        public FieldOffsetAttribute(int value) {…}
        public int Value { get {…} }
    }
}
```

The `FieldOffset` attribute may not be placed on a field declarations that is a member of a class.

B.10 The Guid attribute

The Guid attribute is used to specify a globally unique identifier (GUID) for a class or an interface. This information is primarily useful for interoperability with COM.

```
namespace System.Runtime.InteropServices
{
   [AttributeUsage(AttributeTargets.Assembly
                 | AttributeTargets.Class
                 | AttributeTargets.Interface
                 | AttributeTargets.Enum
                 | AttributeTargets.Delegate
                 | AttributeTargets.Struct)]
   public class GuidAttribute: System.Attribute
   {
      public GuidAttribute(string value) {…}
      public string Value { get {…} }
   }
}
```

The format of the positional string argument is verified at compile-time. It is an error to specify a string argument that is not a syntactically valid GUID.

B.11 The HasDefaultInterface attribute

If present, the HasDefaultInterface attribute indicates that a class has a default interface.

```
namespace System.Runtime.InteropServices
{
   [AttributeUsage(AttributeTargets.Class)]
   public class HasDefaultInterfaceAttribute: System.Attribute
   {
      public HasDefaultInterfaceAttribute() {…}
   }
}
```

B.12 The ImportedFromTypeLib attribute

The ImportedFromTypeLib attribute is used to specify that an assembly was imported from a COM type library.

```
namespace System.Runtime.InteropServices
{
    [AttributeUsage(AttributeTargets.Assembly)]
    public class ImportedFromTypeLib: System.Attribute
    {
        public ImportedFromTypeLib(string value) {…}
        public string Value { get {..} }
    }
}
```

B.13 The In and Out attributes

The In and Out attributes are used to provide custom marshalling information for parameters. All combinations of these marshalling attributes are permitted.

```
namespace System.Runtime.InteropServices
{
    [AttributeUsage(AttributeTargets.Parameter)]
    public class InAttribute: System.Attribute
    {
        public InAttribute() {…}
    }
    [AttributeUsage(AttributeTargets.Parameter)]
    public class OutAttribute: System.Attribute
    {
        public OutAttribute() {…}
    }
}
```

If a parameter is not decorated with either marshalling attribute, then it is marshalled based on the its *parameter-modifiers*, as follows. If the parameter has no modifiers then the marshalling is [In]. If the parameter has the ref modifier then the marshalling is [In, Out]. If the parameter has the out modifier then the marshalling is [Out].

Note that out is a keyword, and Out is an attribute. The example

```
class Class1
{
    void M([Out] out int i) {
        ...
    }
}
```

shows that the use of out as a *parameter-modifier* and the use of Out in an *attribute*.

B.14 The IndexerName attribute

Indexers are implemented in some systems using indexed properties. If no IndexerName attribute is present for an indexer, then the name Item is used by default. The IndexerName attribute enables a developer to override this default and specify a different name.

```
namespace System.Runtime.InteropServices
{
    [AttributeUsage(AttributeTargets.Property)]
    public class IndexerNameAttribute: System.Attribute
    {
        public IndexerNameAttribute(string indexerName) {…}
        public string Value { get {...} }
    }
}
```

B.15 The InterfaceType attribute

When placed on an interface, the InterfaceType attribute specifies the manner in which the interface is treated in COM.

```
namespace System.Runtime.InteropServices
{
    [AttributeUsage(AttributeTargets.Interface)]
    public class InterfaceTypeAttribute: System.Attribute
    {
        public InterfaceTypeAttribute(ComInterfaceType value) {…}
        public ComInterfaceType Value { get {…} }
    }
}
```

B.16 The MarshalAs attribute

The MarshalAs attribute is used to describe the marshalling format for a field, method, or parameter.

```
namespace System.Runtime.InteropServices
{
    [AttributeUsage(AttributeTargets.Method |
              AttributeTargets.Parameter |
              AttributeTargets.Field)]
    public class MarshalAsAttribute: System.Attribute
    {
        public MarshalAsAttribute(UnmanagedType unmanagedType) {…}
        public UnmanagedType ArraySubType;
        public string MarshalCookie;
        public string MarshalType;
        public VarEnum SafeArraySubType;
        public int SizeConst;
        public short SizeParamIndex;
        public int SizeParamMultiplier;
    }
}
```

B.17 The NoIDispatch attribute

The presence of the NoIDispatch attribute indicates that the class or interface should derive from IUnknown rather than IDispatch when exported to COM.

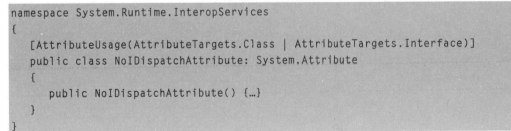

```
namespace System.Runtime.InteropServices
{
    [AttributeUsage(AttributeTargets.Class | AttributeTargets.Interface)]
    public class NoIDispatchAttribute: System.Attribute
    {
        public NoIDispatchAttribute() {…}
    }
}
```

B.18 The PreserveSig attribute

The PreserveSig attribute is used to indicate that the HRESULT/retval signature transformation that normally takes place during interoperability calls should be suppressed.

```
namespace System.Runtime.InteropServices
{
   [AttributeUsage(AttributeTargets.Method | AttributeTargets.Property)]
   public class PreserveSigAttribute: System.Attribute
   {
      public PreserveSigAttribute(bool value) {…}
      public bool Value { get {…} }
   }.
}
```

B.19 The StructLayout attribute

The StructLayout attribute is used to specify the layout of fields for the struct.

```
namespace System.Runtime.InteropServices
{
   [AttributeUsage(AttributeTargets.Class | AttributeTargets.Struct)]
   public class StructLayoutAttribute: System.Attribute
   {
      public StructLayoutAttribute(LayoutKind value) {…}
      public CharSet CharSet;
      public bool CheckFastMarshal;
      public int Pack;
      public LayoutKind Value { get {…} }
   }
}
```

If LayoutKind.Explicit is specified, then every field in the struct must have the StructOffset attribute. If LayoutKind.Explicit is not specified, then use of the StructOffset attribute is prohibited.

B.20 The TypeLibFunc attribute

The `TypeLibFunc` attribute is used to specify typelib flags, for interoperability with COM.

```
namespace System.Runtime.InteropServices
{
   [AttributeUsage(AttributeTargets.Method)]
   public class TypeLibFuncAttribute: System.Attribute
   {
      public TypeLibFuncAttribute(TypeLibFuncFlags value) {…}
      public TypeLibFuncFlags Value { get {…} }
   }
}
```

B.21 The TypeLibType attribute

The `TypeLibType` attribute is used to specify typelib flags, for interoperability with COM.

```
namespace System.Runtime.InteropServices
{
   [AttributeUsage(AttributeTargets.Class | AttributeTargets.Interface)]
   public class TypeLibTypeAttribute: System.Attribute
   {
      public TypeLibTypeAttribute(TypeLibTypeFlags value) {…}
      public TypeLibTypeFlags Value { get {…} }
   }
}
```

B.22 The TypeLibVar attribute

The `TypeLibVar` attribute is used to specify typelib flags, for interoperability with COM.

```
namespace System.Runtime.InteropServices
{
   [AttributeUsage(AttributeTargets.Field)]
   public class TypeLibVarAttribute: System.Attribute
   {
      public TypeLibVarAttribute(TypeLibVarFlags value) {…}
      public TypeLibVarFlags Value { get {…} }
   }
}
```

B.23 Supporting enums

```
namespace System.Runtime.InteropServices
{
   public enum CallingConvention
   {
      Winapi = 1,
      Cdecl = 2,
      Stdcall = 3,
      Thiscall = 4,
      Fastcall = 5
   }
   public enum CharSet
   {
      None,
      Auto,
      Ansi,
      Unicode
   }
   public enum ComInterfaceType
   {
      InterfaceIsDual = 0,
      InterfaceIsIUnknown = 1,
      InterfaceIsIDispatch = 2,
   }
   public enum LayoutKind
   {
      Sequential,
      Union,
      Explicit,
   }
   public enum TypeLibFuncFlags
   {
      FRestricted = 1,
      FSource = 2,
      FBindable = 4,
      FRequestEdit = 8,
      FDisplayBind = 16,
      FDefaultBind = 32,
      FHidden = 64,
      FUsesGetLastError = 128,
      FDefaultCollelem = 256,
      FUiDefault = 512,
      FNonBrowsable = 1024,
      FReplaceable = 2048,
```

```
      FImmediateBind = 4096
}
public enum TypeLibTypeFlags
{
   FAppObject = 1,
   FCanCreate = 2,
   FLicensed = 4,
   FPreDeclId = 8,
   FHidden = 16,
   FControl = 32,
   FDual = 64,
   FNonExtensible = 128,
   FOleAutomation = 256,
   FRestricted = 512,
   FAggregatable = 1024,
   FReplaceable = 2048,
   FDispatchable = 4096,
   FReverseBind = 8192
}
public enum TypeLibVarFlags
{
   FReadOnly = 1,
   FSource = 2,
   FBindable = 4,
   FRequestEdit = 8,
   FDisplayBind = 16,
   FDefaultBind = 32,
   FHidden = 64,
   FRestricted = 128,
   FDefaultCollelem = 256,
   FUiDefault = 512,
   FNonBrowsable = 1024,
   FReplaceable = 2048,
   FImmediateBind = 4096
}
public enum UnmanagedType
{
   Bool       = 0x2,
   I1         = 0x3,
   U1         = 0x4,
   I2         = 0x5,
   U2         = 0x6,
   I4         = 0x7,
   U4         = 0x8,
```

(continued)

(continued)

```
    I8            = 0x9,
    U8            = 0xa,
    R4            = 0xb,
    R8            = 0xc,
    BStr          = 0x13,
    LPStr         = 0x14,
    LPWStr        = 0x15,
    LPTStr        = 0x16,
    ByValTStr     = 0x17,
    Struct        = 0x1b,
    Interface     = 0x1c,
    SafeArray     = 0x1d,
    ByValArray    = 0x1e,
    SysInt        = 0x1f,
    SysUInt       = 0x20,
    VBByRefStr    = 0x22,
    AnsiBStr      = 0x23,
    TBStr         = 0x24,
    VariantBool   = 0x25,
    FunctionPtr   = 0x26,
    LPVoid        = 0x27,
    AsAny         = 0x28,
    RPrecise      = 0x29,
    LPArray       = 0x2a,
    LPStruct      = 0x2b,
    CustomMarshaler = 0x2c,
  }
}
```

C. References

Unicode Consortium. *The Unicode Standard, Version 3.0*. Addison-Wesley, Reading, Massachusetts, 2000, ISBN 0-201-616335-5.

IEEEE. *IEEE Standard for Binary Floating-Point Arithmetic*. ANSI/IEEE Standard 754-1985. Available from http://www.ieee.org.

ISO/IEC. *C++*. ANSI/ISO/IEC 14882:1998.

OWNER REGISTRATION CARD   *Register Today!*   0-7356-1448-2

Return the bottom portion of this card to register today.

Microsoft® C# Language Specifications

FIRST NAME   **MIDDLE INITIAL**   **LAST NAME**

INSTITUTION OR COMPANY NAME

ADDRESS

CITY   **STATE**   **ZIP**

( )

E-MAIL ADDRESS   **PHONE NUMBER**

U.S. and Canada addresses only. Fill in information above and mail postage-free.
Please mail only the bottom half of this page.

For information about Microsoft Press®
products, visit our Web site at
mspress.microsoft.com

||||||

I||ıluıIıdıIılıluıluıIıllılılılıIılıIılIıluılllıuılIıl